THE TWELVE CAKES OF CHRISTMAS

THE TWELVE CAKES OF CHRISTMAS

AN EVOLUTIONARY HISTORY, WITH RECIPES

*Helen Leach, Mary Browne
& Raelene Inglis*

OTAGO

Published by Otago University Press
Level 1, 398 Cumberland Street, Dunedin, New Zealand
PO Box 56, Dunedin, New Zealand
E: university.press@otago.ac.nz F: 64 3 479 8385
www.otago.ac.nz

First published 2011
Copyright © Helen Leach, Mary Browne, Raelene Inglis 2011
ISBN 978 1 877578 19 9

Publisher: Wendy Harrex
Cover & internal design: Fiona Moffat
Printed through Condor Production Ltd, Hong Kong

Frontispiece: Stained glass window in Old St Paul's, Wellington. Photo by Mary Browne.
Back cover photos of authors are by Janey Thomas (Mary Browne and Helen Leach) and Scott Inglis.

Contents

Preface   *9*

1 Origins of the Christmas cake   *11*
The evolution of fruit cakes in prehistory
Cakes and ingredients in ancient Greece and the Roman Empire
English cakes from the fourteenth to sixteenth centuries

2 In search of the seventeenth-century twelfth cake   *25*
Samuel Pepys's twelfth cake
The seventeenth-century twelfth cake
CAKE 1. SIR KENELM DIGBY'S RECIPE 'TO MAKE AN EXCELLENT CAKE' (1669)
ICING FESTIVE CAKES IN THE SEVENTEENTH CENTURY

3 Eighteenth-century twelfth cakes and the baking revolution   *41*
Recipes for eighteenth-century fruit cakes
CAKE 2. HANNAH GLASSE'S RECIPE 'TO MAKE A RICH CAKE' (1747)
ICING FESTIVE CAKES IN THE EIGHTEENTH CENTURY

4 From twelfth cake to Christmas cake   *57*
Twelfth cake recipes in the nineteenth century
Nineteenth-century recipes for Christmas cakes
Changes in fruit cakes in the nineteenth century
CAKE 3. ISABELLA BEETON'S 'CHRISTMAS CAKE' (1861)
ICING FESTIVE CAKES IN THE NINETEENTH CENTURY

5 Christmas cakes in twentieth-century New Zealand   *77*
Christmas cake size and ingredients in the twentieth century
Types of twentieth-century Christmas cakes
Variations in twentieth-century Christmas cake ingredients

6 Christmas cakes from the last hundred years   95

The cake that put on weight
CAKE 4. EDMONDS' CHRISTMAS CAKE
A 'Black Cake' transformed – Mrs Harman & Mrs Gard'ner's recipe
CAKE 5. CHRISTMAS OR WEDDING CAKE
TO ICE OR NOT TO ICE – CHRISTMAS CAKES IN THE TWENTIETH CENTURY
A home-grown country cake? Tui's & Aunt Daisy's blackcurrant cakes
CAKE 6. HOWICK CHRISTMAS CAKE
Making do with fewer eggs
CAKE 7. 2-EGG CUSTARD CHRISTMAS CAKE
A trans-Tasman import?
CAKE 8. GINGER ALE CHRISTMAS CAKE
Breaking with tradition – the pineapple Christmas cake
CAKE 9. DARK CHRISTMAS CAKE
One challenge and four solutions
CAKE 10. SWEETENED CONDENSED MILK CHRISTMAS CAKE
One Christmas cake, ten names
CAKE 11. CHRISTMAS JEWEL CAKE
Making 'healthy' Christmas cakes
CAKE 12. FESTIVE FRUIT CAKE

7 So what Christmas cake will we make this year?   *161*

RECIPES FOR ICINGS
HINTS FOR MAKING RICH FRUIT CAKES

Notes   *170*

Bibliography   *175*

Index   *186*

The twelve cakes of Christmas
Updated and photographed by Mary Browne

1	Excellent Cake (1669)	32
2	Rich Cake (1747)	48
3	Mrs Beeton's Christmas Cake (1861)	68
4	Edmonds' Christmas Cake (1908 [1974])	100
5	Christmas or Wedding Cake (1904 [1951])	106
6	Howick Christmas Cake (1935)	116
7	2-Egg Custard Christmas Cake (1948)	123
8	Ginger Ale Christmas Cake (1943 [1972])	128
9	Dark Christmas Cake (1935 [1968])	136
10	Sweetened Condensed Milk Christmas Cake (1968 [2000])	142
11	Christmas Jewel Cake (1987)	151
12	Festive Fruit Cake (2002)	156
	Recipes for Icings	163
	Hints on making Rich Fruit Cakes	167

Granddaughters prepare a Sweetened Condensed Milk Christmas Cake in Mary's kitchen. Alice pours the sweetened condensed milk into the large saucepan while Hannah waits to add the golden syrup and butter (see recipe on page 142).

Preface

This book arose from more than ten years' exploration of the potential of recipes for studying the history of domestic life. We started with a pilot study in 2002, in which one of the present authors, Raelene Inglis, wrote her BA Hons research essay on the theme 'Recipes as Material Culture'. The term 'material culture' is applied by anthropologists to the artefacts that humans make to facilitate their lives – from tools required for obtaining food and fuel, clothes and structures to keep us insulated from climatic extremes, to the items we fashion for social and religious reasons. Helen Leach supervised this research project, which was designed to test the notion that even though prepared dishes of food are very short-lived items of material culture – because we eat them – recipes encode their distinctive features, and can be studied as proxy-artefacts. Human cultures never stand still, but adapt of necessity to changing environments and social circumstances. Archaeologists have found that artefacts provide good examples of cultural evolution, changing their form and function through time. As proxy-artefacts, recipes should be equally adaptive.

Raelene's preliminary study confirmed that certain types of recipes are very responsive to external economic changes. We wondered whether a more traditional recipe type, for example the Christmas cake, would be more resistant to change. This question inspired another round of data collection and analysis, resulting in the article 'The Archaeology of Christmas Cakes' published in the American journal *Food and Foodways* in 2003. The period we covered was 1901 to 1980. After discovering much more variation than expected, and clear evidence of trends in cake sizes and ingredients, we resolved to expand the study in future. In the meantime, Raelene undertook research for her doctoral thesis, completed in 2007, which explored the ways in which cookery knowledge and recipes are transmitted between and within generations. Her topic formed part of a Marsden-funded project on the development of New Zealand's culinary traditions, led by Helen Leach.

With that completed, we returned to the evolution of New Zealand Christmas cakes. The statistical analysis now covers the whole of the twentieth century and over 800 recipes – this has been Raelene's particular contribution. Helen has expanded the section of the 2003 article outlining the history of Christmas cakes prior to the twentieth century. Many more international sources are now accessible online and, even more important, some are searchable. Helen has also used the data to identify recipe 'lineages'. For the first time, it is possible to take a recipe from a 1990s cookbook and track its forebears, in some cases for two centuries or more. This approach underpinned Helen's study of the evolution of New Zealand pavlova recipes, published in *The Pavlova Story* (Otago University Press, 2008). It has now provided some exciting new findings on the origins of New Zealand Christmas cakes.

We have always maintained that hours spent researching and writing the history of recipes generate an appetite that deserves to be satisfied. In addition, making old recipes teaches us about the working conditions of our ancestors, and the ingredients that were available to them. But we do not expect readers to learn the hard way. With the experience of making twelve classic pavlovas behind her, Mary Browne (Helen's sister) bravely embarked on the making of twelve classic Christmas cakes, ranging in age from the seventeenth century to the twenty-first. Her years of experience as a food-writer have resulted in a set of cake recipes up-dated for modern cooks with a taste for history. She was also responsible for the photographs of each cake, before family and friends claimed their share as Christmas cake connoisseurs.

Many people have contributed to this book and we thank them for sharing their knowledge. We should like to single out a few from whom we have received special assistance: food-writers Joan Bishop, Tui Flower, and Jill Brewis; former members of our Marsden research team, Jane Teal and Janet Mitchell; the always helpful staff at the Hocken Collections, the University of Otago Library (especially Teresa Smith and Donald Kerr), and the Dunedin Public Libraries Heritage Collection. We should like to acknowledge the many donors of old cookbooks and recipes – without them the analysis could not have proceeded. They include Reva Calvert, the Curwood family, Janet Goddard, Frank Leckie, Adele McKirdy, Diane Milne, Margaret Philip, Alison Roxburgh, Ann Sharp, Thelma Sheat and Helen Sise.

Finally we should like to thank Wendy Harrex for encouraging us to return to Christmas cakes and with Fiona Moffat making this book a celebration of their fascinating history.

Helen Leach, Mary Browne, Raelene Inglis
JULY 2011

1
Origins of the Christmas cake

> Thinking about Christmas? Before you start counting
> shopping days, remember your Christmas cake –
> the earlier it is made, the better it will be.[1]

This timely advice appeared in the November pages of the first volume of *Alison Holst's Kitchen Diary*, published in 1978. Her audience of home cooks expected to make a Christmas cake every year, as did their mothers and grandmothers. We like to imagine that our more distant ancestors also baked Christmas cakes – in short, that this is one of the most conservative items in our culinary tradition. But when we went in search of a recipe entitled 'Christmas Cake' that our great-great grandmother might have made before she emigrated to New Zealand in 1850, we could not find one, at least not under that name.

The earliest British fruit-cake recipe we have found with the name 'Christmas Cake' was Mrs Beeton's of 1861. But this does not mean that Christmas cakes were 'invented' in the 1850s–1860s. Like the pavlova cake, a re-named meringue cake of the late 1920s,[2] Christmas cakes were known by other names before 1861. Some early names were specific, like 'Twelfth Cake', and others more generic, like the seventeenth- and eighteenth-century recipes entitled 'A Rich Cake' or 'An Excellent Cake'.

In order to study the evolution of the New Zealand Christmas cake in all the forms in which it now exists, we cannot rely solely on the name of the recipe. So how can we separate out the cake recipes that led to our modern Christmas cakes? For a start we should look for key characteristics that distinguish modern Christmas cakes from everyday fruit cakes, for example more fruit and nuts, more spices, and the addition of spirits. But wedding and christening cakes include many of those expensive ingredients, and we know from some recipe books that the same recipe could serve for all three. What defines a rich fruit cake as a Christmas cake is its attachment to a festive season as indicated in its name, or by the section of cookbook in which its recipe appears, or by the commentary that accompanies it. To qualify as a possible ancestral Christmas cake, a fruit cake recipe must not only contain expensive ingredients, but show evidence of an association with the Christmas season. Such evidence can be found back to the seventeenth century.

Our study began with data entry in a spreadsheet, recording the source, date, name, ingredients and method of mixing of historical recipes for rich cakes. We began with published recipes that date to the seventeenth century, concentrating on those considered likely to be associated with the celebrations of the twelve-day-long Christmas season, especially those marking its end on Twelfth Night (5–6 January). Except during Cromwell's regime, Christmas Day in the seventeenth century might be marked by a special dinner as well as church services. Christmas puddings were served at these dinners, as they had been for several centuries before, but not cakes. In contrast, Twelfth Night marked a return to secular life, free of religious restrictions. It was on this night that the dividing of the twelfth cake initiated parties, enlivened by role-playing and drinking. The twelfth cake was the only cake closely associated with Christmas over the seventeenth and eighteenth centuries.

The Twelfth Night ceremonies continued into the early decades of the nineteenth century when Christmas Day began to acquire its present customs. As the twelfth cake lost its significance under that name, the Christmas cake hesitantly emerged, eventually consolidating in a form that was closer to the recipes for plum cakes and wedding cakes than for the twelfth cake. Our spreadsheets documented this transition in Britain, and the subsequent proliferation of Christmas cakes in New Zealand in the twentieth century. We used the same selection criteria for each century, and this allowed us to trace lineages of recipes.

The notion of a recipe lineage may seem strange but the study of the pavlova cake demonstrated that recipes are handed down from one generation to the next, as well as shared within generations. Many forms of transmission operate, from grandmothers to grandchildren in home kitchens, from teachers to pupils, from cooking demonstrators and television personalities to their often-vast audiences, and from newspapers, magazines and printed cookbooks to their readers who may be local or international. We shouldn't forget the recipes that pass between friends over a cup of tea, or those that are printed on the outside of a can or packet. Home cooks feel no constraint to reproduce any of these recipes exactly. From the first time they make the newly acquired recipe, they are likely to introduce some changes to accommodate personal or household tastes, the equipment available in their kitchen, or their food budget. If they pass their version on, more changes can be expected. Spreadsheet programs that offer filtering and sorting tools are very good at isolating these lineages of related recipes, and allowing us to track the changes.

One of the outcomes of spreadsheet analysis of Christmas cake recipes was that we were able to identify major types and the variants of those types, as well as document how long they were in circulation, and when new ones first appeared. Some innovative cake types became briefly fashionable, while other types represent classic forms made for more than two centuries. We have selected twelve cake recipes to represent the key types and some of the most distinctive variants, and adapted these for making in a twenty-first-century kitchen. Our aim was to achieve a version that reproduces as accurately as possible the taste and texture of these historical cakes. You will not need a seventeenth-century bread oven, nor a kitchen maid with the arm strength of a shot-put champion, sufficient to beat an eighteenth-century cake mixture for the requisite hour. We have reduced nineteenth-century recipe sizes to suit contemporary households rather than prolific Victorian families. Cooking instructions of the early twentieth century involving multiple layers of paper both inside and outside the cake tins have been modified to suit our thermostatically-controlled ovens and new types of bakeware.

Many people with an interest in food history are content to browse old recipes and read modern commentaries about their significance. We like to go further than this, and believe that recipes are actually invitations to cook. A recipe encodes the flavour and texture of a dish-in-waiting. Unlike most forms of historical evidence relating to the family or household, such as letters, diaries, wills, newspapers and photographs, the contents of recipe books offer a unique opportunity to taste history. We should warn you that the older the recipe, the harder it is to replicate the dish in a modern kitchen with today's ingredients. But increasingly, food historians are working out the modern equivalents of old measurements and technical terms, as well as differences in the composition of important constituents like flour.

The twelve cakes we have selected for adaptation to twenty-first-century kitchens start with an example from the seventeenth century and finish with a new cake from 2002, a taste of the future. They are not necessarily the best of their type, either as recipes or the cakes made from them, but are faithful interpretations of historically important forms. They provide edible accompaniments to our story of a festive cake and its evolution.

The evolution of fruit cakes in prehistory

The evolution of life starts not with cakes but soup – a primordial soup of single-cell prokaryotes – about 3500 billion years ago. Just as evolutionary biologists study the preconditions for life, we should ask when conditions were right for a fruit cake like our Christmas cake to emerge.

Obviously the foundation of such a cake is flour extracted from certain species of plants that store energy in the form of starch. However, not all plants are suitable. Although it would be possible to make a Christmas cake using potato flour, it would be exceedingly dense and crumbly. In our culinary tradition and those of Europe and western Asia, cakes and leavened breads exist because of the special characteristics of wheat flour. The proteins (gliadin and glutenin) in the starchy endosperm of the wheat seed respond in a unique way to beating or kneading – they develop the ability to trap air from beating, or gas produced by multiplying yeast fungi. Rye and barley have the same proteins but in much lower quantities.

Wheat (*Triticum* spp.) and barley (*Hordeum* spp.) were possibly the earliest cereals to be harvested in the Middle East. Eaten raw, they are much less nutritious than if they are ground into fine particles and then subjected to heat to rupture the starch cells. By 20,000 years ago, at the Ohalo II site on the shores of the Sea of Galilee, a group of hunter-gatherers were crushing wild cereal seeds on flat basalt stones – starch grains from barley and possibly emmer wheat have been identified on their grindstones.[3] Arrangements of stones showing signs of burning have been found near the huts at this site, and researchers believe that the products of grinding were cooked on top of hot stones. Before humans had heat-proof vessels in which porridges or gruels could be cooked, we must assume that they mixed the wild cereal flour with water, and formed flat cakes or breads. These could be baked on pre-heated stones in a cooking hearth. Why do we assume these breads were flat? This is the best shape when there is a single source of heat such as a bake-stone. The heat penetrates the centre of the dough quickly and evenly, especially if the flatbread is turned. It is also the most likely shape for dough that has not been leavened (e.g. by yeast) and cannot rise. So the first prerequisites for a primitive bread or cake – cereal flour and suitable cooking equipment – were met by 20,000 years ago, some 10,000 years before cultivation of cereals got underway.

Technology for handling cereals continued to improve over the intervening period. Around 9000 BC, a small rectangular room in one of the sixty buildings in the prehistoric settlement of Jerf el Ahmar in Syria caught fire and the pisé roof structure collapsed on to the floor.[4] The debris buried and preserved three saddle querns (grindstones shaped like saddles), two flat polished stone plates each 60 cm in diameter, three limestone basins, a small limestone bowl, several stone pounders and a hearth. Not only is this the earliest 'kitchen' yet found with its equipment *in situ*, but on one of the querns were two cakes made of finely ground seeds of a type of wild mustard (a *Brassica* or *Sinapis* species). Such seeds are rich in oil, as well as having a spicy flavour. We don't know whether these cakes were the residue from pressing out the oil, or whether they were made for consumption. The longer one was 8.5 x 3 x 3 cm, and the shorter 7 x 3 x 2.5 cm. In another part of the kitchen, the remains of coarsely milled wild barley seeds were found close to the limestone basins, in which they might have been soaked. Despite our uncertainty about the dishes made from these plants, we can say that the cooks at this early village produced oil-seed cakes in their kitchens and had stone bowls in which to soak and mix foodstuffs, well before the first appearance of pottery.

Butter is another ingredient that we regard as essential to a good fruit cake because it contributes to the 'mouth-feel' and keeping qualities. Evidence for the milking of cows, in the form of fatty residues with a distinctive carbon isotope signature, has been found in more than a hundred pieces of broken pots from northwestern Anatolia (Turkey) from sites dated to 6500–5000 BC in the early Neolithic period. Cattle bones found in these ancient villages confirm their dependence on herding.[5] Similar residues have been identified in pots from Southeast Europe and as far west as Britain by 4500 BC. In fact, dairying reached Britain with the very first farmers.[6] It seems that British farmers kept their butter fat in small pots. Throughout the cooler parts of Europe, butter became a significant source of storable fat for communities living in regions where traditional oil-producing plants such as olives could not be grown.

Although butter was a product of temperate regions, we should not forget that the fruits and nuts in our fruit cakes came chiefly from the warmer zones of the Eastern Mediterranean and Middle East. They include what we call raisins and currants (both of which are types of dried grape), and nuts, especially the almond. Nor should we ignore the wines added to early fruit cakes. Where were grapes first harvested, and where and when were they domesticated?

The distribution of the wild grapevine (*Vitis vinifera* subsp. *sylvestris*) stretched from Spain to Iran and as far north as the Caucasus. It prefers well-watered regions with warm summers and cool winters, growing along river valleys in close association with deciduous or semi-deciduous forest.[7] Whether wild or domesticated, the grapevine is a climber, using trees as a framework from which to seek the sun.

Humans had probably eaten grapes long before cultivation began around 4500 BC, even though the wild fruits are small and acidic. Because unpicked grape clusters sometimes dry on the vine in hot summers, gatherers would have been familiar with the keeping qualities of the shrivelled grapes we call raisins or currants. Recent chemical analyses of the residues in a pot recovered from Hajji Firuz, an early farming village in Iran's northern Zagros mountains, identified a calcium salt of tartaric acid, a component of grapes.[8] A tree resin was also present, indicating that the practice of making resinated wine (to prevent it from turning into vinegar) was already underway by 5000 BC. Since wine and/or spirits are commonly added to fruit cakes, we can tick off another precondition, the availability of fermented wines.

The grapes used to make the wine in Hajji Firuz were probably still morphologically wild and the site lay within the natural range of the wild grapevine. However, archaeologists have recovered pips and grape residues from later sites around 3500 BC that lie well beyond the range of the wild grapevine.[9] This indicates that cultivation and transport of seeds were underway, processes that would change the shape of grape pips and eventually the plant's mode of reproduction, to the point where domesticated varieties became dominant.

We now know that wine was made much earlier than previously thought, but what about raisins? Distinguishing the remains of raisins from the residues of grape-pressing is by no means straightforward, but the absence of artefacts essential to wine-making on an archaeological site strengthens any argument for raisin production. In the period known as the Early Bronze Age in the Middle East (starting around 3300 BC) there is good evidence for the production of raisins from the domesticated grape (*Vitis vinifera* subsp. *vinifera*). The site of Tell es-Sa'idiyeh in the Jordan valley revealed a small storeroom containing numerous artefacts such as ceramic jars, platters, bowls and jugs.[10] Fire had destroyed the structure, leaving behind not just these artefacts but also the remains of charred cereals (wheat and barley), legumes (lentils, chickpeas and fava beans) and fruits (grapes, figs, a pomegranate and some olives). Whole grapes were identified, as well as pips. The archaeobotanists working on the assemblage wanted to know whether the grapes had been fresh or pre-dried at the time of the fire. They heated some fresh modern grapes in a kiln but these disintegrated into pulp. Only charred modern raisins replicated the appearance of the ancient fruit. Under the scanning electron microscope they could see crystalline features on the ancient specimens, that may have formed as sugars deposited on the skins during the drying. It is very likely that the burnt storeroom included a quantity of raisins, appreciated for their sweetness in an era when only honey offered this quality in concentrated form. Archaeologist Naomi Miller has recently argued that the driving force behind the domestication of the grapevine was not the desire for wine (which could be made from wild grapes) but for sweeter fruit, including raisins.[11]

Nuts have been included in our rich fruit cakes for as long as we have had printed recipes. Although walnuts and hazelnuts are widely distributed in Europe, the almond (*Amygdalus communis*) has been the more common ingredient in rich cakes. It is not native to Europe, and is not easy to grow in northern regions like Britain. Perhaps that is the reason for its popularity in festive cakes – it is included because it is an expensive, imported luxury. What is known of the almond's origins? Unlike the grape, the wild almond kernel is not just bitter but very toxic if more than a few are consumed at once.[12] Two nut-shell fragments were found at the Ohalo II site, 19,000 years ago, but the almond's role at that time is unclear. A single dominant gene controls sweetness in almonds, so we must presume that at some point in prehistory a mutation occurred and humans discovered that the resulting almond tree had sweet kernels. It could not be propagated by cuttings, but only by seed. Given that the mutant sweet almond had to be pollinated by a bitter almond tree, since almonds are not commonly self-fertile, there was a 50:50 chance that a resulting seedling would be bitter. Where did this remarkable discovery occur? Answering this question has been complicated by the need to distinguish truly wild species from feral almond trees that are common between the Mediterranean and Central Asia. One view is that the bitter almond ancestor grew wild in the Levant countries (between Turkey and Jordan), while another places it between the Black Sea and the Caspian.[13] In either case, it would have overlapped with the wild grapevine. Archaeological finds of what appear to be domesticated almonds become common in the Levant in sites from the Bronze Age (3300–1200 BC). By that time, orchardists were not only selecting for sweetness and larger size in almonds, but also for thinner and softer shells. Large domesticated almonds were included among the foodstuffs in Tutankhamun's tomb, dated to 1325 BC.[14]

So far we have traced several key ingredients of our rich fruit cake back beyond the invention of writing: wheat, butter, raisins, wine and almonds. Each of these first appears in the Middle East, especially the northern regions. But there are four other items, eggs, citrus peel, sugar and spices, which have different places of origin and enter our story in the Classical era just over two thousand years ago.

Cakes and ingredients in ancient Greece and the Roman Empire

If we restrict our search to the eggs of the hen, then the wild ancestor of our domestic chicken was the red jungle fowl of Asia (*Gallus gallus*). It did not reach the Middle East until the end of the Bronze Age. A recent study of mitochondrial DNA (passed down through females) has supported the view that domestication took place in several places from India to China.[15] The earliest centre may have been China, with some Indian sites containing chicken bones by 2000–3000 BC.[16] The earliest evidence in the Middle East is from Tell Sweyhat in Syria (around 2400 BC). However, chickens were not common for another thousand years. Phoenician colonists played an important role in distributing them around the Mediterranean. The early domesticated fowl may have been kept for cock-fighting, while its plumage made it a showy bird for sacrifices. Evidence for laying hens finally appears a few hundred years before the Christian era. About 350 BC Aristotle included the hen in his study of the animal kingdom, noting that a large hen could lay up to sixty eggs per year, while the smaller Adrian hen could lay every day.[17] This observation tells us how far down the path of domestication the barnyard hen had travelled. Marcus Varro, a Roman writer on agriculture, described several different breeds in the first century BC, advising that some were only well suited for fighting or looking handsome. A good laying hen was 'usually of a reddish plumage, with black wing feathers', and full-bodied.[18]

The first of the citrus fruits from which peel is preserved reached the Mediterranean world a few centuries after the domestic hen. The citrus fruit peels that were added to rich fruit cakes in eighteenth-century England were from the citron (*Citrus medica*), orange (*C. sinensis*) and lemon (*C. limon*). Citrus species originated in Asia, between China and eastern India, with the orange and lemon likely to be natural hybrids rather than wild species.[19] In fact, the citron was a parent of the lemon. Of these three sources of peel, only the citron was known in ancient Italy.[20] It reached the Classical world, along with the peach and apricot, after Alexander opened up trade routes to the east. The Roman recipe book that appeared under the name of the famous gourmet, Apicius, contains brief instructions for preserving citron fruit by sealing it in a vessel. The juice may have served to strengthen vinegar or as a medicine,[21] but there is no confirmation in this late fourth-century AD cookbook that the peel was used in food. In any case, the Romans had no cane sugar in which to candy the peel and mollify its bitterness.

ORIGINS OF THE CHRISTMAS CAKE

Many of the ingredients of the later Christmas cake were available to cooks in ancient Rome and Greece, although the spices of exotic origin were used more for their perfume than for food. Clockwise from the top: butter, wheat grains and flour, egg, wine grapes, honey, almonds, dried grapes (currants and raisins), ground ginger, cinnamon sticks; centre: citron. Photo: Mary Browne.

The lack of cane (or beet) sugar for sweet cakes seems not to have hampered Greek or Roman cooks. Honey was widely produced and Apicius included it in a recipe for safflower cakes and in instructions for preserving fruit. Extensive use was made of sweet wines, including wines made from raisins. Such wines were important additions to fruit cakes more than a millennium later. However, the composition of honey, in which the sugars fructose and glucose predominate, means that in baking honey is not a straightforward substitute for cane sugar, which is primarily composed of sucrose. It was not until the Arabs established themselves around the Mediterranean that cane sugar became a regular, though expensive, commodity.

The final group of ingredients in our rich fruit cake are the spices. English recipes from the seventeenth and eighteenth centuries list cloves, cinnamon, mace, nutmeg and ginger, all derived from south or southeast Asia. Roman access to these spices improved in the first century BC when they took over control of the Greek trade routes to the Far East.[22] Cloves were first listed on a Roman customs list of AD 176, but these aromatic buds were imported not as foods, but as ingredients for incense and perfumes. Cinnamon was believed by the Romans to come from Ethiopia, when in fact it is the bark of several species of tree of the genus *Cinnamomum* native to southeast Asia. Despite its expense, Romans used it more widely than cloves – in perfumes, wines and some savoury dishes. While nutmeg and mace were missing from Roman cuisine, ginger was an ingredient in several of Apicius's recipes, although the Romans did not know its place of origin.[23]

Having worked our way through the ingredients of the rich fruit cake that eventually became our Christmas cake, we can now consider when conditions were right for its evolution. The conclusion is inescapable that Romans and Greeks had access to most of the ingredients, but that peoples living before the Classical era would not have been able to replicate the spicy flavour or texture of the fruit cake. They certainly had suitable wheat flour, dried raisins of various types, almonds, honey and sweet wine for several millennia, but few ancient cultures around the Mediterranean made butter, and even fewer had access to eggs until the Roman era. This does not mean that the Greeks and Romans didn't make cakes or sweet breads. Numerous named varieties are mentioned in Classical works, but did any have a relationship to our Christmas cake?

There is one possible candidate – Roman cakes called *mustacei* were made from bread wheat flour, moistened with freshly pressed grape juice (known as must) which still contained the crushed pips and grape skins; fats in the form of lard and cheese were added, along with anise and cumin seeds, and the grated bark of a bay twig. According to Cato's book on agriculture, which supplies the recipe, they were shaped and baked on a bed of bay leaves.[24] In appearance, these cakes would have looked speckled like an early fruit cake, especially if the grapes had purple skins. There is no explicit direction in Cato's recipe that they should be left to rise, but natural yeasts would have been present in the must and modern commentators think these cakes would have risen.[25] Roman breads were not leavened until the practice of making sourdough was introduced at the outbreak of the Third Macedonian War (171–168 BC).[26] Cato died in 149 BC so would have been aware of the new process. The significance of this speculation about yeast in must cakes needs to be explained. As will be seen when we describe Twelfth Night cakes in seventeenth-century England, these rich fruit cakes were leavened by ale yeast, and were essentially an enriched bread.

We know something about the occasions when must cakes were served from the poet Statius, who lived in the late first century AD. He described in verse the annual celebrations held in honour of Saturn each December. Saturnalia, as the festival was called, was like a carnival, opening with a sacrifice at the Temple of Saturn, followed by a public banquet. On the menu were 'soft cakes [*gaioli*] and honey cheese fritters ... and cake [*mustaceus*] made with wine must'.[27] Families also celebrated Saturnalia in their private homes with an interesting inversion of the roles of slaves and their masters – slaves wore their masters' robes and were served food by them.[28] Role-playing was a characteristic feature of Twelfth Night ceremonies held over a millennium later in Western Europe. It is claimed that many of the festivities connected to the medieval Christmas period are derived from the Roman winter festival of Saturnalia.[29] If role-playing continued for over a thousand years, then perhaps the festive cake associated with it was equally persistent.

What made must cakes a special treat in Rome was probably not the grape residue in the must or the spicy seeds, but the generous quantity of lard and cheese incorporated in them, contributing a smooth, rich 'mouth feel'. In the Roman provinces of Britain and northern Europe, this quality would be achieved by using butter. The Romans attempted to establish vineyards in Britain but had no long-term success, so the grape pips found in latrines in their military outposts and towns were probably not from fresh grapes but from raisins. Archaeobotanists working on these British and Dutch sites have identified a suite of plant foods imported from warmer parts of the Roman empire: figs were especially common, followed by olives and dried grapes, while almonds were present but rare.[30] Since imports are often considered luxury foods,[31] it is reasonable to propose that a festive cake for a Saturnalia feast in Londinium (London) would include some of these luxuries.

English cakes from the fourteenth to sixteenth centuries

The collapse of Roman power and the subsequent Dark Ages have left us with sparse records of British cookery until the late medieval period. A few clues can be assembled from literature, monastic account books and archaeology. From Chaucer's *Canterbury Tales* comes the story of a cheating miller who told his wife to make a cake with the half-bushel of flour he had stolen from two naïve clerks. If the fourteenth-century bushel of southeast England was 56 lbs, then a cake requiring 28 lbs of flour was as large as any made in the seventeenth century.[32] Though the figure may be a literary exaggeration, the story suggests that large cakes existed at that time. No cake recipes are found in late medieval cookbooks, probably because these were written by and for cooks in wealthy households, and not by the professional bakers or pastry-cooks who made the cakes.[33] However the ingredients in other recipes include all the key elements of a seventeenth-century rich fruit cake – from the basics (wheat flour, eggs, butter, and ale yeast) to the luxury imports (almonds, raisins, currants, sugar, cinnamon, cloves, ginger, nutmeg, mace, and Spanish wine).[34] Grape pips derived from raisins have been recovered from late medieval York, while figs and mace have been identified in the fifteenth-century drains of Paisley Abbey in Scotland.[35] It would be unwise to assume from our lack of cake recipes from this long period that a festive cake containing imported luxury ingredients did not exist.

Recipe books are more prevalent in the sixteenth century, although they continue the focus on meat or Lenten dishes served in well-to-do households. By the Elizabethan period, the lady of the house was responsible for preserving exotic fruits; these books often contain a selection of recipes for candying orange peel (probably from the bitter Seville orange that was so valued for marmalade), as well as the peel of lemon and 'pomecitron' (citron fruit).[36] Given the prevalence of these recipes, we might expect candied peel to become more common in baking. A recipe exists for 'A buttered Loafe', originally published in 1584, which gives an indication of the range of spices then available: 'Take very fine flowre and yolks of Egs, sweet butter, yest, cloves, mace, sugar, sinamon, ginger, and woork it togither and make them in little loves …'.[37] It is clear that these loaves were raised by the action of yeast, as was their daily bread. We need to remind ourselves that the fruit cake of the seventeenth century was also leavened by yeast and the practice would continue into the eighteenth and nineteenth centuries.

William Shakespeare contributes some important information on the elusive Elizabethan cake. In two of his plays, *Twelfth Night* and *King Henry the Eighth*, he couples 'cakes and ale' when referring to festival fare, which would have included that served during the revelries of the twelve days of Christmas.[38] From the play *Troilus and Cressida*,[39] we find that Shakespeare was well aware of the steps involved in preparing a cake from wheat flour, spelling out the need for patience at each stage, from grinding the flour, bolting it (to make it as fine and white as possible), leavening it (with yeast), kneading, making up the cake, heating the oven, baking the cake and cooling it. In *The Taming of the Shrew*,[40] having your project fail is likened to finding that your 'cake is dough', perhaps because it did not have long enough in the oven, or was made with contaminated flour.

Curiously, the play *Twelfth Night* is not about this festival, although the audience would have seen a connection through the allusions to 'cakes and ale', role-playing, masquerading, and the heavy drinking of Sir Toby Belch and Sir Andrew Aguecheek. So how did the play get its name? One scholar has argued that its first production was in honour of Queen Elizabeth and the Duke of Bracciano on Twelfth Night in 1601, while others think the content would have been regarded as improper in front of the Queen.[41] The earliest reference to an actual performance is from 2 February 1602. Whatever the explanation, we know from many sources that the celebrations of the twelve days of Christmas were as unruly under the Tudors as they would become again after the Restoration of the Monarchy in 1660.[42]

We have now reached the seventeenth century, when for the first time we have recipes that are likely to have been followed in making the twelfth cake, together with some accounts of the celebrations. From what we have described already, it is clear that the twelfth cake did not suddenly emerge in the seventeenth century, but has a history that may go back several centuries, if not two thousand years. The strength of the case for such great antiquity depends on the continuity of the tradition of Saturnalia from the Roman era, through its transformation into a mid-winter Christian festival. Although the church adjusted this festival's place in the calendar, many elements of the Saturnalia kept reappearing – too many for coincidence. We should like to think that the rich fruit cake was also part of this tradition.

2

In search of the seventeenth-century twelfth cake

> Now, now the mirth comes
> With the cake full of plums,
> Where Beane's the *King* of the sport here;
> Beside we must know,
> The Pea also
> Must revell, as *Queene*, in the Court here.
>
> – from Robert Herrick's poem *Twelfe night, or* King *and* Queene, written about 1630–40[1]

This verse needs some explanation. For a start, Robert Herrick's cake wasn't full of plums, but of dried fruits like currants and raisins. The word 'plum' applied originally to both fresh plums and the dried plums that we now call prunes. But by the early seventeenth century, the 'plum' in both 'plum cake' and 'plum pudding' had extended its meaning to include dried fruit in general, especially raisins and currants. Herrick's cake also contained two tokens: a bean and a pea. Whoever found the bean in his or her portion acted the role of king for the rest of the Twelfth Night festivities, while the finder of the pea became queen. At court, even royalty joined in the ensuing rollicking role-playing.

Herrick refers to a single cake, which must have been of considerable size. Thanks to Ben Jonson, Shakespeare's contemporary and rival, we have some more details from a masque that he wrote for the Christmas celebrations at the court of King James the First in 1616. Masques were short allegorical entertainments that used professional actors, singers and dancers for the major roles, but included courtiers in non-speaking parts. Costuming and sets were highly elaborate. Ben Jonson's masque for this occasion was called *Christmas, His Masque*, and began with Father Christmas introducing his ten children: Mis-rule, Caroll, and Minc'd Pie through to Wassall and Baby-Cake. The latter two are the most interesting, in the light of Shakespeare's allusions to 'cakes and ale'. 'Wassall', or wassail, was warm spiced ale served in a large bowl with the pulp of roasted apples floating on top. 'Baby-Cake' came at the rear of the procession of Christmas's children: 'Last, Baby-cake, that an end doth make/Of Christmas' merry ...', a reference to Twelfth Night marking the end of the Christmas season. He was dressed like a boy, wearing 'a fine long coat ... his usher bearing a great cake, with a bean and a pease'.[2]

Ben Jonson's and Robert Herrick's clues from the first half of the seventeenth century raise the question: where are the recipes for such large fruit-filled cakes as they describe? Or were these great cakes still made outside the household and therefore not represented in the cookbooks? Publishing in seventeenth-century England must have been affected by the dramatic upheavals that engulfed the country. Within two years of James the First's accession to the throne, the gunpowder plot marked the onset of rising political tensions. His son, Charles the First, faced civil war from 1642, ending with his execution in 1649. But despite Puritan laws to curb Christmas celebrations (including mass), in place from 1644 to 1660, we find a recipe for a very large cake in a cookbook entitled *A True Gentlewomans Delight,* published in 1653. Not surprisingly, the publisher is identified only as 'W. J., Gent[leman]' and no author is named.[3] Elizabeth David argued convincingly that the recipes were probably from a relatively modest household.[4] One of the two cake recipes included in this book is consistent with this view, remembering that even modest households were large until the twentieth century. It was clearly written for an experienced cook, since it omitted the mixing instructions:

> *To make a Cake.*
> Take half a peck of flower, two pound and a half of Currans, three or four Nutmegs, one pound of Almond paste, two pound of Butter, and one pint of Cream, three spoonfuls of Rose-water, three quarters of a pound of Sugar, half a pint of Sack, a quarter of a pint of Yest, and six Eggs, so make it, and bake it.[5]

The other recipe would have made an enormous cake, well-suited for a surreptitious Twelfth Night celebration, though the recipe may well have been passed down from less restrictive times:

> *To make a Spice Cake.*
> Take one bushel of Flower, six pound of Butter, eight pound of Currans, two pints of Cream, a pottle of Milk, half a pint of good Sack, two pound of Sugar, two ounces of Mace, one ounce of Nutmegs, one ounce of Ginger, twelve yolkes, two whites, take the Milk and Cream, and stirre it all the time that it boyles, put your Butter into a bason, and put your hot seething Milk to it, and melt all the Butter in it, and when it is bloud-warm temper the Cake, put not your Currans in till you have made the paste, you must have some Ale yest and forget not Salt.[6]

This recipe is the largest we have found – a bushel of flour weighed 56 lb (25.4 kg) – so mixing would have been very hard work. If made in the same way as most modern Christmas cakes – by creaming the butter and sugar and beating in the rest of the ingredients – it would require all the equipment of a commercial kitchen to have any chance of success. What rendered it feasible for a seventeenth-century cook was that it was mixed in the same way as bread, and indeed its proportion of flour to other ingredients is typical of a rich bread. Even so, the correct order of operations would have been vital, and they are inadequately set out in this recipe. The ale yeast would have been set to work on a small portion of the mixture before the eggs, milk and cream were added. The currants were probably kneaded into the dough after the first rising. Success with this cake required the skills and knowledge of a baker.

Another cookbook that was published in London during the interregnum (1649–60) was entitled *The Queens Closet Opened*; it was claimed to be a transcription of the personal recipes of the exiled widow of Charles the First, Queen Henrietta Maria. Once again we have only the initials of the compiler, W. M., who described himself as a late servant of the queen.[7] Two cake recipes were included, one for small, plain cakes containing currants, and the other entitled '*To make a Cake the way of the Royal Princess the Lady* Elizabeth *daughter to King* Charles *the First*'.[8] Starting with half a peck of flour (7 lb), this recipe made a more substantial cake, but it was hardly a rich cake, with only 4 lb of currants making up the fruit, lacking almonds and wine, and with spices represented only by nutmeg. Although the first appearance of this royalist cookbook was at the height of the interregnum, and the Queen was a Catholic living in exile, it became highly popular, with numerous editions.

Samuel Pepys's twelfth cake

The restoration of the monarchy in 1660 meant that Christmas celebrations and revelry could also return. But in London, at least, the decade would bring both catastrophic plague (1665) and fire (1666). Despite these trials, the people resumed the celebration of Twelfth Night with enthusiasm. The famous diarist Samuel Pepys kept his journal over this decade and left us some more details about the twelfth cake and modification of the rituals associated with it. Even before Charles the Second was installed as King, Pepys and his relatives celebrated Twelfth Night on 6 January 1660 at the house of his cousin Stradwick, 'Where, after a good supper ... we had a brave cake brought us, and in the choosing, Pall [Pepys' sister Pauline] was queen and Mr. Stradwick was king'.⁹ The following year, 6 January fell on a Sunday so the celebrations were deferred by a day. Pepys gave his servants twelve pence (12d.) to buy a cake, then left with his wife for the theatre, and thence to his cousin's:

> And after a good supper we have an excellent cake, where the mark for the Queene was cut; and so there were two queens, my wife and Mrs. Ward; and the King being lost, they chose the Doctor to be King, so we made him send for some wine; and then home.¹⁰

On 6 January 1665, Pepys wrote, perhaps peevishly, that his wife had

> designed much mirth today to end Christmas with among her servants. At night home, being Twelfenight, and there chose my piece of cake, but went up to my vial and then to bed, leaving my wife and people up at their sports, which they continue till morning, not coming to bed at all.¹¹

Mrs Pepys shared her cake with her servants: maid (Mary) Mercer, chambermaid Bess, cook-maid Jane, 'little girl' Susan and Samuel's boy servant Tom Edwards. Did Jane make this cake? We know that she baked one three years later in January 1668. By this time, Pepys was financially secure and seemingly more confident of entertaining in his own home. It was there he held the Twelfth Night party. After dancing and singing till about 12 or 1 am, he provided 'a good sack-posset ... and an excellent Cake, cost me near 20s. of our Jane's making, which was cut into twenty pieces'.¹² In this pre-metric age, twenty shillings (20s.) made one pound (£1) and twelve pence (12d.) made one shilling (1s.).

It was common for guests to tear open their portion of the cake in order to find a token, leading no doubt to much waste. Samuel Pepys, who was a hard-working administrator for the Navy, adopted a much less-destructive method of choosing the king and queen for Twelfth Night in 1669:

> and in the evening I did bring out my cake, a noble cake, and there cut into pieces, with wine and good drink; and after a new fashion, to prevent spoiling the cake, did put so many titles into a hat and so drow [drew] cuts; and I was Queene and The Turner, King ...¹³

Other popular characters from contemporary comedies were included in the draw. In this way the twelfth cake began to be appreciated as a high-quality and expensive cake, not just as a vehicle for tokens. This change also meant that the cake did not have to be completely consumed (or broken up) on just one occasion.

What recipe did Jane, Samuel Pepys's cook-maid, use for making the expensive twelfth cake served in 1668? Her employer was a noted book collector and his library survives intact in Cambridge. Apart from several cookbooks published after the 1660s, it includes two slender recipe books that may have been acquired while the diary was being kept: *The Compleat Cook*,[14] and *The Gentlewoman's Cabinet Unlocked*.[15] The latter has a promising fruit cake recipe:

> *To make a good Cake*
> Take half a Peck [7 lb] of Flower, three pound of Butter, some Nutmeg, Cloves and Mace, Cinnamon, Ginger, and a pound of sugar[,] mingle these well together with the flower, then take four pound of Currants well washed, picked, and dryed in a warm cloth, a little Ale-Y[ea]st, twelve Eggs, a quart of Cream or good Milk warm'd, half a pint of Sack, a quarter of Rose-water, knead it well and let it be very lith, lay it in a warm cloth, and let it lye half an hour against the fire, then make it up with the white of an Egg beaten with a little Butter, Rose-water, and Sugar: put it into the Oven; and let it stand an hour and a half.[16]

In quantity, the resulting cake would certainly have provided twenty generous pieces. Is there any way we can test the theory that Jane used this particular recipe? From Pepys's diary we know that it cost him 'near 20s.'. We decided to calculate the cost of the ingredients needed to make up this recipe, together with six other fruit cake recipes then in circulation, to see which was the best fit in both size and cost. Thanks to the efforts of dedicated economic historians, we have a reasonable idea of the cost of commodities in England at various periods of history. For our purpose we used prices for cake ingredients recorded between 1665 and 1669 (Table 2.1).[17]

Of the seven fruit cake recipes in these recipe books, two are enormous – one starting with 56 lb of flour, and the other 28 lb, far too large for the twenty guests for whom Pepys's cake was baked; another is too small; the other four called for 8 lb or 7 lb of flour. The very large cakes cost nearly 24s. each, but we can discount them for their excessive size. The three medium-sized cakes with secure dates would have cost from nearly 6s. to 8s. each, un-iced. The cake from Pepys's book would have cost considerably more than these because we have to allow for the spices, for which no quantities were given. But if we guess that the spice quantities were similar to those of No. 5, Robert May's '*To make a Cake otherways*' (1660), then the cost of the cake would rise to 11s. 10d., un-iced. Given the price of refined sugar in 1666, 15d. per pound, this cake when iced would clearly have been more expensive than the others. But the total is still not near 20s.

There is a possibility that Pepys's estimate of the cost of his cake was inaccurate, exaggerated perhaps to impress his guests. Alternatively, Jane, the cook-maid, may have used another recipe, but it is hard to imagine how a medium-sized cake could

Table 2.1. Quantities of bulk ingredients and estimated total cost of seven cakes that could have served the Pepys household as twelfth cakes in the 1660s.[18]

Recipe & Date	Flour (lb)	Butter (lb)	Currants (lb)	Cost in shillings & pence
1 *To make a Spice Cake* (1653)	56	6	8	23s. 9d.
2 *To make a Cake* (1653)	7	2	2.5	8s.
3 *To make a Cake the way of the Royal Princess…* (1655)	7	1.5	4	5s. 11d.
4 *To make an extraordinary good Cake* (1660)	28	3	14	23s. 11d.
5 *To make a Cake otherways* (1660)	8	0	3	7s. 3d.
6 *To make a good Cake* (1664?) [in Pepys's library]	7	3	4	8s. 10d. + spices
7 *To make a Cake with Almonds* (1664)	1.5	1	some	2s. 6d. + spices & fruit

have enough of the most expensive ingredients (e.g. musk, mace, cloves, cinnamon) to raise the cost of the cake to 'near 20s.' without making the cake excessively spicy. Only saffron (at 7s. per ounce) could bridge the cost gap, but too much would make the cake taste bitter. Perhaps Elizabeth Pepys inflated the cost of the cake to get some more housekeeping money from her husband. Was this one occasion when the meticulous Samuel Pepys didn't check her kitchen accounts?[19]

Samuel was in the habit of inspecting Elizabeth's accounts on what seems to have been a monthly basis. The diaries mention four occasions when he became angry at the discrepancies he found. On the first, in September 1664, Elizabeth 'confessed that when she doth misse a sum, she doth add something to other things to make it [up]'.[20] A few months later, Samuel found a discrepancy of 7s. In the ensuing row, he called her 'beggar' and criticised her friends. Immediately afterwards he went to his office and went over his own monthly accounts, finding that he was worth £1270, for which he thanked God![21] In May 1666, he found a mistake amounting to 20s. in the kitchen accounts, which made him 'mighty angry'.[22] Later that year, he begrudged Elizabeth's purchase of a lace handkerchief and pinner (a close-fitting cap), not on the grounds of price but as a matter of principle – she had not sought permission.[23]

If Elizabeth subsequently inflated the cost of the twelfth cake by 7s. to obtain a little spending money, she has our sympathy! Speculation aside, even at an estimated 13s., this cake would have cost as much as the daily wages of fourteen building labourers. It was a rich cake in terms of ingredients, and an expensive one – for example, in 1668 the cost of an ounce of cloves was more than a farm labourer would earn in a day.[24] We believe the recipe from *The Gentlewoman's Cabinet Unlocked* would have been perfectly suitable for use as a twelfth cake.

Because the 'good Cake' recipe in Samuel Pepys's cookbook fails to list quantities for the spices, we decided to look for a better example to represent the seventeenth-century twelfth cake in a modern kitchen. The recipe we chose, *To make an excellent Cake*, was one of five fruit cake recipes found in the papers of Sir Kenelm Digby.[25]

TO MAKE AN EXCELLENT CAKE

To a Peck of fine flower, take six pounds of fresh butter, which must be tenderly melted, ten pounds of Currants, of Cloves and Mace, half an ounce of each, an ounce of Cinnamon, half an ounce of Nutmegs, four ounces of Sugar, one pint of Sack mixed with a quart at least of thick barm of Ale (as soon as it is settled, to have the thick fall to the bottom, which will be, when it is about two days old) half a pint of Rose-water; half a quarter of an ounce of Saffron. Then make your paste, strewing the spices, finely beaten, upon the flower: Then put the melted butter (but even just melted) to it; then the barm, and other liquors: and put it in the oven well heated presently. For the better baking of it, put it in a hoop, and let it stand in the oven one hour and half. You Ice the Cake with the whites of two Eggs, a small quantity of Rose-water, and some Sugar.[26]

Digby's collection of recipes was published posthumously by his laboratory assistant George Hartman in 1669. They would have sold readily, for Sir Kenelm was a seventeenth-century celebrity who had led a remarkably glamorous life. In 1606, his father was hung, drawn and quartered after being implicated in the gunpowder plot – Kenelm was only two years old. At the age of fourteen, he travelled with his uncle to Spain on diplomatic business. As a young man he lived in Italy, then returned to England to secretly marry Venetia Stanley, the beautiful mistress of Edward Sackville. She died suddenly in 1633, so Sir Kenelm commissioned a death-bed portrait of her by Van Dyck – his enemies spread the rumour that he'd poisoned her. He was a Herculean figure, fluent in six languages, an avid book- and manuscript-collector, and scientist. What interests us particularly is that he clearly loved food and wrote down recipes most of his life, though not with the intention of publishing them – that was Hartman's idea. Sir Kenelm died in 1665, so the recipes must pre-date the Great Plague of that year.

1

EXCELLENT CAKE

Adapted from 'To Make an Excellent Cake', in *The Closet of the Eminently Learned Sir Kenelme Digbie K*^t. [1669].

The first task was to translate the seventeenth-century recipe. For example, what is a 'peck of fine flower'? Although British measurements varied depending on region, the most likely equivalent of a peck in modern terms is 14 pounds or 6.35 kilograms. 'Flower' is the seventeenth-century spelling of 'flour'. Obviously this would make an enormous cake. Our version is scaled to one tenth. Although yeast is used as a raising agent, the flavour and texture is cake-like rather than what you would expect from a rich, fruited bread. 'Barm of ale' was the source of yeast – we have used bread makers' yeast. A mixture of stone-ground wholemeal and white bread flour is used to replicate household flour of the period. 'Rich Cream Wine' or sweet sherry is the best substitute for 'sack'– a wine reported to taste like a modern sweet fortified wine.

400 g currants
5 tablespoons 'Rich Cream Wine' or sweet sherry
½ teaspoon saffron strands
300 g white bread flour (an additional 100 g is used later)
200 g stone-ground wholemeal flour or roller-milled flour
¼ teaspoon ground cloves
¼ teaspoon ground mace
¼ teaspoon freshly grated nutmeg

½ teaspoon ground cinnamon
250 g butter, melted
1 teaspoon rosewater
100 g white bread flour
½ teaspoon salt
2 teaspoons sugar
2 tablespoons 'Surebake' or 'Breadmaker Yeast'
80 ml cold water
80 ml boiling water

In a small bowl, combine the currants, wine and ground saffron strands (place the strands in a dessertspoon and use a teaspoon to crush to a fine powder). Cover and leave to macerate overnight.

Next day, combine the 300 g of white bread flour and the wholemeal (if using roller-milled flour, sift and discard the large particles of bran left behind in the sifter) with the spices. Leave in a warm place.

Line a 23 cm-round cake pan with baking paper.

Cut the butter into cubes and melt in a small saucepan over gentle heat. Allow to cool to blood heat before adding the rosewater.

In a large warm bowl combine the 100 g of white bread flour with the salt, sugar and yeast. Stir to mix thoroughly. Boil some water in an electric jug or kettle. Add the 80 ml of cold water to the flour mixture, followed immediately with the 80 ml boiling water. Beat vigorously to form a smooth batter. Leave to stand for 5 minutes in a warm place.

Add the currants and soaking liquid to the batter followed by the warmed flours and spices and lastly the melted butter. Knead into a soft dough incorporating any stray currants. A large electric mixer and dough hook will speed this process (about 5 minutes). Shape the dough into a round ball and place in the prepared cake pan. Use your fingers to push the dough to fit the tin evenly.

Cover the cake pan with a plate and leave to rise in a warm place for 1 ½ hours. Preheat the oven to 200°C with a rack in the middle position. If you have a pizza stone place this on the rack before heating the oven (this will imitate the brick floor of a seventeenth-century bread oven).

Place the cake in the oven and bake for 10 minutes. Lower the temperature to 160° C and continue to bake for a further hour. If the top starts to brown excessively before the time is up cover the surface with a doubled piece of brown paper. Insert a wire cake tester to check that the middle is cooked. When cool, wrap in greaseproof paper and store in an airtight container.

ROYAL ICING

1 egg white	½ teaspoon glycerine (this helps
1 teaspoon strained lemon juice	prevent excessive hardening)
2–2 ½ cups sifted icing sugar	

Beat the egg white and lemon juice until frothy. Slowly add the icing sugar beating vigorously until the desired consistency is reached (you may not need all the icing sugar). Add the glycerine and mix in thoroughly.

Cover the cake with a good layer of icing allowing a little to flow down the sides in few places. Let the icing become firm before storing the cake in an airtight container.

Allow a little of the royal icing to flow down the sides.

Gentle heat will help the dough to rise.

Another private recipe collection, made by scientist John Evelyn (1620–1706), a contemporary and correspondent of Samuel Pepys, was published for the first time only in 1997.[27] Evelyn kept a diary for many more years than Pepys, but in his lifetime was known for his published books on topics such as architecture, air pollution, forestry, gardening, town planning, and the art of making salads. His recipes sometimes included the names of the donors, a reminder to us that recipes are not only an invitation to cook, but are also items that are gifted and received, reinforcing bonds within families and between friends. John Evelyn's collection included ten that we would classify as fruit cakes. They cover a range of cake sizes, from those starting with a peck of flour (14 lb in weight) in the case of *'an Excellent Rich Cake'* and *'the lady Harringtons cake'*, down to *'a light plum cake'* with only 3 lb of flour. Collecting recipes does not mean that John Evelyn cooked them; however, he may have taken as keen an interest in what was prepared by his wife and his kitchen staff as Samuel Pepys.

The seventeenth-century twelfth cake

From these and other sources,[28] we have compared twenty-four recipes for fruit cakes, all but one from the second half of the seventeenth century. We have presented the case, with the help of Samuel Pepys, that some are recipes for twelfth cakes, though we cannot be certain that all served that function, since none were given that specific title. Some of the variation in these cakes has already been mentioned, especially that of size. The recipe for the largest cake (*'to make a Spice Cake'*, published in 1653) called for a bushel of flour, weighing 56 lb, while that *'to make a light plum cake'* (probably collected several decades later) required only 3 lb. The remaining recipes show a strong preference for two weights, 14 lb (seven recipes) and 7 lb (seven recipes), corresponding to the measures known as the peck and the half-peck. By our standards, these are all very large amounts of flour to put in a single cake.

Because these cakes were made by bread-making techniques, all of them were raised with yeast. This was usually described as ale-yeast or barm, an indication of the prevalence of brewing in English towns and households. The quantities range from a ¼ pint to 3 pints. Yeast quantities didn't need to be exact, since yeasts multiply if supplied with warmth and food, and provided enough rising time is available they can raise a large amount of dough. The recipes are often vague about the sequence of operations. Some specify two risings, with the yeast in the ale-barm set to work on half the flour at the beginning, while others put all the ingredients together.

ICING FESTIVE CAKES IN THE SEVENTEENTH CENTURY

Although there are few recipes for fruit cake from the first half of the seventeenth century, icings are well represented, because they were applied to a range of dishes. The art of 'encrusting or adorning with crystallizations of sugar', as the *Oxford English Dictionary* defines the term 'icing' was highly esteemed in the sixteenth century for what the Elizabethans called 'banqueting dishes'.[1] Many different items were iced, from tarts to biscuits, and several recipes have survived.[2] One in particular is relevant to the evolution of Christmas cakes, which in their 'traditional' form have two layers of icing – almond icing underneath a layer of white royal icing. Though there is no evidence that this combination was applied to cakes in the seventeenth century, it was the key feature of this recipe published by Sir Hugh Plat in 1602:

To make a Marchpane.

> Take two poundes of Almonds being blanched and dryed in a sieve over the fire, beat them in a stone mortar, and when they be small mixe with them two pounde of sugar beeing finely beaten, adding two or three spoonefulls of Rosewater, and that will keep your almonds from oiling: when your paste is beaten fine, drive it thin with a rowling pin, and so lay it on a bottome of wafers, then raise up a little edge on the side, & so bake it, then yce it with Rosewater and sugar, then put it in the oven againe, and when you see your [marchpane] is risen up and drie, then take it out of the Oven and garnish it with pretty conceipts, as birds & beasts being caste out of standing moldes.[3]

Marchpane was the original English name for marzipan or almond paste. Wafers were very thin cakes, like waffles, made of flour, cream, egg yolks, spices and rosewater, worked into a paste and baked on hot irons.[4]

While twelfth cakes were still torn apart at Twelfth Night parties, there was little point in icing them or applying elaborate decorations, but as this practice declined in the second half of the seventeenth century, there was no reason why they should be treated differently from other expensive items that were iced. Given the fact that Sir Hugh Plat's marchpane was decorated with birds and beasts, it is not surprising that iced cakes were later richly ornamented. Frustratingly, however, there is no description from seventeenth-century sources that their fruit cakes were decorated, nor is there evidence for the underlying layer of almond icing.[5]

Five of Sir Kenelm Digby's fruit cake recipes included instructions for a single layer of icing. Four specified fine or double-refined sugar in amounts from ¾ lb pound to 1 ½ lb. From two to five egg whites were used, along with rosewater or orange-flower water for flavouring. The method was simple, though laborious. The recipe 'To make a Plumb-Cake' ended as follows:

> Then to Ice it, take a pound and half of double refined Sugar beaten and searsed [sieved]; The whites of three Eggs new-laid, and a little Orange-flower-water, with a little musk and Ambergreece, beaten and searsed, and put to your sugar; Then strew your Sugar into the Eggs, and beat it in a stone Mortar with a Wooddden Pestle, till it be as white as snow, which will be by that time the Cake is baked; Then draw it to the ovens mouth, and drop it on, in what form you will; let it stand a little again in the oven to harden.[6]

This recipe clearly belongs to the lineage of what we call royal icing, though that name would not be applied to it until the nineteenth century. Most of the other seventeenth-century recipes for icing follow the same method of beating the whites, flavouring and sugar until very white, then hardening the icing by returning the cake to the oven, taking care not to destroy the snow effect with too much heat. Just one recipe dispensed with the egg white and boiled the sugar and a little rosewater to 'candy height' and then poured it over the cake.[7]

Even though it was not yet on top of cakes, marchpane continued to be popular. It had been widely used in Europe from the fourteenth century and both of its names (marchpane and marzipan) are thought to be derived from the name of the Persian city Martaban from which sweetmeats and preserves were exported to the West in jars.[8] John Evelyn's recipe book contained two recipes for 'Royall Marchpane', one of which departed from Sir Hugh Plat's version by including beaten egg whites with the almonds, rosewater and sugar.[9] This addition is found in the earliest known recipe for almond icing for a cake, printed in 1769.[10] All told, the skills of working sugar were in place well before the seventeenth century, and cooks were already in the habit of icing small cakes with almond paste. The ancestral recipes for royal icing and almond icing were already in circulation, but as yet only one of them had been applied to the forerunner of our Christmas cake.

(26)
Cakes

A Batter Cake

Take 6 pound of currants 5 pound of flower an ounce of Cloves and mace a little cinnamon halfe a pound of pounded and blanchd Almonds halfe an ounce of Nuttmeggs 3 quarters of a pound of Sliced Cittron Lemon and orange peile halfe a pint of Sack a little Honey water a quart of good Ale yest a pint of creame and a pound and an halfe of butter melted therein mix it together in a Kittle over a Soft fier Stirring it with your hands till it is very Smooth Lett it be as hott as you can bear it put it in a hoop with a paper at the bottom.

The Iceing

Beat and Sift a pound Of double refin'd Sugar and put to it the Whites of 4 Eggs putt in butt one att a time with halfe a Spoonfull of Honey water beat them in a bason with a Silver Spoon till it is very light.

Pupils at Edward Kidder's cookery classes, held in London early in the eighteenth century used hand-written recipes such as this 'Batter Cake', a yeast-raised bread-cake, typical of seventeenth-century fruit cakes. The copyist omitted the sugar – based on a 1732 version of this recipe, the amount would have been ½ lb.
H. Leach Collection.

Butter and/or cream contributed richness to these cakes. All but two of the twenty-four recipes called for butter, and these exceptions contained cream. It was important to mix the butter into the flour very evenly. Two methods were employed: rubbing the butter into the flour is specified in seven recipes; melting the butter is found in fifteen. Not a single recipe mentions creaming the butter and sugar, as we do today. This difference relates directly to the proportions of butter, sugar, and flour in the seventeenth-century cake compared to the modern fruit cake. Because this early cake was essentially a fruit bread, it had a low proportion of butter compared to flour, and an even lower proportion of sugar. We calculated these ratios as follows, adding one of our favourite twentieth-century cakes for comparison (Table 2.2).[29]

The most significant difference between the seventeenth-century 'bread-cakes' and those that would gain popularity in the eighteenth century and continue to the

Table 2.2. Ratios between weights of butter and flour, butter and sugar, and butter and dried fruit in 22 seventeenth-century fruit cakes, with a twentieth-century Christmas cake for comparison. (Note: The inclusion of cream would have contributed further milk fats to these cakes, but since we do not know the exact composition of seventeenth-century cream, we decided not to combine the butter and cream in our calculations. We guess that a pint of cream, the quantity called for in seven of the recipes, may have contained 4–6 ounces of butter fat.)

Ratio (by weight)	Highest	Lowest	Mean	20th century cake
Butter: Flour	1: 9.33	1: 1.5	1: 3.98	1: 1.25
Butter: Sugar	1: 0.75	1: 0.04	1: 0.34	1: 1
Butter: Fruit	1: 5	1: 1.25	1: 2.86	1: 4.88

present, lies in the proportion of sugar. Price must have been an important factor. While butter cost Elizabeth Pepys around 8d. per pound in 1666, and 6d. in 1668, the refined sugar most suitable for the cake would have cost her 15d. per pound.[30] Today the price of butter is five times that of sugar!

With ale-yeast providing the leavening for the seventeenth-century fruit cakes, there was no need to call on egg whites to hold air incorporated by whipping. In fact, only five of the twenty-four recipes used the same number of whites as yolks. It was not that they were beating them separately, just removing about half of the whites when they opened the eggs. There would have been plenty of recipes for using the left-over whites – although meringues had not yet been introduced from France, snows and other egg-white desserts were very popular. As for the yolks, they would have contributed both colour and thickening to the cake. However, eggs were not mandatory – four of John Evelyn's cake recipes did not include them.

Although there were no liquid essences available in the seventeenth and eighteenth centuries, these cakes would not have lacked flavour. Rosewater was present in half the cakes, and orange-flower water in one other. Sack was as common as rosewater, though it is difficult for us to assess its taste. The term was applied to strong, sweet (probably fortified) white wines from the Canary Islands and Spain (including Malaga and Jerez, from which the later name 'sherry' is derived).

As in today's Christmas cakes, dry spices contributed significantly to cake flavour in the seventeenth century. Cloves, mace, cinnamon and nutmeg were very commonly specified, despite their prices. In 1666, mace was the most expensive at

13 ½d. per ounce, with cloves costing 11 ¼d. Although no cake used more than two ounces of mace, that was more than the daily wages of two building labourers. Whole nutmegs (from the same tree species) were less than half the price of mace. As for saffron, it was so expensive (7s. per ounce) that only three recipes recommended it.

Seventeenth-century cooks had less choice of dried or candied fruit than we do. All of their fruit cake recipes contained currants, but only a third also called for raisins. The quantities seem large, ranging from 2 ½ lb to 14 lb of currants (with a mean of nearly 7 lb), but given the amount of flour in these cakes, they were much less dense than our cakes. The ratio of flour to fruit in the cake with 14 lb of fruit is 1: 0.5, whereas Helen's favourite twentieth-century cake has a flour-to-fruit ratio of 1: 3.9. It has nearly eight times more fruit than its distant ancestor.

Candied peel is listed in only six recipes. Its appearance in the cakes coincides with the proliferation of candying recipes in contemporary recipe books. In *The Queens Closet Opened*,[31] the recipe for *Syrup of Citron Peels* concludes with the prescient remark 'It defendeth from the Plague'. No such claim was made for dates. They were included in only three of the recipes, perhaps because they were relatively expensive, being more than twice the price of currants. Per pound, dates cost as much as almonds (18d. per lb). We think of almonds as an essential ingredient of a Christmas cake, but they were present in only six of the seventeenth-century cakes, where they were always used in 'beaten' or ground form. Cooks did the pulverising themselves, adding rosewater to stop the almonds oiling during the process.

Two other ingredients, musk and ambergris, were optional extras in four of the cakes. Musk was derived from a glandular secretion of the male musk-deer, while ambergris formed in the intestines of the sperm whale. Both were used in the manufacture of perfumes, and their presence in seventeenth-century cookbooks is considered a survival from sixteenth-century or earlier cuisines.[32] Today they are illegal or unobtainable.[33] In the 1670s, cooks paid 4d. per grain of musk, so it is not surprising that it soon vanished from the recipes.

The final question must be this: would we recognise these seventeenth-century fruit cakes as the ancestors of our Christmas cakes? Obviously the occasion for serving them has moved to the start of the Christmas season, and some radical changes have occurred in their methods of mixing and proportions. But evolution can accelerate or slow down, depending on the stability of the environment. In the seventeenth century, we have seen the making of twelfth cakes extend to home kitchens, with recipes increasing in the cookbooks written for women like Elizabeth Pepys and her cook-maid Jane. The next step is to show the evolution of the 'bread-cake' into an even richer cake during the eighteenth century.

3
Eighteenth-century twelfth cakes and the baking revolution

An universal Quarrel consequently ensued; and the whole Cake was cut slashed, hacked, and mangled, and tost about, and crumbled, and broke to Pieces in the Fray

– from Letter to the Printer, *St. James's Chronicle or the British Evening Post*, 12–14 January 1762

Fortunately for the cake and the feelings of the cook, this dreadful event was a bad dream. On the previous Twelfth Night, the author of the letter, 'Cosmopolita', had been watching his family engaged in what he called 'the old *Christmas* Game of *chusing King and Queen*'. That night when he fell asleep:

> I imagined the EARTH to be a TWELFTH-Cake; the Surface of which was marked out with Lines drawn in various Colours, like those upon our Maps, and scored (like a College Pound of Butter) ready to be cut into different Slices, which were adorned with the Flags, Streamers, and ensigns of several Potentates, who stood round it in order to draw the Lots, which should entitle each to their respective Share.[1]

The King of England drew Lord of the Sea, 'a very rich, though but small Portion of the Cake'. Progressively the other leaders drew their shares, of such varying sizes and quality that general discontent arose and fighting broke out. Obviously 'Cosmopolita' was not writing about the cutting of twelfth cakes but expressing his feelings about a global conflict we now refer to as the Seven Years' War. From 1756 to 1763, European powers fought over their territories and trading outposts, not just in Europe but in Africa, America and Asia. Although allegorical, the description of the cake is very useful – we learn that it contained 'plums' (dried fruit) and 'sweetmeats' (candied peel), sugar and spices, and that it was iced and decorated with flags. We know that flags were stuck into other Twelfth Cakes. A poem entitled 'Christmas Holidays', published about three years later, began with this verse:

> *Behold, at length, Twelfth-night arrives,*
> *So pleasing to us all;*
> *The glorious cake with flags appears,*
> *Within the spacious hall.*[2]

In the first half of the previous century, Twelfth Night characters were symbolised by tokens buried within the cake – beans, peas and cloves. Samuel Pepys tried out the new practice of drawing the characters by lots in 1669 and this allowed him to increase the number of characters substantially. We don't know whether women could play men's roles in Pepys's times, but this was not possible a century later. One account from 1774 states 'After Tea Yesterday a noble Cake was produced, and two Bowls containing the fortunate Chances for the different Sexes'.[3] By the end of the eighteenth century, hosts could purchase a booklet of cards with illustrations of twenty-six characters to be drawn as '*The Chances; or, sport for Twelfth-Night*'.[4] As expected, the King and Queen came first. On later pages we find topical characters such as the grasping lawyer Counsellor Double Fee, the gin-swigging Jenny Juniper, and Doctor Poison Guts.

Twelfth cakes were increasingly adorned with figures as well as flags. These were composed of sugar or painted sweetmeats,[5] or later of wax or plaster.[6] Judging by the advertisements in the London newspapers, pastry-cooks supplied many of the twelfth cakes eaten in that city. Under the heading 'Twelfth Day', Mrs Trusler begged leave 'to acquaint the Nobility, Gentry and others, that she has made a large Assortment of rich Cakes for this Day; and as they are superior to any Twelfth Cake, she hopes for the Honour of their Commands'.[7] One cake mentioned in 1769 weighed in at 45 lb, and had been made and decorated by a pastry-cook.[8]

We need to ask, however, whether the cake and role-playing were as common elsewhere in Britain as in London, and who partook. A Twelfth Night party was held in 1771 at the country seat of Edmund Williams, Esquire, in Berkshire. The account of the event tells us that when supper was over, the twelfth-cake was shared, 'with the customary Scene of Frolic'.[9] But is there evidence that the middle classes held similar parties? Just as in the seventeenth century, there are some potentially useful eighteenth-century diarists who regularly listed the dishes they had for dinners and suppers. One was shop-keeper and local official, Thomas Turner, of East Hoathly in Sussex, who wrote his diary from 1754 to 1765.[10] He described countless evenings spent with friends playing cards and drinking (to excess), and itemises every Christmas dinner – however, there is not a single reference to a Twelfth Night party or twelfth cake, or to a cake served on Christmas Day.

An even more dedicated recorder of his household's food and drink was Norfolk parson James Woodforde, whose diary covers the period from 1758 to 1803. He received a 'small plumb cake' at the time of conducting a funeral in 1765,[11] and was served a 'Plumb Cake' at a Shrove Tuesday supper in Brasenose College in Oxford in 1775.[12] He was given portions of wedding cake in 1794[13] and 1795 – the latter had been sent from London and had 'Very curious devices on the Top of the Cake'.[14] Did he have plum cake at Christmas as well? On 30 December 1790, a visitor to his house ate 'some plum Cake and drank some Rum and Water'.[15] This sounds remarkably like the context in which we bring out our Christmas cakes. He also recorded a well-established Oxford college tradition of serving cake after dinner on Christmas Day: 'After the second course there was a fine plumb cake brought to the sen[io]r Table as is usual on this day, which also goes to the Batchelors after'.[16] Woodforde's diary entries suggest that there were many occasions through the year when a plum cake was appropriate, including Christmas, and that in his social circle in Norfolk, Twelfth Night revelries did not take place.

Fruit cakes were clearly proliferating, both socially and in the number of occasions on which they were served. We should expect to see a greater variety of recipes for cakes to cover all these contexts, from the large expensive twelfth cake down to the small plum cake given to the parson before a funeral.

Recipes for eighteenth-century fruit cakes

It is time to examine the composition of these eighteenth-century plum cakes. Compared to the seventeenth century, there were many more recipes for fruit cakes in circulation, and not just because more cookbooks had been published. While the cookbooks of the 1650s and 1660s offered only one or two cake recipes (until Sir Kenelm Digby provided six in 1669), by the mid-eighteenth century, cake recipes were numerous enough to warrant their own chapters or sections.[17]

One particularly popular recipe book, written by E[liza?] Smith and first published in 1727, had reached its fifteenth edition by 1753. By then its section entitled 'All Sorts of Cakes' contained forty-one recipes for large cakes, small cakes, buns, gingerbreads, enriched breads, and biscuits, as well as two recipes for icing. Focusing on the sixteen large cakes in this 1753 edition, nearly all fall into just two categories: eight 'plumb' or fruit cakes, and seven seed cakes – the seeds were from the caraway herb. Not only is there a greater choice of recipes for readers wanting to make these popular cakes, but some new methods of aerating the mixture were available – creaming the butter, and beating eggs with sugar.

Creaming the butter was a novel method first adopted in the eighteenth century. Yet this innovation in home baking was not flagged in the recipe books, instead it was concealed within the recipe wording. Instructions such as 'Take four pounds of butter, beat it in your hands till it is very soft like cream' can be found in three of Smith's seed cake recipes and in one fruit cake recipe entitled '*Another Plumb Cake with Almonds*'.[18] Today, this same method is often worded as 'Cream the butter and sugar till light and fluffy'. Since it is found in the majority of recipes for Christmas cakes that we have recorded, it can be regarded as a key element. Not a single seventeenth-century cake recipe of any type required creaming the butter. In fact, all seventeenth-century fruit cakes were raised with yeast, just as an enriched bread might be. The best way of incorporating butter into a yeasted bread or cake is to melt it in the liquid ingredients, or to rub it into the flour before the dough is mixed.

In her study of eighteenth-century British cooking, Gilly Lehmann emphasises the beating of the eggs as the new way of lightening the cake.[19] It is true that many of the seventeenth-century fruit cakes had no eggs at all, and that others with eggs did not stipulate beating. However towards the end of the century, recipes start to recommend this step,[20] and given the number of eggs involved it would have added to the lightening effect brought about by the yeast. However the next innovation, creaming the butter, rendered aeration by yeast unnecessary.

Finding the source of this revolutionary technique has proved difficult, but we have established when it first began to spread through English cookbooks. In 1705, William Salmon issued the third edition of his *The Family-Dictionary: or, Houshold Companion*. It was greatly enlarged compared to the original 1696 edition, and the number of cake recipes had been increased from three to six. One of the new recipes not only called for the butter to be creamed and eggs to be beaten, but also adopted the equal proportions of butter, sugar and flour that later typified the famous pound cake:

> *Cakes, Queens, call'd Portugal Cakes*: Take a pound of the finest Flower you can get, well dry'd; and a pound of Loaf-sugar beaten and sifted; mingle them together, then take a pound of Dish-butter, and clap them in your Hands, with Rose-water till it come to a Cream; then strew in your Sugar and Flower by degrees till it be half in, and keep it working with your Hands; then put in the yolks of six, and the whites of five Eggs, beat with two spoonfuls of Sack: Then by degrees work in the other half of your Flower and Sugar, and when your Oven is hot, put in a pound of Currans ready wash'd, pick'd, and dry'd over the Fire, your Pans must be ready butter'd, then fill them half full, and sift double refin'd Sugar over them, let the Oven be pretty hot, then set up the Lid.[21]

'Dish-butter' refers to butter sold in lumps weighing 24 ounces.[22] The 'Lid' may have been a domed copper cover placed over items in the oven to prevent over-browning.

William Salmon (1644–1713) described himself as a Professor of Physick, and a large proportion of his dictionary was devoted to his remedies – quackery by today's standards. There is no evidence that he was a cook, and it is possible that the work was simply issued under his name, which was well known because of his prolific output. Whoever inserted this particular recipe, and its source, are unclear. We know, however, that cakes of that name were made in the late-seventeenth century. There is a recipe in John Evelyn's manuscript cookbook, initially with the heading *'A sort of fine Cakes that keepe well'* with *'Portugall Cakes'* subsequently added to the title. The recipe has 1 lb each of butter, sugar and flour, like Salmon's, but uses a different number of egg yolks and whites, with the currants treated as an optional extra. Instead of beating the butter to a cream, the cook was told to 'work in the butter into the flower till it is as fine as crumes of bread'[23] – in our terminology, to rub the butter into the flour. The title of Evelyn's recipe captures the essential difference between a pound cake mixture and the old yeasted cake: the pound cake retains its soft 'mouth feel' and resists mould growth, while the yeasted cake goes stale and mouldy like bread.

So far as we know, Salmon's (1705) recipe for Portugal Cakes was the first published in an English cookbook to follow the pound cake principle, and it was the first to adopt creaming of the butter. Other cakes soon expanded their method of aeration to include creaming. In the enlarged fourth edition of his *England's Newest Way in All Sorts of Cookery ...*, published in 1717, Henry Howard recommended creaming the butter in *'How to make Shrewsbury Cakes'* and *'How to make a good Seed-cake'*.[24] These were clearly transitional recipes because he also added a little barm (yeast) to both. Soon that ingredient would be dropped from the recipes.

The lineage that would lead to the twentieth-century Christmas cake is more recognisably modern once the method of creaming the butter spread to plum and other rich fruit cakes during the eighteenth century, and brought about an adjustment of ingredient proportions, away from those adapted to yeasted breads and closer to those in long-keeping pound cakes. The mysterious E(liza?) Smith must take credit for the prototype, first published in the second edition of *The Compleat Housewife* in 1728. All that is known of the author is that she was a woman with thirty years' experience while 'constantly employed in fashionable and noble Families', presumably as a cook.[25] The fifth edition appeared in 1732, with fifty more recipes that she submitted to the publisher just before her death.[26] She was not alive to see the next thirteen highly successful editions, published up to 1773. Several editions of her work were also published in America.

The recipe from the 1728 edition that is most relevant to our story had an unassuming title:

> *Another Plum-Cake with Almonds*
> Take four pounds of fine Flour dried well, five pounds of Currants well picked and rubbed, but not washed; five pounds of Butter washed and beaten in Orange-flower Water and Sack; two pounds of Almonds beaten very fine, four pounds of Eggs weighed, half the Whites taken out; Three pounds of double-refined Sugar, three Nutmegs grated, a little Ginger, a quarter of an ounce of Mace, as much Cloves finely beaten, a quarter of a pint of the best Brandy: The Butter must be beaten to Cream; then put in your Flour, and all the rest of your things, beating it till you put it in your Oven; four hours will bake it, the Oven must be very quick; put in Orange, Lemon-peel candied, and Citron as you like.[27]

The proportions of the main ingredients, though not equal as in a pound cake, would in fact have produced a richer result, further enhanced by the large quantity of ground almonds. Unlike seventeenth-century rich fruit cakes, this cake has less flour than butter, and less sugar than would be present in later fruit cakes. For the first time we see brandy, with the old-fashioned sack relegated to washing the salt from the butter before it is creamed. The mixing instructions are not very explicit – for example, does one beat the eggs? – and so we chose to adapt a later version of the recipe, modified and improved by the most important cookbook writer of the eighteenth century, Hannah Glasse.

The life story of Hannah Glasse starts with her illegitimate birth in Northumberland in 1708, followed by upbringing in her father's relatively well-to-do home.[28] Sent to London to live with her grandmother, Hannah secretly married a junior army officer. After a few years in employment in Essex, and the birth of three children, they moved back to London. Her husband's business failures left Hannah to find ways of supporting the steadily growing family herself – *The Art of Cookery Made Plain and Easy* was the result. First published in 1747, the year her husband died, the author was identified simply as 'A Lady'. In fact, Hannah Glasse was a hard-working housewife and entrepreneur, although she would have understood the needs of 'ladies' through her family connections and upbringing. This cookbook was aimed at the growing numbers of women who could employ a servant to cook, but who needed to supply their cook with clearly written recipes to follow. As a book that went into multiple editions and was still in print in the nineteenth century, it should have brought its author financial success. In fact, Hannah lost the copyright in 1754, after the fifth edition was prepared, when she became bankrupt.[29]

Several scholars have meticulously compared Hannah Glasse's recipes with those of earlier writers. From a comparison with thirteen books published before 1747, Jennifer Stead found that 263 out of Hannah's 972 recipes had been taken from or were based on these sources. Later, Priscilla Bain added another 79 to the list.[30] We need to note that copying was common in eighteenth-century food-writing, and adding the original 'author's' name to a recipe did not occur until late in the century (in particular by Mary Cole in 1789, pp. 54–5). Hannah did not deliberately re-write the beginning and ending of a recipe to conceal its origins as some writers did, nor did she claim originality for the entire collection as the most blatant copiers were to do.[31] She borrowed the recipes of popular dishes and improved them.

The recipe '*To make a* Rich Cake' needs to be added to the list of recipes borrowed and revised by Hannah Glasse. Her source was the recipe we discussed earlier, '*Another Plum-Cake with Almonds*' from an edition of E. Smith's *The Compleat Housewife*. The recipe starts with a similar instruction:

> *To make a* **Rich Cake.**
> Take four Pound of Flower well dried and sifted, seven Pound of Currants washed and rubb'd, six Pound of the best fresh Butter, two Pound of Jordan Almonds blanched, and beaten with Orange Flower Water and Sack till they are fine, then take four Pound of Eggs, put half the Whites away, three Pound of double refin'd Sugar beaten and sifted, a quarter of an Ounce of Mace, the same of Cloves and Cinnamon, three large Nutmegs, all beaten fine, a little Ginger, half a pint of Sack, half a Pint of right French Brandy, Sweetmeats to your liking, they must be Orange, Lemon, and Citron. Work your Butter to a Cream with your Hands before any of your Ingredients are in, then put in your Sugar, mix it well together; let your Eggs be well beat, and strain'd thro' a Sieve, work in your Almonds first, then put in your Eggs, beat them all together till they look white and thick, then put in your Sack and Brandy and Spices, and shake your Flour in by Degrees, and when your Oven is ready, put in your Currants and Sweetmeats as you put it in your hoop; it will take four Hours baking in a quick Oven, you must keep it beaten with your Hand all the while you are mixing of it, and when your Currants are well wash'd and clean'd, let them be kept before the Fire, so that they may go warm into your Cake. This Quantity will bake best in two Hoops.[32]

Apart from the clear instruction 'The Butter must be beaten to Cream', E. Smith assumed her readers would know how to mix all the ingredients. In contrast, Hannah Glasse wrote out every step. There are too many points of similarity in

RICH CAKE

Adapted from *'To make a Rich Cake'*, in Hannah Glasse's *The Art of Cookery Made Plain and Simple'* (1747). Our recipe is scaled to one quarter of the original. The generous quantities of spices, orange-flower water, ground almonds and brandy give this extra large cake a delightful aroma and flavour. Depending on the size of your cake mixer you may find it necessary to transfer the creamed mixture to a larger bowl before folding in the ground almonds and remaining ingredients.

450 g bread flour	8 eggs, size 6 (4 whole eggs plus 4 yolks – 4 whites will not be used)
1 teaspoon each of ground mace, cloves, cinnamon, and nutmeg	225 g ground almonds
¼ teaspoon ground ginger	⅓ cup 'Rich Cream Wine' or sweet sherry
700 g butter	⅓ cup brandy
350 g sugar	800 g currants
1 teaspoon orange-flower water	100 g chopped citrus peel

Line the base and sides of a 30cm-round cake pan with a double layer of brown paper and a single layer of baking paper. Preheat the oven to 150°C with a shelf in the middle position.

Sift the flour and spices.

Soften the butter in a large bowl and cream with the sugar until light coloured and fluffy. Add the orange-flower water. Gradually add the 4 whole eggs, beating vigorously after each addition. If curdling appears add a spoonful of the sifted flour and spices. Add the yolks with a little more flour if necessary. Beat well until the mixture is creamy and thick.

Fold in the ground almonds and lastly add the sifted flour and spices alternately with the wine or sherry and the brandy. Lastly fold in the currants and peel.

Spoon into the prepared cake pan, smooth the surface and place in the preheated oven. Bake for 2–2 ½ hours. (Details on how to test when a cake is cooked are given on page 168.)

Place on a rack to cool. Cover with a teatowel and leave in the pan until cooled to room temperature. Wrap in greaseproof paper and store in an airtight cake container or seal well in aluminium foil.

Rich Cake served with the traditional drink Wassail, made from roasted apples and ale.

these two recipes for the charge of borrowing to be dismissed. But the deliberate changes made by Hannah Glasse, especially in the method of mixing, turned Smith's innovative but poorly-written recipe into the prototype for many Christmas cake recipes of our times.

The Art of Cookery Made Plain and Easy reached its twentieth edition by 1791, with numerous pirated versions also in circulation. This saturation gave its recipes tremendous influence. As well, many other writers borrowed from Hannah Glasse, including James Jenks, author of *The Complete Cook*, published in 1768. He described himself as a cook, and began his book with instructions concerning the daily tasks of housemaids and kitchen maids. But his prime audience was the cook-maid for whom the recipes were assembled. One recipe entitled '*A* Rich Cake' begins with the step 'Take six pounds of the best fresh butter'.[33] Then follows a re-arranged version of Hannah Glasse's '*To make a* Rich Cake'. Jenks increases the almonds from 2 lb to 3 lb, but retains the same quantities of butter, flour, sugar, and fruit. He omits the instruction to leave out half the egg whites. We suspect that was a mistake in the light of his instruction to use two ounces each of mace, cloves, and cinnamon – Hannah Glasse and E. Smith had stipulated just quarter of an ounce of each spice in their recipes. The cost of two ounces of mace alone would have been 32d., equivalent to the price of 5 lb of butter. The flavour would have been overwhelming.

Though this recipe is probably an unreliable adaptation of Hannah Glasse's version, it includes a very valuable piece of information just before the instructions for icing the cake – Jenks writes 'This is called a *twelfth cake* at *London*'. At last we can directly assign a recipe to the twelfth cake served at the end of the Christmas holiday. It is not a traditional recipe that could have been made in the seventeenth century because it is not raised with yeast. In fact, it is up-to-date with the latest methods of aerating a cake by creaming the butter, and beating the eggs before mixing them in. Just as the Twelfth Night festivities evolved through time, so too did the twelfth cake.

Within a year of publication of Jenks's twelfth cake, there is evidence that the pound cake principle had infiltrated recipes for rich fruit cakes. In 1769 E. Taylor, a resident of Berwick-upon-Tweed in Northumberland, published *The Lady's, Housewife's and Cookmaid's Assistant*. It contained a recipe entitled 'A rich CAKE made in the pound way'. Unlike most pound cakes that contain 1 lb of each of the main ingredients, this started with 4 lb. Instead of creaming the butter by itself and then stirring in the sugar, this recipe instructed the cook to 'Take four pounds of butter, work it to a cream, add to it four pounds of lump sugar pounded; beat the

ICING FESTIVE CAKES IN THE EIGHTEENTH CENTURY

As we recorded fruit cake recipes from the eighteenth century, a period that saw the important transition from bread-cakes to the much richer fruit and pound cakes, we noticed that icing recipes became more common and more varied. In the seventeenth century, nearly all icings had been a combination of egg whites beaten with powdered sugar and flavourings, such as rosewater or orange-flower water, hardened by returning the cake to the oven. This early form of royal icing continued in the eighteenth century and was the icing on the very first cake recipe to be identified as a twelfth cake. Published in 1768 by James Jenks, it was actually a modified version of Hannah Glasse's recipe 'To Ice a Great Cake', printed in 1747 in the second edition of her influential book. This is how Jenks presented the icing recipe, as an attachment to his instructions for making 'A Rich Cake ... called a *twelfth cake* at *London*',

> In order to ice it beat up the whites of 24 eggs with a pound of double refined sugar beaten and sifted very fine, till it looks very white and grows thick. Spread this with a feather or a fine brush over the top of the cake, after it is taken out of the tin hoop: and set it thus iced before a clear fire, at a proper distance, and keep turning it round for fear of discolouring it. But the best way to harden this ice [is] in an oven, for about an hour.
> *N.B.* this is the way to *ice* all cakes.[1]

For obvious reasons we have not tested this recipe. The proportion of egg whites to sugar seems excessive, compared to preceding recipes of this type, where three egg whites were sufficient to make an icing from 1 lb sugar. However we have seen the recipe in at least five other cookbooks between 1768 and 1843,[2] and it occurs in the first five editions of Hannah Glasse's book issued during the period when she held the copyright.[3] If there had been an error, she would surely have corrected it.

An eighteenth-century shift in the method of mixing the early type of royal icing saw the egg whites whipped to a stiff froth before the sugar was incorporated. This variant was more popular than the original version, especially in the first half of the eighteenth century, and we have found its recipe accompanying those for an array of fruit cakes, from 'Plum', 'Excellent Plum', and 'Great', to 'Rich Great'. For very large cakes, this new type of royal icing was strengthened by the addition of some fine starch. The starch variant appears in the earliest recipe for a cake icing to be placed on top of an almond icing. At last we have the prototype for our traditional Christmas cake, with its two delicious layers of icing – except that it was not for a Christmas cake but the famous 'Bride Cake', first published by Mrs Elizabeth Raffald in 1769:

To make **ALMOND-ICEING** *for the* **BRIDE CAKE**

BEAT the whites of three eggs to a strong froth, beat a pound of Jordan almonds very fine with rose water, mix your almonds with the eggs lightly together, a pound of common loaf sugar beat fine, and put in by degrees; when your cake is [baked] enough, take it out and lay your iceing on, then put it in to brown.

To make **SUGAR ICEING** *for the* **BRIDE CAKE.**

BEAT two pounds of double refined sugar, with two ounces of fine starch, sift it through a gauze sieve, then beat the whites of five eggs with a knife upon a pewter dish half an hour; beat in your sugar a little at a time, or it will make the eggs fall, and will not be so good a colour, when you have put in all your sugar, beat it half an hour longer, then lay it on your almond iceing, and spread it even with a knife; if it be put on as soon as the cake comes out of the oven, it will be hard by that time the cake is cold.[4]

Icings of the royal type predominated in the eighteenth century; however cooks knew of other ways of making icing. We found two butter icings composed of 'thick butter' and 'fine sugar', applied to small cakes,[5] as well as two simple frostings where cakes straight from the oven were washed over with beaten egg white, dusted with fine sugar, and in one case returned to the oven to 'ice'.[6]

By the end of the eighteenth century there were rich cakes with both almond and royal icings, but none were specifically identified as twelfth cakes. In fact, the one twelfth cake recipe that gave directions for icing used the seventeenth-century version of royal icing as a single layer. We know from newspapers that many highly decorated twelfth cakes were the work of professional pastry-cooks. However, decoration wasn't limited to twelfth cakes. At the end of the eighteenth century we find in the work of Edinburgh cookery teacher, Mrs Frazer, evidence that plum cakes and seed cakes could also be enhanced. After giving the recipes for these cakes, she wrote,

If you choose to ornament the cake, put a crown in the middle, and other small fancy figures on the top; waving small shells up and down the sides of it, and placing within the crown a bunch of artificial flowers of different colours; the crown, figures, and shells are of sugar paste, the flowers and leaves of different coloured paste, and the stalks of lemon-peel.[7]

sugar and butter together a quarter of an hour'.[34] Eventually this would lead to the modern instruction: beat the butter and sugar to a cream, or in our abbreviated terminology, to cream the butter and sugar.

One last eighteenth-century baking innovation relevant to the fruit cake needs to be introduced – the practice of separating the eggs and beating the yolks separately from the whites. This should add even more air to a cake, provided that the stiffly beaten whites are gently folded in just before the cake is spooned into the tin. The effectiveness of the eighteenth-century version of this technique would need to be tested by experiment, for in the recipes where it is found, the beaten whites are added to the sugar and butter mixture at an earlier stage, before the flour and fruit.[35] The innovation is evident in three cake recipes provided by Mrs Elizabeth Raffald in her influential book, *The Experienced English Housekeeper*, first published in 1769 and still in print in the early nineteenth century. Not all Christmas cake recipes advocate separating the whites from the yolks, but the practice clearly has a long tradition, and would prove especially popular in America.

In conclusion, we know that in the eighteenth century rich fruit cakes were made for numerous occasions – from weddings to funerals, for Twelfth Night festivities and even for Christmas supper in an Oxford college and Christmas entertaining in a Norfolk village. Many recipes were in circulation, some for the old-style yeasted bread-cakes that prevailed in the seventeenth century, others for quite new cakes with very different proportions. Although London pastry-cooks made rich fruit cakes for sale, especially for Twelfth Night, the increasing number of cake recipes in cookbooks written for housewives and cook-maids leaves no doubt that cakes were cooked in home kitchens. It is in these recipe books that we see the revolution in mixing methods that led to our present procedures.

The new-style rich fruit cakes deserved their name, for they were decidedly richer than the yeasted cakes, where flour constituted the main ingredient. The new eighteenth-century cakes sometimes had a greater weight of butter than flour, and the proportion of sugar increased significantly during the course of the century. As the pound-cake principle became popular, the proportion of eggs increased. Instead of being an optional ingredient as in the seventeenth century, eggs were now essential for the aeration of the mixture, along with the creaming of the butter. The new eighteenth-century recipes may have made smaller cakes than the largest seventeenth-century examples, but they would have been denser, higher in kilocalories, and much longer-lasting.

The green Colour.

Trim the leaves of spinach, boil them a moment in water, and drain them very well to pound; sift the juice in a sieve for use.

Of these cardinal colours, you may make any alteration in imitation of painters, by mixing to what shade you please; but taste and fancy must be your guides upon those occasions.

OF CAKES.

General Observations upon Cakes.

ALWAYS have every thing in readiness before you begin to make any kind of cakes, then beat your eggs well, and never leave them till they are finished, as by that means your cakes will not be so light. When you put butter in your cakes, be particularly careful in beating it to a fine cream before you put in your sugar, otherwise double the beating will not have so good an effect. Rice-cakes, seed-cakes, or plum-cakes, are best baked in wooden garths; for when they are baked in pots or tins, the outsides of the cakes are burned, and they are so confined that the heat cannot penetrate into the middle, which hinders its rising.

A Bride Cake.

Take four pounds of fine flour well dried, four pounds of fresh butter, two pounds of loaf-sugar; pound and sift fine a quarter of an ounce of mace, and the same quantity of nutmegs; to every pound of flour put eight eggs; wash and pick four pounds of currants, and dry them before the fire; blanch a pound of sweet almonds, and cut them lengthways very thin, a pound of citron, a pound of candied orange, a pound of candied lemon, and half a pint of brandy; first work the butter with your hand to a cream, then beat in your sugar a
quarter

quarter of an hour, beat the whites of your eggs to a very strong froth, mix them with your sugar and butter; beat your yolks half an hour at least, and mix them with your cake; then put in your flour, mace, and nutmeg; keep beating it till your oven is ready, put in your brandy, and beat your currants and almonds lightly in; tie three sheets of paper round the bottom of your hoop, to keep it from running out; rub it well with butter, put in your cake, and lay your sweetmeats in three lays, with cake betwixt every lay; after it is risen and coloured, cover it with paper before your oven is stopped up; it will take three hours baking. *Raffald*, 265.

A pound Cake.

Take a pound of butter, beat it in an earthen pan with your hand one way, till it is like a fine thick cream; then have ready twelve eggs, but half the whites; beat them well, and beat them up with the butter, a pound of flour beat in it, a pound of sugar, and a few carraways. Beat it all well together for an hour with your hand, or a great wooden spoon; butter a pan and put it in, and then bake it an hour in a quick oven.

For change, you may put in a pound of currants, clean washed and picked. *Glasse*, 281. *Mason*, 400. *Farley*, 292.

A good Plum Cake.

Take three pounds of flour, three pounds of currants, three quarters of a pound of almonds, blanched and beat grosly, about half an ounce of them bitter, a quarter of a pound of sugar, seven yolks and six whites of eggs, one pint of cream, two pounds of butter, half a pint of good ale yeast; mix the eggs and the yeast together, strain them; set the cream on the fire, melt the butter in it; stir in the almonds and half a pint of sack, part of which should be put to the almonds while beating; mix together the flour, currants, and sugar, what nutmeg, cloves, and mace are liked; stir these to the cream, put in the yeast. *Mason*, 400.

Another way.

To a pound and a half of fine flour well dried, put the same quantity of butter, three quarters of a pound of currants, washed

A CHRISTMAS CAKE

IN FOUR QUARTERS.

BY

LADY BARKER,

AUTHOR OF "STORIES ABOUT:—" "STATION LIFE IN NEW ZEALAND," ETC.

SECOND EDITION.

WITH ILLUSTRATIONS.

London and New York:

MACMILLAN AND CO.

1872.

Following her return to England in 1868, Lady Barker wrote her well-known *Station Life in New Zealand* and, soon after, a book for children called *A Christmas Cake in Four Quarters*. The title page of the second edition (1872) includes one of the first illustrations of a Christmas cake. Courtesy of the Heritage Collection, Dunedin Public Libraries.

4
From twelfth cake to Christmas cake

On 18 December 1820, Mr G. Button of Fleet Street, London, presented 'an ornamented twelfth cake' to 'her Majesty', which he described in a self-promotional letter to the *Times* as

> very large, and exceedingly rich, ... most beautifully and tastefully ornamented, with Justice standing on a rock, trampling venomous reptiles under her feet, in allusion to her Majesty's late sufferings and trial. On each side of the rock were horns of plenty, richly overflowing with great abundance of delicious fruits. The surrounding edges of the cake itself formed a complete coronet ...[1]

As well as having his cake accepted by royalty, Mr Button had the honour of kissing 'her Majesty's' hand. The cake's recipient must have been Caroline, the estranged consort of George the Fourth who had ascended the throne in January 1820. George immediately tried to get a bill through Parliament that would have annulled their marriage and stripped her of her title. It proved a deeply unpopular move – to the extent of inspiring Mr Button's cake decorations.

Just as confectioners supported wronged royal consorts, so royal patronage helped to prop up the twelfth cake during the first half of the nineteenth century. Newspapers regularly reported on the twelfth cakes made for the monarch, culminating in the cake made for Queen Victoria in 1849 by Mr Mawditt, 'the Royal confiseur'. It had sixteen figures on top including a violinist and harpist, all dressed in eighteenth-century costume. The setting was an *al fresco* meal under trees, complete with miniature decanters and glasses.[2]

Compared to the flags of the eighteenth century, the cake decorations of the nineteenth century became infinitely more varied and rendered the quality of the cake itself unimportant. Decorated twelfth cakes were displayed in the windows of the pastry-cooks' shops, attracting large crowds. As the gaslights were turned on at dusk on 'Twelfth Day', they lit up

> countless cakes of all prices and dimensions, that stand in rows and piles on the counters and sideboards, and in the windows. The richest in flavour and heaviest in weight and price are placed on large and massy salvers; one, enormously superior to the rest in size, is the chief object of curiosity; and all are decorated with all imaginable images of things animate and inanimate. Stars, castles, kings, cottages, dragons, trees, fish, palaces, cats, dogs, churches, lions, milkmaids, knights, serpents, and innumerable other forms in snow-white confectionary, painted with variegated colours ...[3]

The figures were crafted from sugar by specialist confectioners and were normally purchased from them by the pastry-cooks. Unlike the edible figures, the colours that made them so attractive to children were obtained from numerous sources, both animate and inanimate, and not all proved to be harmless.

The early nineteenth century saw a dramatic change in the pigments available for artists and fabric manufacturers, and led to the replacement of fugitive colours chiefly derived from plants and insects, to those which were permanent. The chemists devised bright new pigments including emerald greens (composed of copper acetoarsenite), chrome yellow and chrome orange (lead chromate). Without any regulations concerning the adoption of these compounds as food colourings, it is not surprising that poisonings occurred. They came to public attention in the 1840s as doctors began to report cases of children becoming violently ill after consuming painted figures from twelfth cakes.[4] Some survived, but there were many fatalities. *Punch* took up the cause in 1851 and the *Lancet* published the first of several articles in 1854.[5] Green colouring was considered the most poisonous, even in minute doses. In 1858, 44 twelfth-cake ornaments were purchased from a shopkeeper and analysed. Although only one showed traces of copper acetoarsenite, over half tested positive for lead chromate. In the words of the *Lancet* reporter, 'Again, we ask, how long is this wholesale poisoning to be permitted to continue?'.[6] The twelfth cake was in danger of being doomed by association.

From newspapers, we know that royal recognition of the festival and its cake continued for the first half of the nineteenth century. One early account shows that the twelfth cake also acted as an incentive for various forms of lottery. As Prince of Wales, the future George the Fourth was patron of a birthday celebration in honour of his mother, held in the huge Rotunda at Ranelagh Gardens on 23 January each year between 1799 and 1803. For a half guinea, guests were served a 'supper' at one o'clock in the afternoon and the first four hundred received a ticket for a prize draw of fifty twelfth cakes.[7] Given the date of the Queen's birthday, these twelfth cakes would have been consumed after Twelfth Night – or Twelfth Day as it was increasingly known – thereby disconnecting their consumption from the traditional festivities. No mention was made of any hidden tokens, nor of the ring, thimbles or coins that were still baked in the twelfth cakes in some counties in the west of England.[8]

This practice reached Australia, however, and by 1848 such items were an incentive for purchasers of pieces of a 230 lb cake, on sale in Sydney for 2s. per pound. Baked within this cake were seven gold wedding rings and five silver thimbles. The pastry-cook responsible, Thomas Goudie, justified calling this twelfth cake a 'Christmas cake' for he had baked it to celebrate 'Old Christmas' on 6 January.[9] We found that one Sydney pastry-cook, M. Gill, was advertising stocks of 'Christmas Cakes' from 1835. He was not referring to 'Old Christmas', as is made clear by this advertisement published on 30 December 1841:

> M. G[ill] begs to call the attention of the public to his splendid variety of ornamental CHRISTMAS CAKES and in a few days will be seen a most extensive display of grand TWELFTH-NIGHT CAKES, which for richness and workmanship, are unequalled by the minor shops in the business. A variety of well executed Twelfth-Night Characters on sale.[10]

There is no doubt that the Christmas cake was a distinct category in Australia by the 1830s, earlier than is apparent in any London newspapers.

Like their English kin, the Australians held raffles for giant cakes. We have found early advertisements for the raffle of a '60-pound Twelfth cake' in Brisbane in 1847 and for 'magnum giant cakes' worth five guineas from Sydney in 1848 – tickets were one shilling.[11] Such cake lotteries continued up to the 1870s. However, by the 1850s the cakes that were being raffled were increasingly described as Christmas cakes.

New Zealand confectioners also included rings in their large cakes and, in Charles Canning's advertisement from Auckland in 1857, we find the cake referred to not as a twelfth cake but as a 'Monster Christmas Cake, weighing 300 lbs, and containing 18 Plain Gold Rings, ready for sale on Thursday, 24th Dec., in quantities from 1 pound upwards, at 2s. 6d. per pound'.[12] This promotion continued through the 1860s – however by 1866 Canning's monster cake contained only twelve rings.[13] A New Plymouth advertisement from D. Callaghan in 1869 could offer only four gold rings for the same price.[14] A year later he baked 'seventy pieces of gold and silver coin, consisting of half-sovereigns, half-crowns, shillings, and sixpences' into a 'Splendid Christmas Cake' and cut it on Christmas Eve.[15] By 1882, the purchaser of a pound of Christmas Cake from Mr B.C. Lawrence's shop in Waitara acquired a ticket naming a prize 'such as silver sugar basins, cream jugs, purses, work-boxes, money-boxes, and other numerous articles'.[16] In the advertisements from Australia, we see a remarkably smooth transition in the date for cutting the cake or drawing the raffle, from 6 January to 24 December, as well as a parallel shift in the name from twelfth cake to Christmas cake. By the time New Zealand pastry-cooks were advertising in the 1850s, none of them referred to the twelfth cake at all.

In England, the replacement of the twelfth cake by the Christmas cake was slower than in the colonies. Instead, cakes of both names appear to have co-existed for several decades. The old-style twelfth cake was the focus of a court case involving a Frenchman, Louis Dethier, who was charged in late December 1860 at Bow Street Court with conducting an illegal lottery for twelfth cakes.[17] He had rented and staffed an office and claimed to have purchased £10,000 worth of twelfth cakes. The public bought tickets at 1s. each, not just for cakes but for cash prize draws to take place on ten consecutive days, with twenty thousand tickets allotted for each draw, and £1,000 worth of prizes to be won on each day by 1201 lucky punters. Since the income (if all the tickets were sold) would exactly match his claimed outlay, where would Dethier's profit lie? According to the Court of Bankruptcy news nine days later, 'his 2,700 cakes are about to be offered to the public otherwise than by lottery'.[18] Dethier (a liar as well as a potential fraudster) chose this outcome to avoid a prison term.

The 'Monster Twelfth Cake' persisted in British newspaper advertisements until the 1870s, but commentators showed little affection for it. The cake had received bad publicity for its association with the deaths and poisoning of children, and for its connection with dodgy lotteries. In 1854, in his weekly journal, *Household Words*, Charles Dickens criticised the misuse of terms such as 'monster', 'mammoth' or 'leviathan', noting that 'every confectioner's new year's raffle was a monster twelfth cake'.[19] He would have not have appreciated the name of the massive cake exhibited at the Crystal Palace in December 1857.[20] Weighing in at four hundredweight [203 kg], it was called Leviathan, perhaps after the massive ship then being completed in London to the plans of Isambard Brunel. Significantly, the Crystal Palace cake was not called a twelfth cake, but a 'Christmas Cake'. In 1860, further raising the profile of the Christmas cake, one of the pantomimes playing at the Theatre Royal in Marylebone was entitled 'The Little Mouse Who Built a House in a Christmas Cake'.[21]

In her book on English Christmas traditions, entitled *Cakes and Characters*, Bridget Ann Henisch plotted the decline of Twelfth Day characters and role-playing, noting that the twelfth cake 'was claimed by Christmas as its own' and was subject to a 'triumphant transformation'.[22] The examples that we have quoted show that some of the roles of the twelfth cake were indeed taken over by the Christmas cake, especially in New Zealand and Australia. Henisch believes that the increasing emphasis on Christmas Day in Victorian Britain was a driving force behind the change. Christmas Day became the day on which presents are given – it was formerly a New Year's Day activity. Christmas cards and Christmas crackers became fashionable in the 1840s, together with the Christmas tree, an introduction from Germany.[23] But although Christmas became the more important family festival, we have already seen that the twelfth cake had a role extending beyond 6 January and its festivities. In the first half of the nineteenth century, its name epitomised a giant cake with elaborate decoration, accepted by royalty, and carrying the chance of good fortune. Changes to Christmas should not have brought about its decline. In our view, it was the bad publicity of the 1850s that led to the disappearance of the twelfth cake in its monstrous, sometimes toxic form. The Australasian newspapers' practice of reprinting items from English papers made the scandal of the poisonous figurines as well known there as in Britain.

In the previous chapter, we showed that even in the eighteenth century plum cakes were cut and offered to visitors and guests at Christmas time, serving a similar role to our all-purpose Christmas cake. They were made from a variety of recipes with a range of names. Did this group of cakes become the Christmas cakes of the second half of the nineteenth century, or was it a slimmed-down version of a twelfth cake that underwent the transformation? An equally interesting question concerns the contributions of the professional pastry-cook and home cook to the emergence of the new Christmas cake. With these issues in mind, we turned to the nineteenth-century recipes.

Twelfth cake recipes in the nineteenth century

In 1768, when James Jenks revealed that his 'Rich Cake' was called a twelfth cake in London, cooks wishing to make a twelfth cake probably used a variety of recipes with epithets like 'rich', 'excellent', 'great' and 'extraordinary' in their titles. It wasn't until the nineteenth century that recipes were actually named 'Twelfth Cake'. Ironically this would also be the last century in which these cakes were commonly made. The first nineteenth–century recipe with this title, found by food historian Alan Davidson, was in a family recipe book dated 1811, under the name 'A Very Rich Twelfth Cake'.[24] The cake was of the old-style, raised by yeast and almost identical in ingredients and quantities to '*An extraordinary plum-cake*', published in 1749 in the third edition of Charles Carter's *The London and Country Cook*.[25] The same recipe had appeared in 1762, this time with the name '*A rich* PLUM-CAKE'.[26] We have recently located an earlier recipe for 'Twelfth Cakes' in the second edition of John Mollard's *The Art of Cookery Made Easy and Refined*. Published in 1802, this old-style recipe called for yeast and the mixture was baked in several hoops before being iced with sugar.[27]

By contrast, William Kitchiner's recipe for 'Twelfth Cake', first printed in 1823, was based on the pound-cake principle and his cake would have acquired lightness from over twenty minutes of mixing, together with the large number of eggs.[28] By our standards it was a big cake, with 2 lb each of flour, sugar, and butter, and 4 lb of currants, all supported by eighteen eggs. Kitchiner described it as 'twelve or fourteen inches over' – in our units, 30–36 cm in diameter. However, his book was addressed to housewives, not to professional cooks. For the latter, a twelfth cake was distinguished by its decorations, not by its recipe. The view expressed by Eleanor Parkinson, a confectioner from Philadelphia, was probably typical. She wrote in 1849: 'Twelfth [Cake]. – Prepare your mixture as for pound-cake, plum-cake, or bride-cake, which[ever] you please ...'.[29] The exceptionally large cakes that were displayed in pastry-cooks' windows were probably still made from a yeast-raised dough, because it is easier to mix in bulk.

Kitchiner's *The Cook's Oracle* was a very influential book. Written by a practical cook and inventor, the recipes were carefully explained and supplied with commentary. Not surprisingly, it remained in print after his death in 1827, both in Britain and America. Other writers borrowed its twelfth cake recipe. In most cases they kept its name, although Esther Copley wrote in *The Housekeeper's Guide* (1838) that the addition of one pound of Smyrna raisins 'advances it to be dignified with the style and title of a bride or wedding cake'.[30] Under its original title, it was included in an Anglo-Indian cookbook published in 1864,[31] and survived to appear in *Cassell's Dictionary of Cookery*, a voluminous work from the mid-1870s that reprinted many recipes from older cookbooks.[32] The editor of this work increased the number of eggs from eighteen to twenty.

What intrigued us most were the two publications that printed Kitchiner's 'Twelfth Cake' recipe with new names. One was the first known fruit-cake recipe to have 'Christmas Cake' in its title. Under the name 'The Housewife's Christmas Cake', Kitchiner's recipe was published in Elizabeth Ellet's *The Practical Housekeeper; A Cyclopaedia of Domestic Economy* in 1857.[33] The compiler of this large and expensive American work clearly thought the recipe had more appeal as a Christmas cake than twelfth cake. To suit her readers, she doubled the amounts of

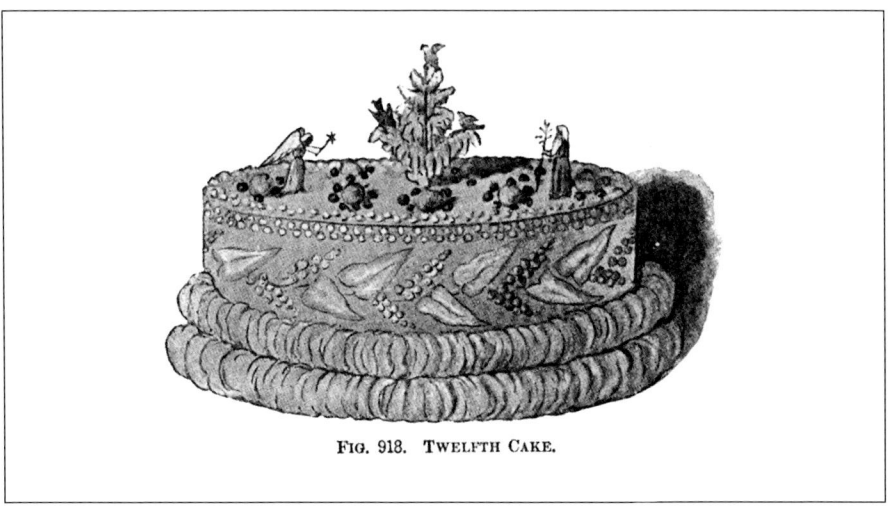

FIG. 918. TWELFTH CAKE.

Theodore Garrett's *The Encyclopaedia of Practical Cookery*, published about 1894, included one of the last illustrations of a twelfth cake and three twelfth cake recipes dating back to the 1820s. Courtesy of the University of Otago Library.

the spices and brandy. Another name change is evident in the Christchurch *Star*, which published Kitchiner's recipe as 'Yule Cake' in 1905 and again in 1906.[34] Rather than copying directly from Kitchiner, its source was probably *Cassell's Dictionary* or Theodore Garrett's eight-volume work *The Encyclopaedia of Practical Cookery*, which reprinted all of Cassell's twelfth cake recipes. Garrett believed that the twelfth cake 'seems to have a charmed life, and dies hard' compared to the Twelfth Night cards and characters, but his twelfth cake recipes were almost the last we found.[35]

In the course of recording all the nineteenth-century twelfth cakes that we could locate in different cookbooks and newspapers – seventeen overall – Kitchiner's was the only one that was later re-named 'Christmas Cake', a finding that must cast some doubt on the assertion that twelfth cakes were transformed directly into Christmas cakes. Most twelfth cake recipes appeared in cookbooks produced in the first half of the nineteenth century, and were last reprinted in compendiums from the second half. They seldom survived the end of the Victorian era. Chronologically, they match the evidence for the decline in twelfth cake raffles and the giant cakes with elaborate decorations. If twelfth cake recipes were not recycled, then what were the sources of our Christmas cakes?

Nineteenth-century recipes for Christmas cakes

In Britain, the earliest recipe we could find with the title 'Christmas Cake' was published in 1858, one year after Elizabeth Ellet's 'Housewife's Christmas Cake' appeared in America. From a snippet view of the first few lines of the recipe – 'Christmas Cake For A Party' – it sounded promising. But when we obtained a copy of the page, it proved to be a cake used for a trifle. The writer, Eliza Warren, instructed her readers to 'beat [it] well with a wooden spoon in a pan for a full hour, *without ceasing*'. Without a raising agent, this cake was probably doomed. Eliza gave up on it with the following remark: 'Many persons prefer to buy a cake from the confectioners; it is less trouble, and certain to be good; whereas cakes depend so much on the beating and baking that they frequently turn out failures'.[36] This disastrous Christmas trifle-cake bears no resemblance to the Christmas cake of our story.

The first recipe with the title 'Christmas Cake' to be published in Britain is from the famous Mrs Isabella Beeton. It looks very different to recipes for the rich cakes of the seventeenth and eighteenth centuries:

CHRISTMAS CAKE.

1754. Ingredients. – 5 teacupfuls of flour, 1 teacupful of melted butter, 1 teacupful of cream, 1 teacupful of treacle, 1 teacupful of moist sugar, 2 eggs, ½ oz. of powdered ginger, ½ lb. of raisins, 1 teaspoonful of carbonate of soda, 1 tablespoonful of vinegar.

Mode. – Make the butter sufficiently warm to melt it, but do not allow it to oil; put the flour into a basin; add to it the sugar, ginger, and raisins, which should be stoned and cut into small pieces. When these dry ingredients are thoroughly mixed, stir in the butter, cream, treacle, and well-whisked eggs, and beat the mixture for a few minutes. Dissolve the soda in the vinegar, add it to the dough, and be particular that these latter ingredients are well incorporated with the others; put the cake into a buttered mould or tin, place it in a moderate oven immediately, and bake it from 1¾ to 2¼ hours.

Time. – 1¾ to 2¼ hours. *Average cost*, 1s 6d.[37]

Published as a single volume in 1861, *The Book of Household Management* came out initially as a series of pamphlets, with the first issued in November 1859. Isabella worked on their content until December 1860.[38] These dates are important to the question – where did Mrs Beeton get her Christmas cake recipe from? At this point we need to explain that we have not found any British prototype despite extensive searching. In 2003, when we first wrote about the history of Christmas cakes, we

When cut, Mrs Beeton's 'Christmas Cake' looks more like the soft gingerbread from which it was derived, than a rich fruit cake. Photo: Mary Browne.

asked if Mrs Beeton's version was a 'depauperate Twelfth Cake', and dismissed it as 'meagre'.[39] In fact it was neither – Mrs Beeton's 'Christmas Cake' was actually a soft gingerbread of a type developed in America since the 1820s but not yet common in Britain. We believe that she copied it from a Boston publication, Ballou's *Dollar Monthly Magazine*, specifically from the issue for June, 1859. In its column for 'The Housewife' was the following recipe:

Holiday Cake.

Five teacupsful of flour, one of melted butter, one of cream, one of treacle, one of brown sugar, two eggs, one ounce of powdered ginger, half a pound of chopped raisins, four teaspoonfuls of carbonate of soda mixed with a tablespoon of vinegar – vinegar and soda last. Bake two hours in a slow oven.[40]

This was not a well-written recipe, but then American housewives probably knew how to make soft gingerbread. We think Isabella tested it, then improved the mixing instructions, as well as reducing the amount of baking soda and ginger. It was a new cake with a new name, and was popular enough to be copied.

Within two or three years it had reached Otago in New Zealand among the hand-written recipes of new immigrant Alexander Stuart.[41] In Australia, it was contributed in 1895 to the famous *Cookery Book* of the Presbyterian Women's Missionary Association of New South Wales.[42] New Zealand's *Clutha Leader*

1114   *Recipes for Making Bread, Biscuits and Cakes.*

2462.—RICH BRIDE OR CHRISTENING CAKE.

Ingredients.—5 lbs. of the finest flour, 3 lbs. of fresh butter, 5 lbs. of currants, 2 lbs. of sifted loaf sugar, 2 nutmegs, ¼ oz. of mace, ¼ oz. of cloves, 16 eggs, 1 lb. of sweet almonds, ½ lb. of candied citron, ½ lb. each of candied orange and lemon peel, 1 gill of wine, 1 gill of brandy.

Mode.—Let the flour be as fine as possible, and well dried and sifted; the currants washed, picked and dried before the fire; the sugar well pounded and sifted; the nutmegs grated; the spices pounded; the eggs thoroughly whisked, whites and yolks separately; the almonds pounded with a little orange-flower water; and the candied peel cut in neat slices. When all these ingredients are prepared, mix them in the following manner:—Begin working the butter with the hand till it becomes of a cream-like consistency; stir in the sugar, and when the whites of the eggs are whisked to a solid froth, mix them with the butter and sugar; next, well beat up the yolks for 10 minutes, and adding them to the flour, nutmegs, mace and cloves, continue beating the whole together for half an hour or longer, till wanted for the oven. Then mix in lightly the currants, almonds and candied peel, with the wine and brandy; and having lined a hoop with buttered paper, fill it with the mixture, and bake the cake in a tolerably quick oven, taking care, however, not to burn it; to prevent this, the top of it may be covered with a sheet of paper. To ascertain whether the cake is done, plunge a clean knife into the middle of it, withdraw it directly, and if the blade is not sticky and looks bright, the cake is sufficiently baked. These cakes are usually spread with a thick layer of almond icing, No. 2432, and over that another layer of sugar icing, No. 2436, and afterwards ornamented. In baking a large cake like this, great attention must be paid to

BRIDE CAKE.

CHRISTENING CAKE.

The 1899 edition of Mrs Beeton's *The Book of Household Management* provided illustrations of the elaborately iced 'Rich Bride or Christening Cake', but no image of her 'Christmas Cake', a modified American gingerbread. H. Leach Collection.

Coffee Cake. 1115

the heat of the oven; it should not be too fierce, but have moderate heat to bake the cake through.

Time.—5 to 6 hours. **Average Cost,** 2s. per lb.

2463.—CHRISTMAS CAKE.

Ingredients.—5 teacupfuls of flour, 1 teacupful of melted butter, 1 teacupful of cream, 1 teacupful of treacle, 1 teacupful of moist sugar, 2 eggs, $\frac{1}{2}$ oz. of powdered ginger, $\frac{1}{2}$ lb. of raisins, 1 teaspoonful of carbonate of soda, 1 tablespoonful of vinegar.

Mode.—Make the butter sufficiently warm to melt it, but do not allow it to oil; put the flour into a basin, add to it the sugar, ginger and raisins, which should be stoned and cut into small pieces. When these dry ingredients are thoroughly mixed, stir in the butter, cream, treacle, and well-whisked eggs, and beat the mixture for a few minutes. Mix the soda with the dry ingredients, being very careful to leave no lumps, and stir the vinegar into the dough. When it is wetted, put the cake into a buttered mould or tin, place it in a moderate oven immediately, and bake it from $1\frac{3}{4}$ to $2\frac{1}{4}$ hours.

Time.—$1\frac{3}{4}$ to $2\frac{1}{4}$ hours. **Average Cost,** 1s. 6d.

2464.—COCOA-NUT MACAROONS.

Ingredients.—$\frac{1}{2}$ lb. of flour, $\frac{1}{2}$ lb. of butter, 6 oz. of grated cocoa-nut, 6 oz. of sifted sugar, 4 eggs.

Mode.—Beat the sugar and butter together; add the cocoa-nut and the flour by degrees, then the eggs, still beating the mixture. Drop it in spoonfuls on a buttered baking-tin, and bake in a quick oven.

Time.—About 8 minutes to bake the cakes. **Average Cost,** 1s. 4d.

Sufficient for 30 cakes.

Seasonable at any time.

COCOA-NUT MACAROONS.

2465.—COFFEE CAKE.

Ingredients.—1 teacupful of brown sugar, 1 teacupful of golden syrup, $\frac{1}{2}$ teacupful of butter, $\frac{1}{2}$ teacupful of lard, 1 cup of cold coffee, 2 eggs, 1 cupful of currants, 1 cupful of stoned raisins, $\frac{1}{2}$ teaspoonful of nutmeg, $\frac{1}{2}$ teaspoonful of cloves, $\frac{1}{2}$ teaspoonful of cinnamon, 1 teaspoonful of bi-carbonate of soda, flour.

Mode.—Wash the fruit and dry it. Then mix all the ingredients with sufficient flour to bind it. Bake 1 hour in a quick oven.

Time.—1 hour. **Average Cost,** 1s.

Seasonable at any time.

MRS BEETON'S CHRISTMAS CAKE

Adapted from 'Christmas Cake', in Isabella Beeton's *The Book of Household Management* (1861).

A warm, mellow-flavoured cake that tastes and looks just like a large ginger cake! This cake will stale more rapidly than a modern fruit-rich cake. It freezes well and can be lightly toasted to serve with butter and cheese or with fresh or cooked fruit and cream or yoghurt. Bananas and stewed apples are favourite accompaniments.

- 500 g plain flour
- 2 tablespoons ground ginger
- 160 g soft brown sugar
- 230 g raisins (chopped if large)
- 180 g butter
- 200 ml cream
- 300 g treacle
- 2 eggs, size 7
- 1 teaspoon baking soda
- 1 tablespoon malt vinegar

Prepare a 20cm-round cake pan by lining the base and sides with a double layer of brown paper and a single layer of baking paper or greased greaseproof paper. Preheat the oven to 170°C with a shelf in the middle position.

Sift the flour and ginger into a large bowl. Add the brown sugar and raisins, breaking up any lumps of sugar or clumps of raisins. Mix thoroughly.

In a small saucepan gently heat the butter until barely melted. Cool a little before adding the cream and treacle. Whisk the eggs until thick. Add the butter mixture and mix well. In a cup, dissolve the baking soda in the vinegar (it will froth). Add to the other liquid ingredients and stir well to thoroughly mix.

Pour the liquid ingredients into the dry ingredients and stir until well combined (do not overmix).

Spoon into the prepared pan and smooth the surface. Place in the preheated oven and bake for 1 ¾–2 hours. (Details on how to test when a cake is cooked are given on page 168.)

Place on a rack and leave to cool to room temperature. Turn out on to the cake rack. Wrap the cool cake in greaseproof paper and store in an airtight cake container.

The open book is Isabella Beeton's *The Book of Household Management* (1899).

published it in December 1899 in their recipes column with the flour measurement converted from teacups to breakfast cups.[43] In December 1929, as the Depression set in, the *N.Z. 'Truth'* published a version with cup measurements.[44] A year later, the *Evening Post* published the same recipe under the title 'Economical Christmas Cake'.[45] Its subsequent disappearance in New Zealand suggests that this depressing new name might have played a part. In Australia it has lasted much longer, showing up in 1969 in the *Willow Cookery Book*, produced by the makers of a popular brand of bakeware.[46] With the name 'Christmas Cake (1) (Good Dark Cake)' it may still be made in Australian kitchens. We decided that this recipe's history alone justified its selection as the nineteenth-century Christmas cake for our book. As a bonus, it turned out to be delicious.

A genuine British recipe, Mary Jewry's 'A Rich Plum Cake' doubtless reached New Zealand in one of the editions of *Warne's Model Cookery and Housekeeping Book*.[47] This work was a popular source of recipes for local newspapers in the late-nineteenth century. Renamed 'A Rich Christmas Cake' and then simply 'Rich Christmas Cake', it was printed by the *Otago Witness* in 1883, the Hawke's Bay *Bush Advocate* in 1891, and Wellington's *Evening Post* in 1892.[48] Not one of these papers saw any problems with this recipe, and nor did the compiler or original publisher. Throughout its history, the recipe failed to give any instructions as to what to do with the twelve egg whites (which should have been whisked and folded in), and what was worse, it required the addition of half a pound of spice, when half an ounce must have been intended. Regardless of its flaws, it provides us with an excellent example of the renaming of an existing plum cake recipe as a Christmas cake.

A similar fate affected the recipe for 'Rich Plum Cake', first published in 1820 by a famous London confectioner, William Jarrin.[49] Over four decades later it became 'Christmas Yule Cake' in the very first Australian cookbook, *The English and Australian Cookery Book* by Edward Abbott, published in 1864.[50] Then after another thirty-three years, it was published again (with the sugar omitted) in the *Otago Witness* as 'Christmas Cake'.[51]

Yet another 'Rich Plum Cake', published originally in Arthur Payne's *Choice Dishes at Small Cost* in 1882, was renamed Christmas Cake by both the *Clutha Leader* in 1891 and a Perth newspaper, the *Western Mail,* in 1892.[52] While Payne's cake was of British origin, three other identical Christmas Cake recipes printed in Australia and New Zealand in the late-nineteenth and early twentieth centuries were derived from a Philadelphia publication, *Peterson's Magazine*, where the recipe had been entitled Plum Cake.[53] It contained a small quantity of poisonous bitter almonds.

ICING FESTIVE CAKES IN THE NINETEENTH CENTURY

Judging by their titles, several recipes from the first half of the nineteenth century were suitable for icing twelfth cakes. Dr William Kitchiner, the physician, had left cakes out of the first edition (1817) of his cookbook, being more concerned with the proper composition of dinner dishes. By 1823 the fifth edition contained an Appendix with a recipe for a large 'Twelfth Cake'. He directed readers to a separate recipe for icing it, entitled 'Icing, for Twelfth or Bride Cake'. The egg whites for this seventeenth-century version of royal icing were not separately whisked – everything was beaten together till thick, including 'as much powder Blue as will lie on a sixpence'.[1] We were brought up to observe the maxim that substances stored in the laundry were not for use in the kitchen. In the eighteenth century when it was first mentioned in a recipe, 'powder' or 'stone blue' was a washing whitener, and was made from an extract of the indigo plant mixed with starch.[2] Unlike some of the synthetic blues manufactured for laundry use later in the nineteenth century, Dr Kitchiner's icing whitener was probably safe to use. It is interesting that Kitchiner believed that one cake recipe would serve both for a twelfth cake and wedding cake, and that one icing was suitable for both. While the wedding cake was to be plain-iced, the twelfth cake's iced surface should be ornamented 'with Gum Paste, or fancy articles of any description'.[3]

Most examples of royal icing from nineteenth-century sources required the cook to beat the egg whites to a stiff froth before slowly adding the powdered sugar – this was the method that became popular in the eighteenth century. But not one of these recipes was actually called 'Royal Icing'. Instead it might be described as 'A Fine Icing for Cakes', or in America, as 'Cake Frosting'. The earliest recipe to be named 'Royal Icing' was published by confectioner William Jarrin in 1827, but he made no mention of egg whites, and gave no guidance on quantities.[4] A recipe from I. Roberts in *The Young Cook's Guide* (1836) is more typical:

Royal Iceing

Take two pounds of double refined sugar, pound and sift it through a silk sieve; put it into a basin, wet it with the juice of a lemon, a little orange-flower water, and white of egg; beat it with a spaddle, and when of a thick consistence, and perfectly white, it is fit to use in building pieces, motées, iceing of cakes, or any other purpose which may be required.[5]

Before writing this manual, Roberts had been cook to the Duke of Gloucester. The reference to 'pieces, motées' should have read 'pièces montées' or set-pieces, which were elaborate constructions of sugar paste much loved by pastry-cooks and confectioners.

There is no doubt that royal icing was a versatile material in the hands of skilled professionals. John Massey and his son produced a trade manual in 1866 that provides some convincing evidence that cakes made for the Christmas period, and sometimes still called 'Twelfth Cakes', were not sold with a layer of almond icing beneath the royal icing.

No. 122 Twelfth Cake

Make a cake, No. 121, or a plainer mixture would do for this purpose; trim and ice it neatly, as for Wedding Cake, No. 142, omitting the almond icing; ornament it according to fancy with a comic figure in the centre, and bonbons, liqueur ornaments, &c. (which get at the confectioner's), round; fasten them with Royal Icing, No. 145, introducing a little artistic piping in coloured icing between the ornaments.[6]

The Masseys' recipe for royal icing dispensed with the preliminary whisking of the egg whites. Instead the cook was instructed to put three whites into a round-bottomed basin, and add enough icing sugar to form a stiff batter. Two teaspoons of lemon juice were added during the beating, which must be done with a new wooden spoon. The mixture was ready to apply to the cake when the spoon stood upright in the basin.[7]

When a quicker method of mixing royal icing appeared in America, it was greeted enthusiastically. In 1877, Mary Henderson introduced the section on 'Frosting' in her book *Practical Cooking and Dinner Giving*, with the following remarks:

> The old way of making frosting was a half-day's work. I now laugh at the extra exertion once made to be sure that the eggs were sufficiently and properly beaten. The following is the true way to make frosting, which is done and dried on the cake in ten minutes, allowing three minutes for the making:
>
>> Use a heaping tea-cupful of fine pulverized sugar to the white of each egg, or, say, a pound of sugar to the whites of three eggs. Beat the whites until they are slightly foaming only; do not beat them to a froth. The sugar

> may all be poured on the egg at once, or, if considered easier to mix, it may be gradually added. Either way, as soon as the sugar and eggs are thoroughly stirred together, and flavoured with a little lemon or vanilla, the icing is ready to spread over the cake.[8]

Mary Henderson's famous contemporary, Maria Parloa, declared that this new method gave 'a smooth, tender frosting', qualities that made up for the lower volume it produced.[9] Considering the many types of icing to be found in their cookery books, American food-writers were probably good judges. By the late 1880s, their cake icings were often very colourful and were flavoured with an increasing range of essences. Fanny Gillette, author of the *White House Cook Book* wrote 'The flavors mostly used are lemon, vanilla, almond, rose, chocolate, and orange'.[10] The colours were derived from cochineal, indigo, saffron, strained orange rind, spinach juice, and chocolate – all plant-derived, or in the case of cochineal, from an insect. Various shades of pink could be obtained from using strawberry, currant or cranberry juice.

In England at about the same time, Mrs Beeton's *The Book of Household Management* gave recipes for five icings. All but one were royal icings made the old-fashioned way with stiffly beaten egg whites. The fifth was a boiled icing specified for a marble cake.[11] The editor made the interesting comment, 'On very rich cakes, such as wedding, christening cakes, &c., a layer of almond icing ... is usually spread over the top, and over that the white icing ...'.[12] With no mention of Christmas cakes, we conclude that almond icing was still not routinely placed on English Christmas cakes.

In New Zealand, however, the late-nineteenth century saw the adoption of cookery ideas from America as well as from Australia and Britain. Many New Zealand newspapers included recipes in their women's pages, and on-line searching has helped us identify their sources. The most significant example as far as the Christmas cake is concerned is a recipe for a 'Splendid Fruit Cake', published in the *Otago Witness* on 5 December 1885 under the heading 'Christmas Cookery' and sub-heading 'Christmas Cakes'. The recipe was introduced as derived 'from the notebook of a famous Virginia housekeeper'.[13] It was a very large pound-style cake, starting with 3 lb each of butter and sugar. At the end of the recipe was the instruction 'Frost with almond icing'. The American source was *Jennie June's American Cookery Book*, first published in 1866.[14] However the American recipe, though identical in ingredients and method, had a different title – 'A Fine Bride Cake'. The author, Jane Croly, supplied recipes for both the almond icing and what she called 'Sugar Icing', our royal icing. Ten years after its first publication in the *Otago Witness*, the recipe reappeared under the title 'Christmas Cake'.[15] Whether or not New Zealand cooks made this particular cake, with its twenty-four eggs, and expensive sweetmeats, is immaterial. The recipe's history of publication in New Zealand shows how local cooks transformed the wedding cake with its two layers of icing into their Christmas cake. A similar story is apparent in Australian cookery columns from the first decade of the twentieth century.

All told, the 'traditional' Christmas cake, complete with almond icing and royal icing, is not quite as traditional as we once thought. Though the component parts have long histories, putting them all together was not accomplished until the end of the nineteenth century.

No more examples are needed to demonstrate that when home-cooks began to rename familiar recipes as Christmas cakes, the recipes they selected were much more likely to have been called 'Plum Cake', or 'Rich Plum Cake', than 'Twelfth Cake'. This should be no surprise, because twelfth cakes seem to have been the specialty of pastry-cooks and confectioners, and they used whatever recipe – pound, plum, or bride – was most suited to the size of the intended cake. Only Kitchiner's 'Twelfth Cake' recipe seems to have been developed for a domestic setting.

Changes in fruit cakes in the nineteenth century

Of the three most prominent women cookbook writers of the nineteenth century, Mrs Rundell (1808) and Eliza Acton (1845) addressed their advice to 'private families', while Isabella Beeton (1861) wrote for women running a 'household'. Comparing their books, we can trace the labour-saving and cost-cutting changes in cake-making that domestic cooks and housewives adopted during this century. Mrs Rundell provided five recipes for cakes containing dried fruit, ranging from 'A very good common Cake' to 'Plumcake' and 'A very fine Cake'.[54] The last was a variant of a pound cake and relied on the separate beating of twenty yolks and twenty whites for aeration. The other four were raised by yeast in the old way. In size, Mrs Rundell's fruit cakes were similar to those from the late eighteenth century,

In this illustration from Mrs Beeton's *The Book of Household Management* (1899), the wedding and christening cakes (numbers 19 and 7) were iced, but not the plum or fruit cakes (numbers 6 and 22). No Christmas cake was included. H. Leach Collection.

made with from 2 lb to 4 lb of flour. Eliza Acton restricted herself to just two fruit cakes, requiring 1 lb of flour each.[55] One was simply entitled 'Pound Cake' and the other 'White Cake'. Both used about 1 lb of eggs, in one case beaten together, in the other separately. The new raising agent, baking soda, was listed only in her 'Madeira Cake' and 'Soda Cake' recipes.

By the time Mrs Beeton was assembling her household guide, just fifteen years later, cooks were aware that chemical raising agents made domestic cake-making much quicker. It was also more economical as the number of eggs could be drastically reduced. Recipes for fourteen fruit cakes appeared in Mrs Beeton's 1863 edition – nine used baking soda or baking powder, three were raised by yeast, and only two called for prolonged beating of eggs.[56] One of her recipes was called 'Rich Bride or Christening Cake', and one was the gingerbread 'Christmas Cake' discussed earlier. There was a large 'Common Plum Cake' raised with yeast, and 'A Nice Plum Cake' that included baking soda and only small amounts of butter, currants and peel. It would not have appealed to a cook in the colonies looking for a rich plum cake suitable for Christmas.

Other changes in ingredients distinguish the nineteenth-century fruit cakes from those of the eighteenth century. Fewer spices were named individually in the recipes, and it was more common to refer to 'mixed spice'. Ginger became more popular, sometimes teamed up with a new import known as allspice or Jamaica pepper. Almonds that were to be included in the cake were now more often sliced or slivered than ground or pounded into a paste. More recipes called for 'mixed peel' instead of specifying candied citron, orange or lemon peel. Milk was added to the cheaper fruit cakes, further substituting for eggs. Essences had yet to be widely adopted; however 'syrup' (golden syrup) and treacle were available and increasingly added. Treacle not only provided the acid needed to react with the baking soda, but it also contributed a dark colour to the cake crumb.

As the nineteenth century drew to a close, many different fruit-cake recipes had been seconded as Christmas cakes, often by the editors of newspaper cookery columns in need of copy. Most were considerably smaller than the cakes made in the first half of the nineteenth century, and most followed the pound cake principle. This produced a rich cake that would have kept well, but would also have been expensive. Among the numerous cake recipes provided by Mrs Beeton in response to new methods of aeration was a less costly Christmas cake recipe that remained in circulation for over one hundred years. The twentieth century would see even more scope for variation to suit household means, advances in technology and the supply of ingredients.

5
Christmas cakes in twentieth-century New Zealand

In the course of collecting and studying New Zealand cookbooks, we have found that recipes for baking occupy more pages in fund-raising cookbooks than other categories. This is not because local cooks are addicted to home-made cakes and biscuits – though baking is a rewarding activity in every sense – but because baked goods, especially cakes, have a particularly low tolerance to variation in the proportions of their core ingredients. These must be measured out accurately and mixed in the prescribed order. The cake tin should be of the right size for the quantity, and prepared so that the finished product doesn't break apart on removal. The recommended oven temperature and cooking time must be followed, and so on. While most cooks in the twentieth century already knew how to roast meat or make a pot of vegetable soup, very few trusted cake recipes to memory. That is why fund-raising cookbooks contain only small numbers of meat or vegetable dishes compared to a profusion of cakes, puddings and biscuits, where following the recipe really matters.

Within these large baking sections, we nearly always encountered recipes for Christmas cakes. We noticed differences and wondered whether Christmas cake recipes had changed over time in any systematic way, and whether such changes reflected events occurring beyond the home. When we undertook our first study of this cake type, we recorded the quantities of each ingredient in every recipe, in order to assess its contribution to the total cake weight. Obviously we could not make every recipe in order to establish cake weights. Instead we added the weights of all dry ingredients in the recipe, including eggs, and used these as a proxy for the weight of the cake after it was baked. We also had to assign weights to such uncertain quantities as 'a small teacup of sugar'. Once every imperial weight and volume measurement (e.g. pounds and ounces, pints and breakfast cups) had been carefully converted to metrics, statistics were calculated on the basis of 383 Christmas cake recipes printed in 158 community (fund-raising) cookbooks. These books had been published in New Zealand between 1901 and 1980.[1] Many interesting trends were revealed, including some that were clearly linked to economic conditions – in particular those during the Depression and through two World Wars. We felt it would be worthwhile to repeat the analysis with a larger sample, and to cover the whole of the twentieth century.

Since the first study, we have obtained more cookbooks and have recorded recipes from a selection of magazines and newspapers, as well as from the books written by influential food-writers. The original data set has been expanded to 828 Christmas cake recipes covering the whole of the twentieth century. The same questions underpin the new analysis. Did average cake weights change significantly over the course of a very dynamic century, and did the proportions of the major ingredients vary over that period. Did cakes become 'richer', with proportionally more butter or sugar? Did they become 'fruitier'? Did cooks respond to rising egg prices by reducing the number of eggs? In order to have a sample large enough to be examined in five-year blocks, which are more sensitive than the decade intervals we initially used, we treated Christmas cakes as a single 'population'. This was justifiable because cooks think of them as a distinctive type of cake, even though there seems to be an increasing number of variations.

We also undertook a second type of analysis, more suited to identifying recipe relationships and lineages, similar to the study of the pavlova cake.[2] This teases out recipe types and variants and allows them to be followed through time. But before looking at the evolution of these cake types we need to describe the population overall and answer the question: what characterises the cakes that people have associated with Christmas in twentieth-century New Zealand?

Christmas cake size and ingredients in the twentieth century

Starting with size, the statistics show a Christmas cake that became progressively smaller through the course of the century. We now recognise that this continued a trend apparent since the seventeenth century. In the twentieth century the decade of rationing and disruption of supplies associated with World War II obviously had an impact, but total cake weights did not subsequently return to pre-War values. Instead, they continued to drop until the 1970s. A small rise occurred in the later 1980s. Overall, the cakes of the troubled first half of the twentieth century, with its Depression and wars, were consistently heavier than those of the second half. Decreasing household size is probably the best explanation for this trend.[3]

Table 5.1 Total mean cake weights in grams and pounds/ounces, by five-year intervals, based on 828 New Zealand Christmas cake recipes.

1900–4	1905–9	1910–4	1915–9	1920–4	1925–9	1930–4	1935–9	1940–4	1945–9
3208g	3718g	3543g	3465g	3429g	3214g	3320g	3226g	2996g	2832g
7lb 1oz	8lb 3oz	7lb 13oz	7lb 12oz	7lb 9oz	7lb 1oz	7lb 5oz	7lb 2oz	6lb 10oz	6lb 4oz

1950–4	1955–9	1960–4	1965–9	1970–4	1975–9	1980–4	1985–9	1990–4	1995–9
2981g	2807g	2694g	2697g	2505g	2552g	2634g	2806g	2531g	2588g
6lb 9oz	6lb 3oz	5lb 15oz	5lb 15oz	5lb 8oz	5lb 10oz	5lb 13oz	6lb 3oz	5lb 9oz	5lb 11oz

Cake size fell when we might have expected a post-war rebound. This did not necessarily imply that cake composition changed – after all, it is relatively easy to halve a recipe. In fact, we discovered that there were some trends in the relative proportion of ingredients that were quite independent of the decline in size. As will be seen in Table 5.2, four key ingredients (flour, sugar, butter and eggs) contributed progressively less to the total weight of the cake, while a fifth (fruit) became even more dominant through the course of the twentieth century. When we consider how small the fruit portion was in the seventeenth century fruit cakes, we can see that this trend to 'fruitiness' has been underway for three centuries.

Nutritionists can take heart from the fall in saturated fats (chiefly butter) from 15 to 9 per cent, and the apparent halving in sugar. However, dried and candied fruits also contain sugar (62 to 73 per cent), as does the new ingredient of one of the most popular cakes – the condensed milk Christmas cake. Each 395 g tin of sweetened condensed milk contributes 221 g of sugar to the cake. Although some cakes may contain less granulated sugar (the sort measured from a bag), the increase in fruits overall and the addition of this non-traditional sweetened product may make up the difference.

The decline in the percentage of flour in Christmas cakes has been gradual since it peaked in the late 1920s at 21 per cent. We think that the traditional role of flour in the Christmas cake – to hold the fruit and nuts in a moist, even-textured matrix – has diminished as the cake has become fruitier. Today's cakes are solid with fruit, and the

Table 5.2 Percentage contributions of bulk ingredients to total cake weight in New Zealand Christmas cakes, by five-year intervals, 1900–99 (n=828).

	1900–4	1905–9	1910–4	1915–9	1920–4	1925–9	1930–4	1935–9	1940–4	1945–9
Flour	19	18	17	17	17	21	18	18	19	18
Sugar	18	14	16	14	11	13	13	12	15	12
Butter	15	14	13	12	14	13	12	11	12	12
Eggs	13	15	15	14	14	12	11	12	10	10
Fruit	33	36	34	39	40	39	42	41	40	45
Nuts	1	2	5	3	4	3	3	5	3	2

	1950–4	1955–9	1960–4	1965–9	1970–4	1975–9	1980–4	1985–9	1990–4	1995–9
Flour	17	18	19	17	18	16	16	15	16	16
Sugar	12	13	13	12	11	11	10	11	10	9
Butter	12	12	11	11	11	10	11	10	10	9
Eggs	11	11	11	10	10	9	10	10	9	8
Fruit	46	45	44	46	46	49	49	49	48	53
Nuts	3	2	2	3	3	2	1	3	4	5

chunky brazil nut date cake (also known as Cathedral Cake) that we will discuss later can have as little as 100 g of flour mixed with just over a kilo of fruits and nuts.

Of all the bulk ingredients in the Christmas cake, eggs and butter seem to have been most sensitive to market prices. In Chapter 6, we will profile some recipes that were developed to cut down on egg use, especially during the period of rationing and the price rises of the 1950s. From a high point just before World War I, when eggs provided on average 15 per cent of the total cake weight, the figure reached 8 per cent at the end of the twentieth century.

Butter prices were more easily stabilised than those of seasonally affected eggs. Despite price control from 1939 to 1967, the proportion of butter in Christmas cakes drifted down steadily from 15 per cent at the start of the century to 9 per cent at the end. Over the same period, New Zealanders increased their butter consumption at a very steep rate until the late 1960s.[4] The falling contribution of butter to Christmas cakes from the start of the twentieth century was clearly not driven by price or health concerns, but is likely to be a side-effect of the cake becoming more solid with fruit.

After an initial rise at the end of World War I,[5] the contribution of fruit to New Zealand Christmas cakes levelled off at around 40 per cent. At the end of World War II, butter, eggs and sugar remained under rationing, while dried fruits were imported in large quantities from Australian producers.[6] Not unexpectedly, they provided an acceptable way of bulking up the cake – after all, dried fruit had long been the exotic, expensive ingredient of traditional cakes. Once rationing ceased, New Zealand cooks steadily increased the fruit contribution from 46 to 53 per cent by the end of the century. In contrast, nuts have made up from 1 to 5 per cent of total cake weight over the twentieth century, with much fluctuation. We have noted a recent increase since 1985, which may correlate with the rise of the brazil nut date cake, and increasing availability of New Zealand-grown walnuts and hazelnuts.

Types of twentieth-century Christmas cakes

A separate analysis, not attempted in our earlier study, was designed to identify variation in the Christmas cake, and to follow different types through the twentieth century. The data set contained the details of ingredients and method from 713 recipes. In 1900, nearly all Christmas cakes were of the pound type. That statement probably needs further explanation. When the pound cake emerged in the eighteenth century, it required the cook to measure out a pound each of butter, sugar, eggs and flour. The butter was beaten with the sugar until it was creamy and light – hence the instruction that became common in the twentieth century, to 'cream the butter and sugar'. Dried fruit could be added to make a fruit cake, or caraways to make a seed cake. Cooks quickly understood that the pound cake was not so much a recipe as a principle, and they were free to convert it, for example by doubling or halving the quantities or employing other multiples. Furthermore, there was considerable leeway for stretching the relative quantity of two of the ingredients – flour and fruit – without spoiling the texture or flavour of the cake. We found many examples of nineteenth- and twentieth-century Christmas cakes with a pound each of butter, sugar and eggs supporting one and a quarter pounds, or even one and a half pounds, of flour, and up to four pounds of fruit and nuts, without any assistance from chemical raising agents. So how many New Zealand Christmas cake recipes followed the pound-cake principle – that is to say, creaming

Table 5.3 Percentages of five main types of Christmas cake by decade, grouped according to methods of mixing.

	1900–9	1910–9	1920–9	1930–9	1940–9
Pound type (n=574)	93	100	87	97	80
Boil & bake (n=33)					2
Melt butter (n=32)	3		3	2	
Custard (n=28)			3		7
Brazil (n=12)					

	1950–9	1960–9	1970–9	1980–9	1990–9
Pound type	91	76	77	73	60
Boil & bake		5	7	11	9
Melt butter		3	9	8	13
Custard	6	5	3	2	9
Brazil		2	2	3	6

Notes:
Pound type: usually distinguished by the instruction to cream the butter and sugar
Boil & bake: pre-boil all ingredients except eggs, flour and raising agent
Melt butter: dissolve butter and sugar in hot liquid
Custard: make thin custard with eggs and milk and add to dry ingredients
Brazil nut date cake: no butter; stir beaten eggs into fruit/nuts/flour mixture

the butter and sugar, and following the accepted range of proportions? To answer this question, we assigned all recipes in the new data set to type, based on their distinctive methods of mixing.

Five methods of mixing were common, especially from the 1960s onwards, but only one was dominant over the whole century – the pound type. This eighteenth-century type made up 80 per cent of all twentieth-century Christmas cakes in New Zealand. In size, cakes of this type ranged from two-pound cakes (with two pounds of each of the main ingredients), down to quarter-pound cakes with names like 'Small Family Christmas Cake' or 'Economical Christmas Cake'. However, three

Table 5.4 Percentages of the three most common sizes of twentieth-century New Zealand Christmas cake made according to pound-cake principles, by five-year intervals (n=471).

	1900–4	1905–9	1910–4	1915–9	1920–4	1925–9	1930–4	1935–9	1940–4	1945–9
1 lb	50	71	70	69	100	63	54	44	48	50
¾ lb	10	0	0	9	0	17	8	17	22	6
½ lb	10	0	0	9	0	21	19	28	26	44

	1950–4	1955–9	1960–4	1965–9	1970–4	1975–9	1980–4	1985–9	1990–4	1995–9
1 lb	45	30	38	12	26	8	25	23	12	20
¾ lb	8	15	8	12	3	16	11	13	15	13
½ lb	30	33	40	53	39	59	45	46	45	53

sizes predominated – the one pound, the three-quarter pound and the half pound, and their prevalence in each five-year interval reflects the downward trend in size that was evident in the total cake weight statistics. In 1900 there was a 50 per cent likelihood that the cook started making her Christmas cake by softening a pound of butter, ending the process with a cake that weighed over six pounds (2.7 kg). In 1999, her great-granddaughter was most likely to soften 225 g (half a pound) of butter to start her Christmas cake, provided that she had selected a recipe of the pound cake type. However, her resulting cake might weigh 2.125 kg – over four and a half pounds instead of three – because of the greater proportion of fruit in late twentieth-century pound cakes.

Variations in twentieth-century Christmas cake ingredients

We have looked at changes in average cake size, proportions of ingredients and methods of mixing. It is equally important to examine variation because that is the key to the identification of recipe lineages, those strings of recipes that reveal in their measurements and wording that they are in essence the same recipe being passed from one cook to another, sometimes via publication, at other times on a scrap of paper. Variation in nine important cake lineages will be dealt with in the next chapter. Before introducing them, we want to survey variations in the ingredients and their temporal patterns. A convenient format is that of questions and answers.

Is butter or some other type of fat found in all twentieth-century New Zealand Christmas cakes? Excluding the fat component of nuts and eggs, the answer is that only fourteen of the 713 recipes required no fat – one was for an unbaked Christmas cake, one for a cake with sweetened condensed milk (already containing 32 g of fat), and twelve were for brazil nut date cakes. Since nuts are good sources of fatty acids, mostly in the form of polyunsaturated oils, there is no need to add extra fat to a cake that contains three cups of assorted nuts. Of the remaining recipes, 97 per cent called for butter. The exceptions consisted of two recipes from 1905 and 1943 with dripping (the fat left in the pan after roasting meat), one with lard (rendered pig fat) from 1944, and one offering a choice of lard or margarine from 1940. Fifty years later, a 1996 Christmas cake for diabetics called for oil and a 1998 one stipulated margarine. Another twelve recipes recommended half and half mixtures of fats – butter with cod fat or dripping featured in several 1940s recipes. There is no doubt that until very recently cooks preferred butter in their Christmas cakes and would use another fat or oil only under special circumstances – during rationing or for medical reasons. We predict that this strong attachment to butter will weaken during the twenty-first century. Cakes that used two pounds of butter, or in one case three pounds, haven't been made since the Edwardian era. Butter proportions have fallen steadily ever since that time and this trend is likely to continue.

Was sugar added to all the Christmas cakes? The answer is that all but two of the recipes we recorded contained sugar in one or more forms, in addition to the sugars in the dried and candied fruit. The two exceptions, one from 1981 and the other 1998, used artificial sweeteners and were cakes for diabetics. Thirteen recipes made do with the sugar contained within sweetened condensed milk, and one unbaked Christmas cake used the crumbs of crushed sweet biscuits as a base. Brown, demerara or raw sugar was specified for 224 cakes, and caster sugar for thirty-three. Honey as the sole sweetener was found in only seven cakes, all of the unbaked variety with a biscuit crumb base. It was also added to a few cakes that relied on sugar

---

In 1896 this image of Jessie Buckland engaged in Christmas baking in the family's Strath Taieri farm kitchen was submitted to one of *The Australasian* magazine's photographic competitions. The Bucklands' Christmas cake would have included proportionally less fruit than cakes of the twentieth century. A copy of Beeton's *The Book of Household Management* lies open on the table. Courtesy of the Hocken Collections/Uare Taoka o Hakena, University of Otago, Dunedin S10-221 Jessie Buckland, Album 210 p. 5.

or golden syrup as their main sweetener. Where listed, treacle and golden syrup were used alongside white or brown sugar, with golden syrup in nearly a quarter of the cakes and treacle in a tenth. These liquid sweeteners played additional roles, imparting their distinctive flavours to cakes, darkening them in the case of treacle, and activating baking soda through their acidity. Similarly, the inclusion of jam or jelly (in 46 recipes), or marmalade (49) was not primarily for their sweetness. Nearly all the recommended jams were distinctively flavoured and dark-coloured, in particular blackcurrant jam. The marmalade was explicitly identified as a substitute for candied peel in one 1939 recipe, and this justification could apply to about half of the 49 recipes, those with marmalade but no peel. Overall, sweetness is integral to the Christmas cake, but can be achieved with a wide range of sweet substances.

What other substances were added to darken Christmas cakes? Sixteen recipes, published from 1950 to 1999, called for cocoa, or in two cases for chocolate. Coffee was first listed in a 1930 recipe, and nearly half of the fifteen examples with coffee specified coffee essence. Instant coffee seems to have been used for the first time in a 1967 recipe. Eleven recipes referred to gravy browning, caramel or 'Parisian essence' (spiced caramel) – all intended to darken the cake. Until the 1930s, caramel was sometimes made by the cook, by burning sugar – no instructions were supplied. Later it was purchased as a concentrate. Parisian essence is more commonly listed in Australian recipes than in New Zealand, and it is possible that the four recipes containing this substance came from Australian sources.

How many Christmas cake recipes contained no eggs? Only 24 recipes were egg-less, and there were two distinct cake types represented in this total. One with twelve examples was a form of sweetened condensed milk cake, made by the 'boil and bake' method. The other, represented by eight recipes, was the unbaked Christmas cake that clearly would be unacceptable with raw egg included in the ingredients.

How were eggs incorporated in Christmas cakes? Nearly a third of the recipes instructed cooks to break the eggs into the mixture, one or two at a time. This method was the least likely to trap air. Fifteen per cent of the recipes indicated that the eggs should be beaten before adding to the creamed mixture, usually in small quantities alternately with the dry ingredients. Just under 10 per cent of the recipes stated that the yolks should be separated from whites, with the beaten yolks mixed in first, and the whisked whites folded in last of all. This was the method that aerated eighteenth-century pound cakes before chemical raising agents were available, and its persistence into the twentieth century might be considered an anachronism. However, of the 65 recipes that required separation of the yolks and whites, 32 used no baking powder or baking soda – in other words, their lightness still depended on the air beaten into the yolks and whites. Not surprisingly, the majority of these recipes were of pound cake type. Separation of the eggs was reasonably common in the first two decades of the twentieth century, occurring in at least a fifth of the recipes. Although it is still seen in recipes from the 1990s, the frequency is no higher than 3 per cent.

What other raising agents have been used? Just two recipes, from 1944 and about 1947, recommended yeast and one of these also called for baking soda. Nearly a third of all recipes used no chemical raising agent at all, while another third listed baking powder. Just over a quarter of the cakes used baking soda. The remainder required combinations of baking soda and cream of tartar, or baking soda and baking powder. Alison Holst reminded her readers more than once that rich fruit cakes do not need these raising agents, and listed them as optional.[7] The number of recipes with just token amounts of baking powder supports her observation.

What was the role of glycerine and how often was it used? Glycerine is an anti-staling agent that helps cakes to stay moist. We found it listed as an ingredient in 41 recipes, published between 1929 and 1995. Most were for pound cakes, with a small number of 'boil and bake' cakes. Five of the cakes with glycerine contained canned pineapple, and all had a generous allowance of eggs. There seems no functional reason why they should include glycerine. It is worth noting that glycerine is a common cake ingredient in Australia, where it is believed to improve cake quality in hot dry weather – the practice could have been introduced to New Zealand through the cookery columns of Australian women's magazines.

What types of flour have been used in Christmas cakes? The only Christmas cake recipes that omit flour as an ingredient are the unbaked type with crushed biscuit bases – a case of recycled flour, perhaps. Ten recipes specify self-raising flour, eight add a small amount of cornflour to supplement the plain flour, and two replace this cornflour with ground rice. White flour has remained the dominant source of starch in our Christmas cakes. Only sixteen recipes have included wholemeal, wheat germ, wheat flakes, bran or a commercial product like Vi-max or All-Bran. In seven cases, plain white flour has also been used alongside these. The wholemeal recipes cluster during the 1940s and since 1985. Until 1946 New Zealand's milling extraction rate was 73 per cent, which effectively excluded any portion of the vitamin-rich wheat germ or bran layers from the resulting product. The extraction rate was raised to 80 per cent from 1946 to 1949, then lowered to the present 78 per cent.[8] These higher rates ensure useful amounts of vitamin B1 are present in our white flour.[9] Why should wholemeal Christmas cake recipes be more prevalent when white flour was closer in composition to wholemeal than ever before? We can only guess that public health and the food value of staples had become talking points as a result of rationing. The more recent examples of wholemeal in Christmas cakes are in recipes adapted for diabetics.

What nuts have been used in twentieth century Christmas cakes? Overall, just over 60 per cent of the recipes included nuts. The proportion of recipes with nuts in each five-year interval fluctuated quite markedly, reaching 89 per cent in the late 1930s, and slumping to around 40 per cent from 1975 to 1985. The only explanation we can offer is that the tight import controls in place from 1958 to 1975 had depressed demand for almonds and that this had a knock-on effect on recipes over the next decade. Almonds have always been the most popular nut, in keeping with tradition. Only 44 recipes called for ground almonds – for most recipes they were sliced or chopped. Walnuts were included in 14 per cent of the nut-bearing cakes, a distant second to almonds. Were walnuts seen as a cheaper substitute for imported almonds? Only three recipes with walnuts were published before World War II. Disruption to shipping clearly encouraged the use of home-grown walnuts during the 1940s, but cooks continued to use walnuts as economic conditions returned to normal. They were added to the unbaked Christmas cake and were a common ingredient in the brazil nut date cake, making up half of the total quantity of nuts in this unusual cake. Although they served as a substitute in wartime, they have been appreciated in their own right ever since. Other nuts that have played an even smaller role are the brazil nut, the cashew, the hazel and its close relative the filbert.

What dried fruits have been common in Christmas cakes? In the seventeenth and eighteenth centuries, currants and raisins predominated in rich fruit cakes. Sultanas became available in the nineteenth century, and as Australian and Californian dried fruit production expanded, all three dried fruits became the foundation of New Zealand Christmas cakes. The most popular dried fruit of the twentieth century was the naturally seedless sultana, closely followed by currants and raisins. For the first half of the century, recipes usually stipulated the quantities of each type, though

Table 5.5 Percentage of recipes specifying sultanas, raisins, currants or pre-mixed dried fruit, by five-year intervals.

	1900–4	1905–9	1910–4	1915–9	1920–4	1925–9	1930–4	1935–9	1940–4	1945–9
sultanas	45	50	60	69	100	64	85	72	72	79
raisins	73	44	90	74	100	68	85	78	75	58
currants	72	100	80	83	100	64	72	83	75	67
pre-mixed	0	11	10	11	0	14	8	0	22	33

	1950–4	1955–9	1960–4	1965–9	1970–4	1975–9	1980–4	1985–9	1990–4	1995–9
sultanas	61	61	42	58	50	37	33	43	55	52
raisins	52	53	36	54	44	33	31	42	49	48
currants	66	57	46	41	42	33	33	40	43	39
pre-mixed	41	45	56	44	50	69	74	66	51	55

a few left it up to the cook and simply stated the total weight of fruit to be added to the cake. Commercially mixed pre-packed dried fruit was available in New Zealand shops from the 1930s. Wellington grocers, Fuller Fultons, advertised mixed fruit at one shilling per packet,[10] and we know from slightly later advertisements that each packet held a pound. At the same time, raisins and sultanas cost six pence per pound[11] – presumably the inclusion of candied peel and cherries in the mixture accounted for the higher price. Regardless of cost, New Zealand home cooks were keen to adopt pre-mixed fruit. We suspect this was not because it saved them the trouble of buying and measuring out separate amounts, but because the mixed packets contained pre-cleaned fruit. Picking over, washing and drying fruit for cakes had been mandatory since the seventeenth century. Pre-mixed fruit offered a huge saving in time. Its adoption is evident in Christmas cake recipes from the early 1940s onwards.

Only one Christmas cake type contains no raisins, sultanas, currants or mixed fruit. We found nine recipes for a 'White Christmas Cake' where the fruit is usually made up of candied peel, glacé pineapple and cherries. The recipe was contributed to the *New Zealand Woman's Weekly* in 1962 and then appeared in fund-raising cookbooks from Wanaka to the Waikato over the next two decades.[12]

What other dried fruits have been included in Christmas cakes? Dates are listed in just 11 per cent of our recipes overall. Their use increased between 1915 and 1919, and again between 1945 and 1949. Imports from Iraq resumed quickly at the end of 1945, and presumably included dates, which had not been available for several years.[13] Another peak is evident from 1965 to 1975, when dates were often added to pineapple Christmas cakes, and the first brazil nut date cakes made an appearance. Figs were sometimes listed as an alternative to dates. They have never been popular and of the 36 recipes that include figs, 31 were published before 1965. After minimal use for most of the century, prunes appear in eight recipes from the 1990s: in six recipes for unbaked Christmas cakes, and two for brazil nut date cakes. Dried apple is limited to just one recipe from 1996, compared to stewed or grated apple in eight recipes from 1947 to 1992.

Was candied fruit consistently popular over the twentieth century? Combining the figures for candied, glacé, crystallised, and syrup-stored fruits, together with ginger root processed with sugar, we found that overall 58 per cent of recipes listed candied peel as a separate ingredient, and 38 per cent listed cherries. Preserved ginger was used in only 12 per cent of recipes – but we should not forget that a ginger flavour can also be obtained from ground ginger, or from ginger ale. When we add in the cakes made with pre-mixed fruit, which normally contains both peel and cherries, we can say that 96 per cent of our Christmas cake recipes contain one or more of these sweetmeats. The changes in popularity of each type appear in Table 5.6.

The adoption of pre-mixed fruit seems to have affected candied peel use from 1950. Preserved ginger was unaffected by this trend, and its popularity has fluctuated, with a peak in the 1930s and 1940s. Knowing that cherries are an ingredient of mixed fruit, we might have expected their purchase as a separate ingredient to decline in the same way as peel. Instead, cherries became increasingly popular from the late 1960s. Coloured photographs of cakes were the norm in magazines and commercially published books from about the same time – we wonder whether they encouraged cooks to make their own cakes more colourful with extra cherries.

What other ingredients were used to give a citrus flavour? Until the late 1930s, finely grated fresh citrus rind and/or juice were relatively rare additions to our Christmas cakes. Lemon and orange rinds increased in ingredient lists from the late 1940s, and for the rest of the century can be found in from 14 to 30 per cent of cake recipes. From the 1960s, orange was more frequent than lemon, and its juice was

Table 5.6 Percentage of recipes listing candied peel, ginger and cherries, by five-year intervals.

	1900–4	1905–9	1910–4	1915–9	1920–4	1925–9	1930–4	1935–9	1940–4	1945–9
peel	91	89	90	91	100	82	87	89	78	75
ginger	9	0	0	14	0	11	18	17	25	13
cherries	0	6	0	6	0	32	41	39	44	46
	1950–4	1955–9	1960–4	1965–9	1970–4	1975–9	1980–4	1985–9	1990–4	1995–9
peel	61	59	42	49	54	37	30	43	43	39
ginger	5	14	8	15	8	8	8	13	14	10
cherries	39	35	34	56	48	43	38	40	51	45

often included as well as the rind. The old practice of adding orange-flower water survived in only six recipes, of which five were from the first half of the twentieth century.

Did cake mixtures include more liquid through the course of the twentieth century? This is certainly the impression that many older cooks have formed, but it is not easy to quantify with a single measure. If we examine a typical one-pound cake recipe from the Edwardian period, the only liquid present, other than in the ten or twelve eggs, was one or two wineglasses of brandy or sherry. A similar-sized pound cake from the 1990s might have some of the alcohol replaced by orange juice, but has no more liquid. Recipes calling for a cup of water, pineapple or orange juice, or a small bottle of ginger ale, mark a departure from this pattern. However they usually omit alcohol from the mixture, though it may be poured over the cake when taken from the oven. These non-traditional liquids are not normally added to the cake as it is being mixed, but are a means of plumping up the fruit. Two methods are common: soaking the fruit overnight, or boiling it. In both cases the fruit absorbs liquid, and with boiling there is also some evaporation. The resulting cakes may have moister fruit but the batter is not so wet that a longer cooking time is required. More liquid is involved in the processing of the ingredients, but not all of it makes it into the cake batter.

How common was milk and cream in New Zealand Christmas cakes? Nearly a quarter of the recipes contain milk, condensed milk or cream, both fresh and sour. In most cases it was the activator for baking soda, or compensated for a reduction in eggs. However, it became the keynote ingredient in two distinct types of cake that we discuss in the next section of the book: the custard Christmas cake and the different variants of the condensed milk cake. The custard cake was introduced in the late 1920s and the first of the condensed milk type appeared in New Zealand in the late 1960s.

How many Christmas cakes contained alcohol? Collecting the figures is complicated by the fact that some recipes offered alternatives to the usual brandy and/or sherry, and some called for more than one type. Wine, rum, whisky, port and orange liqueur all made an appearance, but brandy predominated as it had since the eighteenth century. It was listed by itself or with sherry or rum in 192 recipes. A simpler way of showing the trends through time is to calculate the percentage of recipes that do not include any alcohol. This exercise clearly shows that in the 1990s we were more likely to put alcohol in or on Christmas cakes than were the cooks of the first three-quarters of the twentieth century.

Despite its name, ginger ale is a non-alcoholic beverage. Thirty-eight recipes used this liquid ingredient to plump up the dried fruit, beginning in 1943. All but three recipes recommended soaking the fruit overnight. The three exceptions speeded up the process by boiling or simmering the fruit in the ginger ale.

What spices were common in twentieth-century Christmas cakes? Over the course of the century, a total of 432 recipes included spices. However 62 per cent of those recipes left the type of spice up to the cook, or recommended the use of commercially available 'mixed spice'. One brand of mixed spice that we use contains coriander, cinnamon, 'pimento' (allspice), ginger, cassia, nutmeg and cloves, but we do not know their proportions, nor whether all of these spices have been included in earlier formulations of mixed spice. Where the recipes specify individual spices, the most common are cinnamon (249 recipes) and nutmeg (242). Less popular are ground ginger (67), mace (54) and cloves (52). Knowing the composition of one brand of mixed spice, we weren't surprised to find that curry powder (in 23 recipes), allspice (17), cayenne or unspecified pepper (8) and even coriander and cardamom (2 each) had been listed. Spice use fell to 40 per cent of recipes in the early 1960s and peaked at 84 per cent in both the late 1930s and 1990s. No obvious correlations with external conditions explain these fluctuations.

Table 5.7 Percentage of Christmas cake recipes not using alcohol, by five-year intervals.

1900–4	1905–9	1910–4	1915–9	1920–4	1925–9	1930–4	1935–9	1940–4	1945–9
55	44	60	49	n.s.	64	69	72	66	63

1950–4	1955–9	1960–4	1965–9	1970–4	1975–9	1980–4	1985–9	1990–4	1995–9
59	67	60	56	50	45	39	34	37	23

What was the contribution of essences to Christmas cakes? Half of our twentieth-century recipes called on the concentrated flavours of essences to enhance the resulting cake. Lemon and vanilla essences were already in use in some late nineteenth-century recipes, and almond essence made its first appearance in a New Zealand Christmas cake recipe in 1915. However, only fifteen cakes from the 105 published during the first three decades of the twentieth century contained essences of any type. Through the course of the twentieth century, vanilla was the most frequently used essence (in 231 recipes), with almond (221) and lemon (177) nearly as common. One group of essences mimicked the flavour of spirits. Whisky essence appears in a 1927 recipe, with rum, brandy and gin essences first mentioned in the 1940s. Needless to say, cakes that contained real spirits did not call for imitation essences. World War II's constraints encouraged the use of fruit-flavoured essences such as orange (in 20 recipes), pineapple (7), and cherry (5). As with spices, some recipes left the choice of essence up to the cook, simply stating 'any or all essences'. Given the number on sale by the 1950s, there was a danger of competition between the flavours. The maximum number of essences recorded in a single cake was seven in a 1955 recipe: half a teaspoon each of vanilla, 'sherry' (cherry was probably intended), pineapple, orange, brandy, lemon, and almond. Multiple essence use continued to the end of the century, although the usual recommendation was for the three that had the longest history: lemon, vanilla and almond.

What about salt? Not a single recipe stipulated unsalted butter, so the contributors of the 205 Christmas cake recipes that listed extra salt, in amounts ranging from a token pinch to one and a half teaspoons were adding a substance that was totally unnecessary. Tradition dies hard, especially in cakes with as long a pedigree as the

Christmas cake. We believe that the salt in just under one third of our twentieth-century cakes is present only because it once had a legitimate role in the bread-cakes of the seventeenth century. Even fruit breads benefit from a small amount of salt. Pound cakes have more than enough salt from the generous proportion of butter they include.

Anything else worth mentioning? Five recipes from 1958 to 1974 made use of candied angelica stems for their interesting flavour and greenish colouring. Four recipes listed coconut, three included bananas, two recommended grated carrot, and one suggested 'any old jam (up to one pot)'. We can think of no other cake with such diversity in ingredients.

6
Christmas cakes from the last hundred years

When it came to choosing specific recipes to illustrate the evolution of the Christmas cake in New Zealand during the twentieth century (and just beyond), we had first to pick out the lineages that were best represented in the cookbooks. In some cases, a cluster of related recipes achieved widespread popularity over a short period. In others, descendants of one ancestral recipe became well entrenched, persisting over many decades, with minor modifications as each generation of cooks adjusted the recipe to their needs. Some recipe groups stood out for sharing a distinctive ingredient or combination of ingredients, or for a radical departure from the usual method of mixing. Unique recipes weren't eligible, though they contributed their data to the statistical analysis.

The cake that put on weight

The honour of being the first Christmas cake chosen to represent the twentieth century went to Edmonds' recipe published in the first edition of *The "Sure to Rise" Cookery Book* in 1908.[1] It fulfilled our selection criteria without difficulty, being not only the first of a very long-lasting lineage, but one widely disseminated through New Zealand. Edmonds' cookbooks have been published for over a century and this recipe appeared in every edition from 1908 to soon after 1980. The Edmonds' cookbook is often claimed to be New Zealand's overall best-seller. Total sales had reached three million copies when the company's centennial edition appeared in 1978 – this marked one hundred years since the founding of T.J. Edmonds, not the printing of the first cookbook. To be fair to its competitors, we should note that the first six editions (1908–36) were sent free of charge to people who wrote for a copy.[2]

One of the strengths of the cookbook has been the numerous revisions, responding to trends in baking and later to a desire by the company to provide an

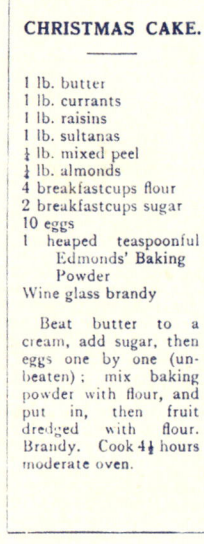

Edmonds provided the first illustration of their popular Christmas cake in 1923, in the fourth edition of *The "Sure to Rise" Cookery Book* (opp. p. 16). H. Leach Collection.

all-purpose cookbook. A comparison of the recipes in the first two editions of 1908 and 1910 with those of the Economy and De Luxe editions of 1955 has shown only eleven recipes survived virtually unchanged – a very low retention rate.[3] Perhaps it would be better described as New Zealand's best-selling cookbook series. Even the Christmas cake recipe was modified, though it is still recognisable as a descendant of this original recipe of 1908:

CHRISTMAS CAKE

1 lb butter
1 lb currants
1 lb raisins
1 lb sultanas
¼ lb mixed peel
¼ lb almonds
4 breakfastcups flour
2 breakfastcups sugar
10 eggs
1 heaped teaspoon Edmonds' Baking Powder
Wineglass brandy

Beat butter to a cream, add sugar, then eggs one by one unbeaten; mix baking powder with flour, and put in, then fruit dredged with flour. Brandy. Cook 4 ½ hours, moderate oven.[4]

The changes to this extremely succinct recipe highlight some of the most important problems faced by the twentieth-century cook. In Edmonds' fifth edition, published about 1931, the four breakfast cups of flour became 2 lb, and the two breakfast cups of sugar became 1 lb.[5] Few housewives had any form of standard measuring cup, and in practice some measured out a heaped or rounded breakfast cup of flour, while others interpreted the quantity as a level measure. This variation could have a profound effect on the success of a recipe. Edmonds' conversion of the four breakfast cups of flour to 2 lb was based on one heaped breakfast cup weighing 8 oz [ounces].[6] Four level breakfast cups – which is how we interpreted the original recipe – should have converted to four times 6 oz, or 1 ½ lb. Edmonds' conversion meant that the cake gained an extra ½ lb.

The next change was to give the oven heat in degrees Fahrenheit. From the late 1920s to the 1950s, New Zealand stove manufacturers had fitted 'heat indicators' to oven doors – these were not thermostats, but thermometers. Oven heat in an electric stove was regulated by turning on top and bottom elements manually. In a coal range, stoking the firebox with shiny coal, adjusting the dampers to send the hot air around the oven box, and controlling the draught were the pre-requisite skills for successful baking. By 1955, as thermostats became more common in electric stoves, Edmonds recommended cooking this cake for 'about 4 ½ hours' at 350 degrees Fahrenheit. This was not a straightforward conversion. Different stove manufacturers and food-writers offered a wide range of equivalents to what had formerly been called 'moderate' oven heat. In her recent study of changing stove technology in New Zealand, Jane Teal found that 'moderate' could be as low as 275 degrees or as high as 375 degrees Fahrenheit.[7] In 1964, the sixth printing of Edmonds' De Luxe edition advised cooking this cake at 350–375 degrees.[8] This would have been a satisfactory temperature for the first hour of cooking, but the temperature should then have been allowed to fall. In the era when this cake was cooked in a coal range, falling oven heat would have been the normal course of events – it was not a good idea to put fresh fuel on while a cake was in the oven. Whether or not Edmonds received letters about burnt or over-browned cakes, they made a major adjustment for the new and revised edition of 1968: this Christmas cake was now to be baked at 250–275 degrees Fahrenheit.[9]

Metrication of household measurements occurred in 1974.[10] Edmonds' 1978 centennial edition inserted the metric equivalents, with the old imperial measurements in brackets.[11] Once again adopting a new system required careful choices, for few cooks have scales capable of measuring 454 g, the equivalent of

1 lb. Edmonds decided to convert 1 lb to 500 g instead of the 450 g that became the usual conversion by the 1980s. Because there were eight ingredients affected by this choice, the cake gained an extra 347 g in the process. As for the baking powder, it was a sensible decision to convert the original heaped teaspoon (of uncertain size) to two metric teaspoons.

We have described what Edmonds did with their own recipe – but in the hands of home cooks and other food-writers even more interesting changes occurred. In one recipe, the wineglass of brandy became 'half a tumbler' – a tumbler was a drinking glass of no set capacity.[12] Others converted the wineglass to a less-risky two or three tablespoons. Some recipes offered alternative alcoholic liquors – rum was the most popular, then whisky, sherry and port. Of the twenty-four versions of the recipe published from 1917 to 1990 (other than in Edmonds' cookbooks), nearly half added cherries, in quantities ranging from 3 oz to 1 ¼ lb. Dates were added to just three recipes. The quantity of almonds was sometimes raised to ½ lb, as was the mixed peel. The lack of spice in the original recipe was quickly amended, with cinnamon, mixed spice, nutmeg, mace and ginger added in various combinations and quantities. However, only a quarter of the recipes added essences, and these were sometimes listed as an alternative to the liquor. From 1929 some contributors made adjustments to the recommended oven temperature, initially changing 'moderate' to 'slow', and later advising readers to reduce the temperature as cooking progressed.

Two very influential cookbooks reproduced versions of Edmonds' original Christmas Cake, which helped to keep it in wide circulation. One was the revised edition of the New Zealand Women's Institutes nationally distributed *Home Cookery Book*, published in 1939.[13] It offered the recipe under the title 'Christmas or Birthday Cake'. The second book was compiled by Mrs Sybil D. Sherriff, who held a Diploma in Home Science, and was President of the Roxburgh Branch of the Women's Division of Federated Farmers. She prepared the book for the GHB (Good Housekeeping Bureau), claimed to be the largest grocery organisation in New Zealand in the 1960s. Three large printings were made of the *GHB Cookery Book* from 1961 to 1968, involving 116,5000 copies. Mrs Sherriff's recipe called for 1 ½ lb flour,[14] which suggests that the four breakfast cups of the original recipe had been converted before Edmonds undertook their own conversion to 2 lb flour in 1931. Mrs Sherriff's recipe halved the amount of almonds, but added crystallised cherries.

Having sketched out the directions Edmonds' Christmas cake took during the twentieth century, we should address its origins. They are much more obscure because the recipe does not have unusual ingredients or distinctively worded instructions to facilitate a search. We know that the early Edmonds' editions share several recipes with *Dr Chase's Third, Last and Complete Receipt Book and Household Physician*, published in America in 1886.[15] Other recipes are shared with early fund-raising cookbooks published in Christchurch in 1903 and Wellington in 1905.[16] However, the closest recipe we have found to Edmonds' Christmas cake is one from the Presbyterian Church of New South Wales Women's Missionary Association's *Cookery Book of Good and Tried Receipts* (1896):

> **PLUM CAKE**
> Take 1 ½ lbs. flour, 1 lb. butter, 1 lb. sugar, 10 eggs, 1 lb. raisins, 1 lb. currants, ¼ lb. cut peel, 3 teaspoonsful baking powder. Beat the butter to a cream, add the sugar, then the eggs, then the flour and baking powder, and lastly the fruit and peel. Line a cake-tin with buttered paper, and bake in a moderate oven.[17]

The Edmonds' cake has three extra ingredients – sultanas, almonds and brandy – perhaps these were added to convert a plum cake into a Christmas cake. Even if no borrowing occurred, we can treat them as typical examples of a class of cake increasingly promoted during the second half of the nineteenth century by the manufacturers of baking powder. Before the first brands came on to the market in Britain in the 1850s, rich fruit cakes based on the pound-cake principle had been raised for over a century by the air trapped in laboriously beaten egg yolks and whites. To achieve this effect, such cakes required large numbers of eggs. The Royal Baking Powder Company of New York explicitly addressed this problem in their cookbook of 1902:

> Eggs are too expensive nowadays to be used as lavishly as they were a generation ago – ten or more to a cake. Not as a substitute wholly, but as an accessory, – as an aid toward producing the lightness and digestibility of the food, – we use the Royal Baking Powder.[18]

In New Zealand, where home egg production was probably much more common than in New York state, the ten eggs of Edmonds' Christmas cake were not excessive, given its total weight. But chemical raising agents were increasingly appreciated for cutting down the mixing time. In Edmonds' cake, the eggs required no prior beating. We recorded twenty-eight Christmas cake recipes from New Zealand books and newspapers over the period 1900 to 1909, and found that only four included baking powder and three, baking soda; so Edmonds' cake was up-to-date with its heaped teaspoon of baking powder.

EDMONDS' CHRISTMAS CAKE

Adapted from 'Christmas Cake (2)', in *Edmonds Cookery Book* (Deluxe Edition 14th printing 1974). Make this large cake several weeks before Christmas, as storage improves both the texture and flavour.

900 g bread flour	450 g butter
450 g currants	450 g sugar
450 g sultanas	10 eggs (size 6)
450 g raisins	2 teaspoons baking powder
120 g peel	¼ cup brandy
120 g almonds, chopped	

Prepare a 26–27 cm diameter-round pan or a 22–23 cm-square pan by lining with a double layer of brown paper and a single layer of baking paper. Preheat the oven to 140°C with a shelf in the middle or slightly below.

Weigh the flour. Combine the dried fruit and almonds in an extra-large bowl or preserving pan. Sprinkle 2 tablespoons of the weighed flour over the fruit and mix through, breaking up any lumps of fruit.

Soften the butter in a large bowl and cream with the sugar until light coloured and fluffy. Add the eggs one at a time, beating well between each addition. If necessary, add a few spoonfuls of the weighed flour to help prevent curdling.

Sift the weighed flour with the baking powder. Fold gradually into the creamed butter mixture. Spoon into the fruit along with the brandy. Fold gently until thoroughly mixed.

Spoon evenly into the prepared cake pan. Smooth the surface with a wet hand. Bake for 4–4 ½ hours. (Details on how to test when a cake is cooked are given on page 168.)

Leave in the pan until cool. Turn out on to a rack or tray. Remove brown paper and baking paper before wrapping in greaseproof paper. Store in an airtight cake container or wrap in foil.

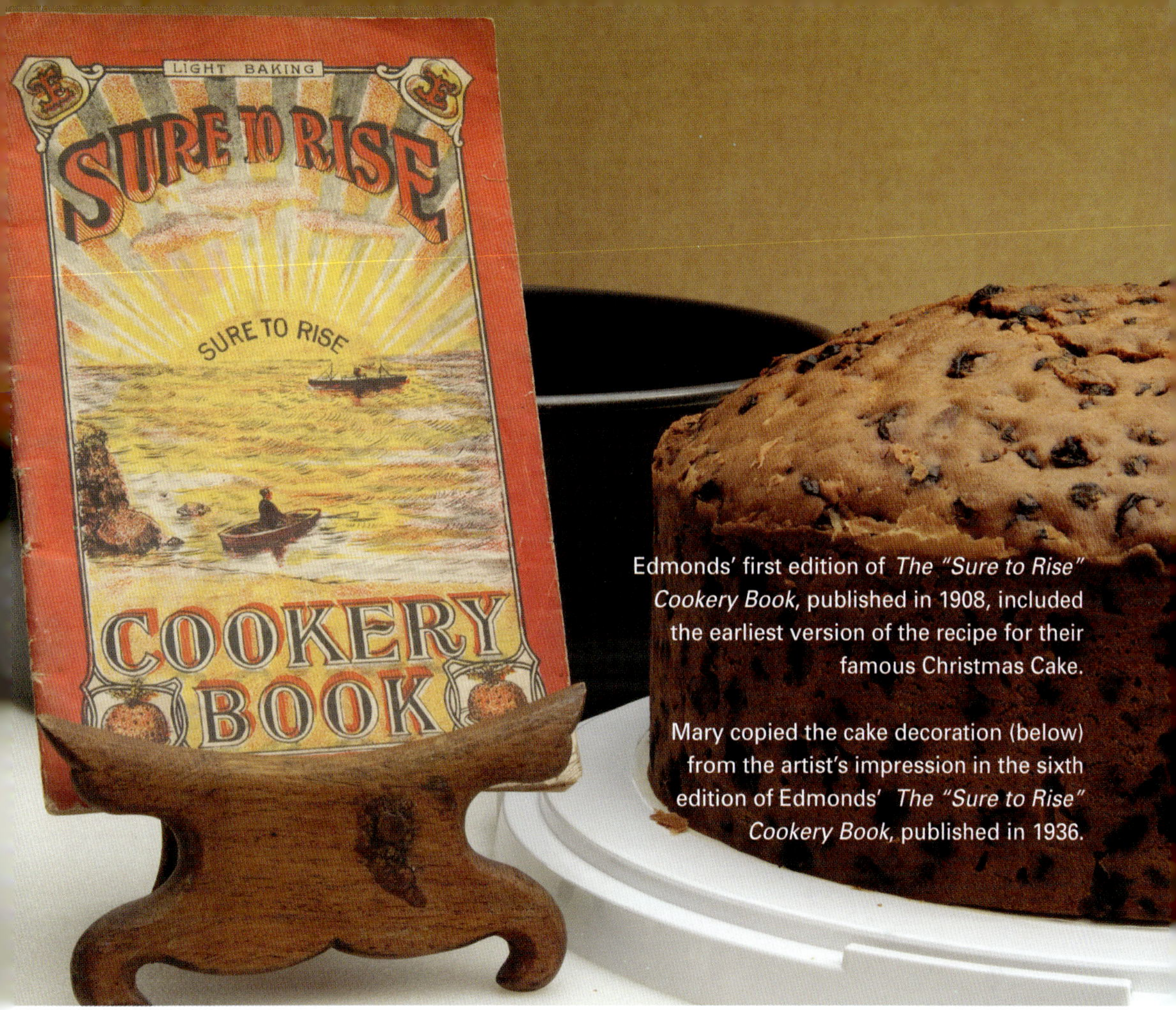

Edmonds' first edition of *The "Sure to Rise" Cookery Book*, published in 1908, included the earliest version of the recipe for their famous Christmas Cake.

Mary copied the cake decoration (below) from the artist's impression in the sixth edition of Edmonds' *The "Sure to Rise" Cookery Book*, published in 1936.

In the naming of one other ingredient – sultanas – this cake was advanced for its time. These seedless light-coloured raisins had been traded throughout the nineteenth century, originally from Turkey. California began production by the 1830s and Australia in the 1870s.[19] Sultanas were more expensive than currants and dark raisins, and this fact may explain why they were slow to appear in recipes. The first New Zealand recipe that we found with sultanas was a 'Raisin Cake' published in 1873.[20] It called for 1 lb 'Sultana raisins'. Throughout the nineteenth century, this was how they were described. It was not until the twentieth century that they became simply 'sultanas'.

A 'Black Cake' transformed – Mrs Harman and Mrs Gard'ner's recipe

In 1904, just four years before Edmonds produced their first cookbook, the Christchurch publisher Whitcombe and Tombs issued the fourth edition of a home cookery manual written by two Christchurch cookery teachers, Mrs R.D. (Alice) Harman and Mrs S. (Elizabeth) Gard'ner. First published in 1900, *The New Zealand Domestic Cookery Book* was in such demand that a new edition had appeared each year.[21] We have not seen the first three editions but know from newspapers that the book was revised and considerably enlarged by the time the fifth edition came out in 1905.[22] By 1904, the Cakes section contained recipes for twelve assorted fruit cakes, one of which was entitled 'Christmas Cake or Bride Cake'[23] – the remainder had names like 'Good Plum Cake', 'Rich Fruit Cake', 'Raisin Cake', 'Sultana Cake', 'Rich Currant Cake', a strong indication of how important the fruit cake was in the Edwardian cook's repertoire.

The 'Christmas Cake or Bride Cake' recipe has many conservative features, reminding us of cakes from as long ago as the eighteenth century. For a start it has no raising agent other than a dozen separately beaten egg yolks and whites. It contained a spice combination that would not have been out of place in the days of Hannah Glasse – mace, nutmeg and cinnamon. Orange-flower water was another ingredient typical of the eighteenth century. The recipe clearly reveals that this is a pound cake with extra fruit and nuts:

Mrs Harman and Mrs Gard'ner's 'Christmas Cake or Bride Cake' would have been suitable for a wedding breakfast such as this English example from the 1890s, depicted in Theodore Garrett's *The Encyclopaedia of Practical Cookery* [1894]. Courtesy of the University of Otago Library.

CHRISTMAS CAKE OR BRIDE CAKE

Flour 1 lb.
Butter 1 lb.
Sugar (sifted) 1 lb.
Eggs 12
Raisins 2 lb.
Currants 2 lb.
Candied peel ½ lb.
Mace 1 tablespoonful
Cinnamon 1 [tablespoonful]
Nutmegs 2 (grated)
Sherry 1 wineglassful
Brandy 1 [wineglassful]
Orange flower water 2 teaspoonsful
Almonds ½ lb.

Mix brandy and sherry together, and put the spice to steep in it over night. Stone the raisins, clean the currants, blanch and chop the almonds, and dredge all lightly with flour. Beat butter and sugar together to a cream, separate the yolks from the whites of the eggs, beat the yolks light, and add them to the butter alternately with the flour, a little of each at a time, till both are well mixed; then beat the whites to a stiff froth, and stir them lightly in; lastly add the fruit and citron. Bake in a slow oven about two hours.[24]

We were keen to know the immediate source of this recipe. It could not be found in recipe columns of nineteenth-century New Zealand newspapers, and so we searched a wide selection of English and Australian cookbooks – but nothing matched. Elizabeth Gard'ner was brought up in Sweden and England and after moving to Tasmania with her civil engineer husband, she took up the position of superintendent at the newly established School of Domestic Instruction in Christchurch in 1895.[25] Unlike Alice Harman, Elizabeth did not have formal qualifications in cookery. Alice held a diploma from the North Midland School of Cookery in England and became the cookery teacher at Christchurch Girls' High School about 1895.[26] Neither teacher had any obvious connection with America, but that was where we found the ancestors of this recipe.

The closest match was in one of the first generation of fund-raising cookbooks to be published: the *Presbyterian Cook Book*, compiled by the 'Ladies of the First Presbyterian Church' in Dayton, Ohio, in 1873.[27] It seems unlikely that this book was owned by either Alice Harman or Elizabeth Gard'ner – we think that there is another American book (yet to be identified) that influenced both the Presbyterian ladies of Dayton and our Christchurch cookery teachers. The 1873 recipe, called 'Fine Fruit Cake', differs only in a few details: it contained no orange-flower water or almonds. Instead of sherry, it called for 'Maderia [sic] wine', and it required 'citron' rather than 'candied peel'. The quantities of the other ingredients were identical. Most convincing was the recommendation to pre-soak the spices – Mrs Harman and Mrs Gard'ner said 'Mix brandy and sherry together, and put the spice to steep in it over night', while contributor Mrs A. F. Payne of Dayton wrote 'Mix a large wine glass of Maderia wine, and one of brandy, together, and steep the spices in it over night'. This instruction to steep the spices in alcohol characterises the eight New Zealand recipes that were probably influenced by Mrs Harman and Mrs Gard'ner's popular manual. In date, they ranged from 1904 to 1988.

The first copy appeared in the Christchurch *Star* in 1904,[28] and was virtually identical to Harman and Gard'ner's recipe. During World War I, a Wellington fund-raising book introduced the first of several changes to the mix of dried fruits – it substituted preserved ginger for candied peel and added half a pound of sultanas, reducing the currants by 1 lb.[29] Another recipe deleted the sherry,[30] but unlike one from about 1947, did not list orange juice as a substitute.[31] The number of eggs was reduced from twelve to ten, and the flour was increased in a 1933 Depression-era recipe.[32] At the same time this recipe added ½ lb cherries, suggesting that economy was not behind the changes. Difficulties with supply probably explain why the orange-flower water was deleted in five of the recipes. Surprisingly, the spices were left unchanged, though three recipes reduced their quantities.

The longevity of Mrs Harman and Mrs Gard'ners recipe was undoubtedly affected not only by the multiple editions of their book – it was still on sale in 1924 – but by the re-appearance of slightly modified versions in three nationally distributed cookbooks. The first was *The Prizewinner Recipe Book*, which appeared about 1933 under the name of Elsie Harvey. Its contents included (unacknowledged) recipes that had won prizes in recipe competitions held by the *New Zealand "Truth"* in 1931. Elsie Harvey and her husband distributed this and her later books by travelling through the country and working through home-based agents. The second influential compiler who kept this recipe in circulation was 'Aunt Daisy' (Maud Basham) in her book *Aunt Daisy's New Cookery No. 6* published about 1947.[33] Daisy's first two books provided the pseudonyms of some of her contributors, but in later cookbooks there is no way to track her sources. The third cookbook with this recipe, *700 Neeco Tested Recipes* (about 1951), accompanied locally made Neeco stoves which were commonly installed in New Zealand homes in the decade after World War II.[34] Because this book was a favourite when we were children, we chose to modernise its version of the recipe.

CHRISTMAS OR WEDDING CAKE

1 lb. flour
1 lb. butter
1 lb. sugar
12 eggs
2 lbs. raisins
1 lb. each of sultanas and currants
½ lb. candied peel

½ lb. almonds
1 tablespoon mace
1 tablespoon cinnamon
2 grated nutmegs
1 wineglass each of sherry and brandy
2 teaspoons orange flower water

Mix brandy and sherry together and steep the spice in it overnight. Blanch and chop the almonds and prepare the rest of the fruit and dredge all lightly with flour. Beat butter and sugar to a cream. Separate egg yolks from whites, beat the yolks till light and add them to the butter alternately with the flour, a little of each at a time, till both are well mixed, then beat the whites to a stiff froth and fold them lightly in. Lastly add the fruit and steeped spice. Bake for 4 ½ hours in oven 350°, top element off, bottom low.[35]

This recipe, that was so successfully transplanted to New Zealand, can be traced back to the early-nineteenth century in America. Table 6.1 (p. 109) shows some of the names under which the recipe appeared, before and after its arrival in this country.

CHRISTMAS OR WEDDING CAKE

Adapted from 'Christmas or Wedding Cake', as published in *700 Neeco Tested Recipes*, [1951]. The original recipe was for a 27 cm diameter-round or 23 cm-square cake. We have halved the quantities to make a 20 cm-round or 18 cm-square cake. The specified spices should be purchased whole, then ground to achieve maximum flavour. Soaking the spices in sherry and brandy produces a delightful mellow taste.

1 ½ teaspoons freshly ground mace	220 g sultanas
1 ½ teaspoons freshly ground cinnamon from a stick of cinnamon	220 g currants
1 freshly grated whole nutmeg	120 g peel
2 tablespoons dry sherry	450 g bread flour
2 tablespoons brandy	220 g butter
120 g whole almonds (blanching optional)	220 g sugar
450 g raisins	6 eggs (size 7)
	1 teaspoon orange-flower water

Mix the sherry and brandy together in a cup. Add the spices and leave to soak overnight.

Prepare a 20 cm diameter-round pan or an 18 cm-square pan by lining with a double layer of brown paper and a single layer of baking paper. Preheat the oven to 140°C with a shelf in the middle or slightly below.

In a large bowl, combine the dried fruit and chopped almonds. Add 3 tablespoons of the weighed flour and stir through, separating any lumps of dried fruit.

Soften the butter in a large bowl and cream with the sugar until light coloured and fluffy. Separate the egg yolks from the whites and beat the yolks until light coloured and thick. Add them to the creamed butter and sugar alternately with the flour 'a little of each at a time'. Beat the whites to a stiff foam (when the beater is removed, the peaks should just fold over). Fold the whites lightly into the cake mixture. Spoon the mixture into the dried fruit along with the spice mixture and the orange-flower water. Fold through gently but thoroughly.

Spoon evenly into the prepared cake pan. Smooth the surface with a wet hand. Bake for 2–2 ½ hours. (Details on how to test when a cake is cooked are given on page 168.) Leave the cake in the pan until cool. Turn out on to a rack or tray. Remove brown paper and baking paper before wrapping in greaseproof paper. Store in an airtight cake container or wrap in foil.

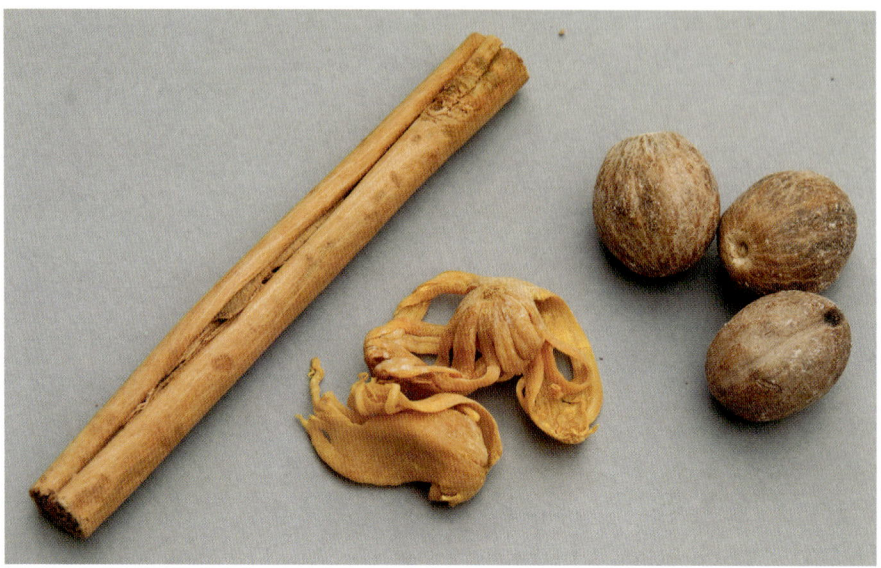

Freshly ground whole spices soaked overnight in sherry and brandy give the 'Christmas or Bride Cake' a deep and mellow flavour. From left to right: cinnamon stick, mace blades, nutmegs. Photo: Mary Browne.

It is clear that this recipe became a designated Christmas cake only after its importation to New Zealand. In America, it was primarily a wedding cake that could double as a 'plum cake', a term that was progressively replaced by 'fruit cake'. In New Zealand, it was a Christmas cake that was equally suitable as a bride or wedding cake.

The term 'Black Cake' was never adopted in New Zealand. By the time organised settlement was underway here, American publications were using other names for the cake, such as 'Wedding Cake'.[37] How did it acquire the name 'Black Cake' in the first place, since it is not an especially dark-coloured cake by modern standards? In his book *Wedding Cakes and Cultural History* (1992), Simon Charsley noted that

> Whiteness ... became a theme of American cake-making as it never did in Britain, with Angel (Food) Cakes as a characteristic development. Recipes were commonly called 'White Cake', providing a sharp contrast with the so-called 'Black Cake'.[38]

In this way the 'Plum Cake' or 'Rich Cake', that had been baked for important events such as Twelfth Night and weddings in eighteenth-century England, acquired a new name on transmission to America to distinguish it from the popular colonial 'white' cakes.

Table 6.1 Variation in the names given to the recipe for Harman and Gard'ners 'Christmas Cake or Bride Cake' before and after 1904.[36]

Date	Recipe Name	Source
1832	Black Cake, or Plum Cake	Eliza Leslie, *Seventy-Five Receipts …*
1840	Black Cake	Eliza Leslie, *Directions for Cookery*
1850	Fruit Cake, or Black Cake	*Miss Beecher's Domestic Receipt Book*
1852	Plum Cake, or Wedding Cake	Sarah Hale, *The Ladies' New Book of Cookery*
1857	Plum New England Wedding Cake	Elizabeth Ellet, *The Practical Housekeeper*
1873	Fine Fruit Cake	*Presbyterian Cook Book* [Dayton, Ohio]
1904	Christmas Cake or Bride Cake	Alice Harman & Elizabeth Gard'ner, *The New Zealand Domestic Cookery Book*
1904	Rich Christmas Plum Cake	*The Star*, 10 December 1904
1915	Christmas Cake	*The Amuri Cookery Book*
1915	Christmas or Bride Cake	*Our Boys' Cookery Book*
[1933]	Excellent Christmas Cake	Elsie Harvey, *The Prizewinner Recipe Book*
[1947]	Christmas Cake (With no Baking Powder)	*Aunt Daisy's New Cookery, No. 6*
[1951]	Christmas or Wedding Cake	*700 Neeco Tested Recipes*
[1952]	Christmas Cake	*Recommended Cooking* [Springs Ellesmere Plunket]
1988	Wedding or Christmas Cake	*Waitaki Favourites* [Waitaki Girls' High School]

We have shown how steeping the spices overnight was a key feature of the New Zealand examples of this recipe. In America, however, we found this instruction only in the most recent recipe, from the 1873 Ohio fund-raiser.[39] The orange-flower water and almonds were absent from all six American examples, so must be attributed to Mrs Harman and Mrs Gard'ner. Twice as much citron was used in four of the American recipes, but the bulk ingredients were almost identical in quantities throughout the history of this cake.

TO ICE OR NOT TO ICE – CHRISTMAS CAKES IN THE TWENTIETH CENTURY

Three editions of Edmonds' cookbooks came out between 1908 and 1914, each with the classic Christmas cake recipe we have profiled, but without a single mention of icing. We know from contemporary newspaper cookery columns that icing was optional, with richer cakes more likely to have the combination of almond icing and royal icing than those entitled 'Plain' or 'Economical Christmas Cake'. In 1923, the fourth edition of Edmonds' cookery book contained a new section, 'Fillings and Icings'. It included a recipe for 'Royal Icing', made with beaten egg white, but there was no recipe for almond icing. The Christmas cake recipe was accompanied by an artist's impression of the finished cake (p. 96).[1] It is covered in white icing with faint ripples. In the centre is a conical mound surrounded by shiny red and green balls. These also mark the outer top edge of the cake, while sprigs of holly with red 'berries' are attached to the bottom edge. When Edmonds' fifth edition appeared, about 1931, the 'Icings and Fillings' section contained a recipe for 'Almond Icing', designated as 'a good foundation for Royal Icing'.[2] For the sixth edition, there was a new illustration of the Christmas cake (p. 101, lower picture) – this shows the two layers of icing in the cut section, along with decorations in pink, red and green.[3]

In contrast, Mrs Harman and Mrs Gard'ner inserted recipes for 'Almond Paste' and 'Royal Icing (Plain)' immediately after their American recipe for 'Christmas Cake or Bride Cake'.[4] The quantities were enough for two layers of royal icing on top of the almond paste. Their royal icing followed the quick method popular in America in the late nineteenth century. While their icing recipes were relatively plain, we encountered several others that incorporated additional substances, such as blueing agents to make the top icing look whiter, citric acid, gelatine, glucose, and glycerine.[5]

In 1955 when Edmonds issued the first of their De Luxe editions, a third type of icing was listed as suitable for a Christmas cake – butter icing. If this type was intended as a substitute for royal icing, then it would have added significantly to the kilocalories in the finished cake.

BUTTER ICING FOR CHRISTMAS CAKE
(will keep)

6 ozs. Butter
1 lb. Icing Sugar
3 tablespoons Wine or Brandy
2 teaspoons Essence of Vanilla

Cream butter with sifted icing sugar; add brandy or wine and vanilla. Beat well.[6]

We know from several other cookbooks that very similar icings, referred to as brandy butter or Vienna icings, were used as single layers on the 'White Christmas Cake', a type of cake in circulation since 1962. In this cake, crystallised pineapple and cherries replaced the dried fruits such as raisins and currants.

As cooks experimented with new styles of Christmas cakes and icings, it was inevitable that the option of no-icing-at-all should be revisited. The no-icing option did not mean a plain top, but substitution with something that was just as decorative as icing. Cooks were instructed to place a layer of almonds (wholes or halves) on top of the batter just before the cake went into the oven. Alternatively, almonds could be attached with an egg white glaze 15 to 30 minutes before the cooking was finished. They could be sprinkled on, or arranged in a formal pattern that sometimes included cherries and other sweetmeats. The first recipe with the instruction 'Put in a lined tin and sprinkle with almonds' appeared in 1961 – it was for a 'Christmas Cake (Light)' in Mrs Sherriff's *GHB Cookery Book*.[7]

The chief proponent of Christmas cakes with such baked-on decorations has been Alison Holst. She wrote in *Meals with the Family*, published in 1967,

> 'Decorating the Christmas cake used to be one of the highlights of our Christmas holidays. We thought that a layer of almond icing and a coat of royal icing were necessities, and I can remember that both needed a great deal of sampling during the icing process!'[8]

After describing how to attach the sweetmeats and nuts, she concluded that 'These decorations can look most attractive on the top of a cake, with the addition of a cake frill and a candle, sprig of holly, or small tinseled decoration.'[9]

> What many of us read between her lines was that we could save time and money with these new cake toppings. To satisfy the traditionalists, she tacked on a recipe for home-made almond icing.
>
> Alison Holst recommended the almond-only, or almond and cherry topping for her 'Pineapple Christmas Cake', which made frequent appearances in *Alison Holst's Kitchen Diary* from 1978 to 1986. When the brazil nut date cake became popular, it lent itself to similar decorative treatment. The trend away from icings has had some other very influential supporters, including food-writers Lois Daish and Elisabeth Pedersen.[10]
>
> We have shown that the combination of almond and royal icings was only prevalent on Christmas cakes from the end of the nineteenth century – so it doesn't really deserve to be called 'traditional'. Its decline in the second half of the twentieth century does not mark the beginning of the end of the Christmas cake, but just another stage in its evolution.

There is a good chance that this recipe was baked for competitions. Today's 'Masterchef' series and similar 'bake-offs' may seem new and fashionable, but a survey of New Zealand newspapers shows that competitive baking was popular throughout the country at the close of the nineteenth century. The categories at the 1890 Geraldine Floral, Horticultural and Industrial Society included 'Best 4 lb currant cake made by amateurs only', while in 1894 the Golden Bay Agricultural & Pastoral Show had separate classes for 'Currant cake' and 'Plum cake'.[40] A Bay of Plenty horticultural show had only three entries for its 'Iced Plum Cake' in 1895,[41] but other shows attracted more. The most interesting venue for competitive baking was the School of Domestic Instruction where Mrs Gard'ner was principal. At the closing ceremony for the year 1899 the results were announced as follows:

> Competition in Cakes and Sweets – Division I., rich Christmas cake, Miss Brownlie; mixed cakes, Miss Rennie; sweets, Norah Merton; iced plum cake, Gladys Thomas. Division II., plain plum cake, Eva Edwards; sponge sandwich, Vale Barns; scones, E. Rutherford.[42]

As the only Christmas cake in the cooking manual written by her principal Mrs Gard'ner and external examiner Mrs Harman, this recipe is surely the one that brought Miss Brownlie success.

A home-grown country cake? Tui's and Aunt Daisy's blackcurrant cakes

Aunt Daisy's recipe appears to be the first of this type, published in 1935, a year before Tui's. However, we need to explain that both 'Tui' and 'Aunt Daisy' often re-published recipes that had been printed in the magazines or newspapers they were associated with, or broadcast on the radio. We think that Tui's 1936 recipe might actually be a little earlier in origin.

The book in which Tui's 'Dark Xmas Cake' recipe appeared, *Tui's Second Cookery Book*, was advertised for sale in 1936 in the widely read *New Zealand Dairy Exporter and Farm Home Journal*.[43] The book was described in the preface as 'a companion volume' to *Tui's Practical Cookery Book*, issued in 1933, and 'rapidly sold out'.[44] 'Tui', the name used by Norah Burnard,[45] editor of the women's pages, explained how the recipes were acquired: 'Each month in the "Dairy Exporter," and each year in "Tui's Annual," the pick of hundreds of tested recipes from country cooks are published, and these provided the first source from which the recipes in this second volume were drawn'.[46] If a section had insufficient recipes, extras were selected elsewhere – however, we don't think there would have been any shortage of cake recipes. It was the 1929 copy of 'Tui's Annual' that published the earliest known recipe for the Pavlova Cake.[47] The *New Zealand Dairy Exporter and Farm Home Journal* was established in 1924 and offered both prizes and payment for the recipes it published every month.[48] It advertised each year for women from country towns around New Zealand to sell 'Tui's Annual' on commission. This would have brought a welcome bonus at an expensive time of year. As yet, we haven't located the 'Dark Xmas Cake' recipe in the journal or annual, but 'Tui's' explanation of her selection procedures suggests it predates 1936.

As you will see, there is no doubt that Aunt Daisy's 'Howick Christmas Cake' is the same recipe, with a few minor adjustments to quantities.[49] The book in which it was first printed, *Aunt Daisy's Book of Special Recipes ...* was Maud Basham's third and it contained recipes from her overseas trip in February–March 1935, as well as from New Zealand contributors. Coming so soon after her first two books, both published in 1934, it seems more likely that the 'Howick Christmas Cake' recipe was sent in during 1935, rather than earlier. If that is the case, the version published by 'Tui' may be the older of the two. Either way, this recipe shows signs of the global Depression to which New Zealand succumbed from 1929 to 1934.

For cooks choosing a cake to make for Christmas entertaining, the Depression encouraged a reconsideration of the old recipes, with their wineglasses of brandy, dozen eggs, generous quantities of butter and almonds, and pounds of dried fruits. These large rich cakes were descended from Edwardian and Victorian times when families had more children – women marrying in 1880 had on average 6.5 children, while those marrying in 1891 had 4.7. For those marrying in 1925, the figure slumped to 2.4.[50] There was a relatively simple solution available for housewives who wanted to down-size their family Christmas cake, and that was to make either a three-quarter or half pound cake. Many of the existing recipes were for preparing pound cakes, and so she could make the conversion directly from the recipe. The imperial measuring system was pre-adapted for this sort of adjustment – instead of 1 lb butter, sugar, flour etc., the cook measured out ¾ lb or ½ lb. Her 'weighing machine' (a balance with a stack of weights and a pan) usually had weights from ½ oz to 4 lb or more, with each weight half the mass of the next one in the sequence. As long as you had learned at school that 16 oz make 1 lb, and that the 8 oz weight was equivalent to ½ lb, halving the quantities of a pound cake was possibly easier than halving 450 grams in your head.

There were certain ingredients, like brandy, that could not be bought in small quantities – in Wellington, a pint bottle of brandy cost 7s. in 1936, seven times the price of a movie ticket.[51] Other ingredients were perceived as expensive, whatever amount was used – candied peel, cherries and almonds were put in this category. For these ingredients, the solution was to make a substitution. The 'Dark Xmas Cake' we have selected not only incorporates an obvious reduction in size from a pound to a three-quarter pound cake, but has several interesting substitutions: in place of brandy or dark rum the recipe calls for five or six tablespoons of blackcurrant jam and in most early versions of the recipe a tablespoon of treacle. In the version published in 1935, home-grown walnuts supplemented the imported almonds. Preserved ginger has been an important ingredient from the beginning, and possibly because of the quantity used, all later versions dispensed with other spices.

671. – Dark Xmas Cake
Guaranteed to keep twelve months. ¾ lb. butter, ¾ lb. sugar, 1 lb. flour, 6 eggs, ¾ lb. sultanas, ¾ lb. seedless raisins or currants, ¼ lb. almonds, ¼ lb. preserved ginger, ½ packet spice, ¾ teaspoon soda, ¼ lb. lemon peel, and lastly five tablespoonsful of black currant jam. Beat butter and sugar to a cream, adding eggs one by one, beating with hand, then add flour with soda, then add fruit, etc., gradually; lastly, add black currant jam. Bake in a dry tin lined with brown paper for about three hours.[52]

Twelve examples of this recipe have been recorded, from the two printed in 1935 and 1936 to one called 'Grandmother's Christmas Cake', submitted by

Scales.—As one of the great elements of success in cooking is preciseness in the proportions of ingredients, the cook should never be without a good pair of scales, and she should keep them in thorough order. In delicate dishes an unequal proportion of an article inserted only to impart a certain flavour, will ruin the dish. The necessity as well as use of scales is therefore obvious.

'Weighing machines' such as this late Victorian example from Mary Jewry's *Warne's Model Cookery* (1893, p. 38) were common in New Zealand kitchens until the 1960s. They made recipe doubling or halving comparatively simple. The 14 lb weight was equivalent to a peck.
H. Leach Collection.

Pat McQuillan to *The NCW Centennial Recipe Book* of the National Council of Women, published in 1996.[53] Seven of the recipes retain the word 'dark' in the title, suggesting that they were descended either from the 1936 version set out above, or from the recipe published as 'Dark Fruit Cake (suitable for Christmas)' in editions of the *Home Cookery Book* of the New Zealand Women's Institutes published from 1939 to 1950.[54] Five recipes noted this cake's keeping qualities. As might be expected from the length of time the recipe has been in circulation, the 1996 recipe has departed from the original in several respects, introducing spices, sherry and essences, and dropping the ginger. We used Aunt Daisy's version of the recipe published repeatedly between 1935 and 1961 as a model for our cake, because it has dropped the imprecise half packet of spice.[55]

HOWICK CHRISTMAS CAKE

¾ lb butter.
¾ lb sugar.
1 lb flour.
¾ lb raisins.
¾ lb sultanas.
¾ lb currants.
½ lb. peel.
½ lb. preserved ginger.

6 eggs.
¼ lb walnuts.
¼ lb almonds.
½ teaspoon salt.
1 small teaspoon baking soda.
1 tablespoon treacle.
6 tablespoons black currant jam.

Cream butter and sugar. Beat eggs well and add separately. Add soda to flour, and then sift into creamed mixture. Then add fruit and treacle and lastly jam. (Sift some of the flour lightly over the fruit before adding to mixture). Cook in a slow oven 5 hours.[56]

6

HOWICK CHRISTMAS CAKE

Adapted from 'Howick Christmas Cake', first published in *Aunt Daisy's Book of Selected Special Recipes From California, Canada, France, Australia and New Zealand* (1935).

At the time when this cake was popular, the jam that distinguishes the recipe would have been homemade. It was economical to use up the jam from the last season or from even older batches. Homemade jam contains less sugar than the purchased product. If blackcurrant jam has to be bought for this recipe, choose a quality product and compare sugar content.

450 g bread flour	340 g butter
340 g raisins	340 g sugar
340 g sultanas	6 eggs
340 g currants	½ teaspoon salt
225 g peel	1 teaspoon baking soda
225 g crystallised ginger, chopped	2 tablespoons treacle
115 g walnuts, chopped	1 cup blackcurrant jam
115 g almonds, chopped (no need to skin)	

Prepare a 25 cm diameter-round pan or 23 cm-square pan by lining with a double layer of brown paper and a single layer of baking paper. Preheat the oven to 130°C with a shelf in the middle or slightly below.

Weigh the flour and set aside. In a large bowl place the raisins, sultanas, currants, peel, ginger, walnuts and almonds. Add 2 tablespoons of the weighed flour and stir through, separating any clumps of dried fruit.

Soften the butter in a large bowl and cream with the sugar until light and fluffy. In another bowl beat the eggs until foamy. Add to the creamed mixture a little at a time and continue beating. If the mixture shows signs of curdling add a spoonful or two from the weighed flour. Beat well. Sift the remaining weighed flour with the salt and baking soda. Fold into the creamed mixture.

Add the treacle and jam to the fruit and stir to mix thoroughly. Lastly add the creamed mixture and fold through gently but thoroughly.

Spoon into the prepared cake pan. Smooth the surface with a wet hand. Place in the oven and bake for 4 to 4 ½ hours. (Details on how to test when a cake is cooked are given on page 168.) Cover with a tea towel and leave in the pan until cold. Turn out on to a rack or tray. Remove brown paper and baking paper. Wrap in greaseproof paper and store in an airtight cake container or wrap in foil.

Blackcurrant jam gives this cake its dark colour.

Blackcurrants are of course not the same as the currants that make up the dried fruit in Christmas and other fruit cakes. Instead of being small black seedless grapes (once known as 'raisins of Corinth' – from which the name is derived), blackcurrants grow on bushes of *Ribes nigrum*. Closely related are the red and white currants from which we make jelly. The blackcurrant has the strongest flavour of the three, as well as deep purple pigmentation, perfect for darkening this cake.

Whoever thought of the idea of adding the blackcurrant's distinctive taste and colour to a Christmas cake is unlikely to be discovered. We favour the view that this particular cake developed in a country district in New Zealand, though not out of the blue. Cooks had been putting blackcurrant jam in puddings for many decades and it was an ingredient of a Christmas mincemeat recipe published in Auckland in 1911.[57] New Zealand readers of the *Australian Women's Weekly* might have spotted a recipe for 'Black Currant Christmas Cake' that won a 1s. consolation prize for a Mrs Day of Queanbeyan in December 1934.[58] The Australian recipe is in no way related to the New Zealand examples – however the idea might well have been the basis of our New Zealand recipe.

Making do with fewer eggs

Everyone has heard of wartime rationing, and there are many people who remember it personally, or who have heard from older generations how hard it was to find exciting recipes for offal (the only unrationed meat), or for cakes with no eggs, no butter and no milk. Fewer people know how long rationing regulations were in place, or that the prices of some key ingredients had fluctuated dramatically before World War II.

Immediately after the end of World War I, the price of eggs rose briefly to such high levels – 5s. per dozen – that 'there was an inclination in most households to abandon the use of this food, except in cases of absolute necessity'.[59] Eggs were considered vital for invalids, and public nervousness about influenza following the 1918 pandemic had driven demand. By 1923, the average price of a dozen eggs had fallen to about the same as 1 lb butter (1s. 9d.), and this relationship continued to the end of the decade. The Depression saw a fall in food prices, but incomes also diminished. Contemporary recipe books suggest that economies were applied just as much in the kitchen as in the public sphere. In the 1930s, there was a noticeable price threshold of 2s. per dozen eggs, above which consumption dropped.[60] Fortunately, Christmas cakes were made at a time of the year when egg supplies were good. From December 1938, butter prices were set at 1s. 6d. per lb. Egg prices, however, were not successfully stabilised despite government efforts, and in 1942 the average price began to climb until by 1949 a dozen eggs were more than twice the price of 1 lb butter.[61] Egg shortages in the early 1940s gave way to comprehensive egg rationing from March 1944.[62] While the price of butter remained fixed through the 1940s, the costs of poultry feed escalated. So even before rationing there were obvious economic pressures encouraging cooks to adjust old recipes or adopt new ones.

The first ration books were issued in April 1942, and sugar rationing commenced at the end of the month. It would last until the end of August 1948. At its most severe, the sugar ration was cut to 10 oz (283 g) per person per week in mid-1945. Special issues of 3 lb sugar at a time were made for jam making. Some of that might have been diverted into baking, but social pressure would have been placed on the housewife who offered any form of rich fruit cake to her friends. From the end of October 1943, butter was rationed to 8 oz (227 g) per person per week. The regulations were finally lifted in June 1950.[63] While they were still in place, we remember being told as small children that we could have butter or jam on our bread, but not both.

We can blame rationing for the rise in the number of cakes after 1942 that replaced some or all of the butter with dripping, or made do without it, as in the 'Economical Chocolate Sponge (Sugarless and Butterless)' in the *War Economy Recipe Book*.[64] Milk and golden syrup substituted for the butter and sugar. Eggless cake recipes were even more common, generally with an increased quantity of milk. The *War Economy Recipe Book* also contained a recipe for 'Cheap Fruit Cake' that called for two preserved eggs. Several products were on sale that people could use to prolong the usable life of surplus eggs for times when their hens had stopped laying. Preserved eggs were also available in grocers' shops. On reading this recipe closely, we realised that this cake had a rather unusual method of mixing:

CHEAP FRUIT CAKE.
1 lb. flour, 6 ozs. butter, 8 ozs. sugar, 2 preserved eggs, 1 lb. currants, ¼ lb. peel, 1 cup sultanas, 2 teaspoons soda, ½ pint boiled milk, 2 teaspoons lemon essence, 1 teaspoon almond essence. Rub butter into flour, soda and sugar, add fruit, etc., beat eggs. Put into boiling milk and beat again, and add to dry ingredients. Mix well and bake 2 ½ hours, according to tin.[65]

Most of us who have grown up making rich fruit cakes at Christmas time know that the butter is creamed with the sugar and that the eggs are added progressively, either beaten or unbeaten, alternating with the dry ingredients. This was the method recommended in the 1950s by British chefs and food scientists for cakes where the weights of the butter and sugar are each more than half the weight of the flour.[66] In a plain cake, the proportions of butter and sugar to flour are much lower and there is a danger that the flour will overwhelm the creamed mixture. So for plain cakes (including those described as 'economical' or 'cheap'), it was common to see the instruction to rub the butter into the flour. Then a well is made in the resulting breadcrumb-like mixture and the liquid ingredients stirred in.

It is not the rubbing-in that is unusual in this recipe but the pre-cooking of the liquid ingredients – the eggs and boiled milk are turned into custard before being added to the dry ingredients. How could this idea have come about? The first recipe we have found that provides a clue was contributed by Mrs Triggs to *The Ideal Cookery Book* published in 1929 to aid the funds of the Wellington Branch of the Plunket Society. The cake is a large one, and if the mixing follows the order of ingredients in the recipe, it is likely that the butter was rubbed into the flour, rather than creamed with the sugar. If this is what was intended, Mrs Triggs' recipe is the earliest known custard Christmas cake.

CHRISTMAS CAKE
Mrs. Triggs, Napier.

Ingredients:
Two pounds flour
One pound butter
One pound sugar
Three pounds seeded raisins
Quarter pound cherries
Quarter pound almonds

Half pound lemon peel
One tablespoon carbonate of soda
One teaspoonful essence almond
One teaspoonful essence lemon
Four eggs well beaten into a pint of boiling milk.

Method:
Mix all dry ingredients and fruit. Then add eggs, milk and essences. Bake in a slow oven – No. 2 – for four hours.[67]

Mrs Triggs' recipe is similar in quantities to Rita's 'Rich Fruit Cake', printed in *Tui's Annual* for 1934, which explicitly refers to rubbing the butter into the flour. Instead of adding the eggs to the boiling milk, however, the 1934 recipe makes the custard within the mixing bowl. Either way, these two recipes are designed to make large fruit cakes with half as many eggs as would normally be used.

Rich Fruit Cake.
A nice dark rich cake which can be made when eggs are scarce. Rub 1 lb. of butter into 2 lbs flour. Add 1 lb. sugar, 2 lbs. currants, ½ lb peel and 2 cups sultanas. Mix well together. Then make a well in centre into which break four eggs. Add essence of

lemon and almond and one pint of boiling milk in which 4 teaspoons of soda have been dissolved. Mix quickly and thoroughly. Pour the mixture, which should be rather thin, into one large or two smaller pans and bake in a moderate oven about 4 hours. – Rita.[68]

The next version of the recipe is found in a cookbook published early in 1941, before rationing began. Christchurch broadcaster, Mrs W.F. (Nan) Kent-Johnston, produced a book entitled *Everyday Recipes* for the many listeners to her weekly 3YA radio show 'Every-day Meals'.[69] During the period of her broadcasts (about 1938 to 1941), she received numerous letters and undoubtedly recipes, some of which may be represented in this book. As a prominent member of women's organisations, she had nation-wide connections. She was also responsible for two fund-raising cookbooks, one compiled for Christchurch Boys' High School, and the other for the Diocese of Waiapu (Napier), where she moved with her husband in 1941.[70]

Interestingly, Nan Kent-Johnston's custard cake recipe was no longer described as 'rich', but as 'economical', even though it retained the large quantities of the 1929 and 1934 examples. It shows the next stage in the evolution of this distinctive recipe:

Economical Fruit Cake.
1 lb butter, 2 lb flour, pinch salt, 1 lb sugar, 4 level teaspoons bicarbonate soda, [cream of tartar – omitted], 4 eggs, 1 pint milk, up to 4 lb fruit, 3 teaspoons essence (1 of almond, 1 of vanilla, 1 of lemon).

Put flour, salt and bicarbonate soda and cream of tartar and sugar in bowl. Rub butter well in. Then add fruit and leave overnight. Next morning bring milk to the boil and pour over beaten eggs, making custard and mix well into dry ingredients. Put into greased and well-lined tin. Bake 4 hours in moderate oven. (A large cake and keeps beautifully).[71]

After rationing began in 1942 and then increased in severity, halved versions of this cake appeared. We have given the recipe from the *War Economy Recipe Book*, and to this can be added one from the ninth edition of *Una Carter's Famous Cookery Book*, also published about 1944.[72] Another was found in *Better Baking*, written between 1946 and 1949 by S. Galloway, a chef employed by Imperial Chemical Industries to help housewives adjust to phosphate baking powders when cream of tartar became unavailable.[73] His recipe used margarine instead of butter, while another contributed by Mrs F.E. Cartner to the *Papanui Parish Cookery Book*[74] called for dripping. This fund-raising cookbook contained four recipes based on the custard principle: two were of the original size, and two the halved version. One carried the title 'Tired Housewife Cake'.[75]

After this inauspicious start, we might have expected the halved recipe to disappear as people tried to forget the hard times. However, in a brave act of culinary propaganda, the cake was given a new name '2-Egg Custard Christmas Cake'. The publication in which it appeared was distributed free in December, 1948 to customers of G.U.S. (Grocers' United Stores Ltd), an organisation covering Canterbury, Marlborough, Nelson and Westland. By now the recipe had been streamlined and simplified, and we have chosen to make it as the representative of its type.

2-EGG CUSTARD CHRISTMAS CAKE

1 lb flour
2 eggs
½ lb butter
Teaspoon baking soda

½ lb sugar
½ pint milk
2 lb mixed fruit
2 teaspoons mixed spices

Method: Rub butter into flour. Add baking soda, sugar, fruit, spice; well mixed. Boil milk and pour into 2 beaten eggs. Let milk and eggs cool a little then add to dry ingredients. Mix well together and bake 2 to 3 hours in moderate oven.[76]

The small version of the custard cake remained in circulation into the 1960s, and there is even a likely descendant in a 1999 cookbook.[77] However, it was the original large version that went on to become famous as the Christmas Cake contributed by Jenny Shipley, then Minister of Social Welfare and Minister of Women's Affairs, to two fund-raising cookbooks from her home region: *The Windwhistle Cookery Book* (1990) and *A Taste of Mid-Canterbury*, published about 1993. Dame Jenny Shipley was the first woman Prime Minister of New Zealand (1997–99). Her cake had outgrown its modest origins – possibly the 'Economical Fruit Cake' recipe in Nan Kent-Johnston's 1941 cookbook – and now included six eggs and ½ lb each of cherries, almonds and mixed peel.[78] How do we know it belongs to this lineage? The answer is that in addition to the method and quantities of the key ingredients, it shares a distinctive combination of three essences: one teaspoon each of almond, lemon and vanilla. The only change has been replacement of the original baking soda and cream of tartar by baking powder.

The final version of this ministerial Christmas cake[79] deserves the prize for the most accurate metric conversion we have ever encountered in a recipe book. Each pound has become 454 g and each ½ lb 227 g. Most digital balances can't weigh this

2-EGG CUSTARD CHRISTMAS CAKE

Adapted from '2-Egg Custard Christmas Cake', in *Approved Recipes and Household Hints* [Grocers' United Stores Ltd.] 1948. This small, moist cake is similar to sultana cakes still popular in rural areas as a 'smoko' standby. Its streamlined mixing method is a bonus. To make it a more festive cake we suggest the following additions – ½ teaspoon each of lemon, almond and vanilla essences, added to the eggs; substituting chopped cherries, peel and almonds for some of the mixed fruit (keep the total weight of fruit the same as the original recipe); and drizzling 2 dessertspoons of a liqueur over the cooked cake.

2 eggs	1 teaspoon baking soda
280 ml whole milk	225 g sugar
450 g bread flour	900 g mixed dried fruit
225 g butter	2 teaspoons mixed spice

Prepare a 20 cm-square or 23 cm-round cake pan by lining the base and sides with a double layer of brown paper and single layer of baking paper. Preheat the oven to 150°C with a shelf in the middle or slightly below.

In a small bowl, beat the eggs until fluffy. Heat the milk to boiling point and pour into the eggs while continuing to beat (the mixture does not thicken). Allow to cool a little while preparing the remaining ingredients.

Weigh the flour and place in a large bowl. Cut the butter into small cubes and rub into the flour until the mixture resembles fine breadcrumbs. Stir in the baking soda, sugar, dried fruit and spice. Mix thoroughly.

Pour the egg and milk mixture into the dry ingredients. Combine thoroughly.

Spoon into the prepared cake pan and spread the mixture evenly. Bake for 2 hours. (How to test when a cake is cooked is explained on page 100.) Leave the cake in the pan until cool. Turn out on to a rack. Remove the paper before rewrapping in fresh greaseproof paper. Store in an airtight cake container or wrap in foil.

Above: The 2-Egg Custard Christmas Cake ready for wrapping.

'Iceland Poppies' cake tin courtesy of the artist, Nancy Tichborne.

Below: A portable Christmas cake adds to the festivities of a family picnic. This one is a Sweetened Condensed Milk Christmas Cake, see p. 142–3.

precisely, but concern for detail must be commended in both the household and national economy.

The custard fruit cake and its Christmas cake variants were cakes whose early evolution occurred in the Depression and World War II. Canterbury cooks seem to have played an important role in the process, though the custard cake was not limited to this region. We have found a few examples of the custard cake recipe in Australian sources,[80] but not beyond Australasia. The ingredient list grew over time, but the method that was so well adapted to an era when eggs were expensive, or rationed, was still valued in later, more affluent times.

A trans-Tasman import?

When it first appeared in Australia, and soon after in New Zealand, the ginger ale cake introduced a new way of preparing the dried fruits as well as a new ingredient. Instead of adding carefully washed, dried, and floured fruit to the mixture, the cook tipped in a saturated mass. This was a revolutionary step because cake recipes had stipulated washed and dried fruit for centuries, and cooks thought they knew why. Was this belief justified? – after all, other culinary principles have been found to be scientifically unsound.[81] To answer this question, we need to look at the way dried fruits for cakes were processed historically.

If we go back to the seventeenth-century recipe possibly used for Pepys's twelfth cake, the instruction was to 'take four pound of Currants well washed, picked, and dryed in a warm cloth'.[82] One of Sir Kenelm Digby's recipes was more explicit about the reason: 'Then have ready twelve pounds of Currants very well washed and pick'd, that there may be neither stalks, nor broken Currants in them'.[83] We suspect that imported currants had more than just stalks to be picked out and removed. But, having been washed clean, why did they need to be dried? The answer is that in a bread-like cake, raised by yeast, dried fruits were usually the last ingredients to be added. If wet, they would have made the dough slippery to handle, if not unmanageably sticky. In some early eighteenth-century recipes, however, the writers implied that washing made the fruit swell up, a desirable outcome. Patrick Lamb listed 'six Pounds of Currans, which must be plump'd before the Fire, after they are wash'd and pick'd'.[84]

The eighteenth-century transition to rich pound cakes, aerated by beaten eggs, brought some changes to this procedure. In one recipe, E[liza?] Smith referred to 'five pounds of Currants well picked and rubbed, but not washed'.[85] For Hannah Glasse, the temperature of the prepared fruit was important: 'when your Currants are well wash'd and clean'd, let them be kept before the Fire, so that they may go warm into your Cake'.[86]

Early in the nineteenth century, another step was added after the preparation of the fruit. In a book entitled *The Female Economist*, Mrs Smith (of whom little is known, not even her first name) recommended flouring the fruit before adding it:

> currants should be well washed, picked, dried in a cloth, and then set before the fire. If damp, they will make the cake heavy; a little flour should be thrown over them before they are put into the cake.[87]

Heaviness was an ever-present threat in the post-yeast era before baking soda was employed. Some later authors, who borrowed from Mrs Smith, accepted her rationale.[88] However 'Meg Dods' (the pseudonym of Christian Johnstone) introduced yet another concern – that of the fruit sinking to the bottom of the cake. She implied that this occurred if the cake was not put in the oven immediately after mixing.[89] The American writer Eliza Leslie offered this and two other reasons for flouring the fruit. In a recipe for a pudding published in 1847 she wrote 'Dredge the fruit thickly with flour to prevent its sinking',[90] a view that is still current today. But in 1850, her words were 'dredge the fruit profusely with flour to prevent its clodding while baking'.[91] Around 1857, she said dredging of the fruit was 'to prevent its sinking or clogging'.[92]

The wide circulation and multiple editions of Meg Dods' and Eliza Leslie's books, among many others, meant that by the end of the nineteenth century everyone knew why fruit should not be added wet, and why it should be floured. In New Zealand, the influential manual, *Colonial Everyday Cookery*, first published in 1901, extended these preparation steps to include raisins and sultanas, and repeated the mantra that rubbing fruit in flour 'prevents it from sinking'.[93] Mrs Harman and Mrs Gard'ner advised that only a '*little* flour' was necessary to prevent the fruit from sinking.[94] Our spreadsheet contains recipes calling for this treatment of the fruit right through to the 1990s, as in this recipe from 1997, which begins

> Wash and dry the fruit if necessary. Measure the flour and mix about half of it with the cleaned fruit.[95]

In view of the fact that the ingredient list calls for 1 ½ kg mixed dried fruit that shouldn't require any pre-washing, we suspect that the recipe instructions originated in an era when fruit was not pre-cleaned and sealed in packages.

A closer look at 80 Christmas cake recipes from the 1990s shows that although many follow the traditional procedure, 35 recipes (44 per cent) either pre-soak or pre-boil the fruit. If the sinking-fruit theory is correct, why don't food-writers who publish such recipes receive complaints? Over the course of the twentieth century, New Zealand cooks increased the proportion of fruit in Christmas cakes to the extent that there is often little cake crumb visible between the fruit and nuts. In the eighteenth and nineteenth centuries, sinking fruit was a real risk – if it went into the cake wet, it may have thinned the batter to the point where it was too runny to hold up the fruit. Lightness is no longer desirable in a Christmas cake, and the cross-section of many modern cakes suggests that the fruit supports itself, like bricks in a wall!

The 'Ginger Ale Cake' was the first popular cake recipe to rethink the necessity for dry, floured fruit. The earliest Australian recipe that we have found was published in *"Woman's" Tested Recipes* in 1939.[96] The magazine *Woman* held an all-Australian cookery contest, selecting the best recipes for publication in this book. Mrs P. A. Clarke of 'Sunnyside', Boree Creek, New South Wales submitted this recipe:

GINGER ALE CAKE

Ingredients. – 1 pint ginger ale, 10 ounces butter, ½ pound sugar, 12 ounces flour, 6 eggs, 1 pound sultanas, ¼ pound peel, ½ pound raisins, 2 ounces cherries, 2 ounces almonds, 1 tablespoon glycerine, 1 tablespoon brandy, ½ grated nutmeg, ½ teaspoon cinnamon, pinch of salt.

Method. – Cut up fruit and soak all night in ginger ale. Cream butter and sugar, add eggs one at a time and beat well. Add fruit, spice, flour, brandy and then the glycerine. Bake 3 ½ to 4 hours. This is something out of the ordinary and makes a good cake for special occasions.[97]

The final comment in the recipe indicates that the recipe was new and unexpected and that the year 1939 must be close to its first appearance in Australia. In 1968, an Australian cookery competition entrant said that he had found the recipe 'folded inside the family Bible' in 1935.[98] Despite extensive searching, we have not discovered a prototype in Britain or America. The recipe began to circulate quickly and early in 1940 the *Australian Women's Weekly* gave consolation prizes to two readers who submitted nearly identical versions of the recipe for publication.[99] One of the recipes increased the butter to 12 oz and expanded the instructions to include lining the tin with paper.[100]

In one other respect the 'Ginger Ale Cake' was unusual – it contained glycerine, a substance that was more likely to be in the bathroom cabinet than in the pantry. Newspaper articles from the 1930s advocated its use in mouth washes, hand creams and scalp tonics, and as a cure for coughs and indigestion.[101] Glycerine is a monoglyceride, related to the true fats, which had been used by bakers since the

GINGER ALE CHRISTMAS CAKE

Adapted from 'Ginger Ale Christmas Cake', in *Souvenir Recipe Book*, compiled by Katharine Scaife and Molly Scurr, published by the Wanaka Improvement Society, 1972.

We can understand why this excellent cake is still commonly made today!

230 g raisins	4 eggs, size 6
230 g sultanas	1 teaspoon vanilla essence
230 g currants	½ teaspoon almond essence
230 g dates, chopped	340 g bread flour
250 ml dry ginger ale	1 teaspoon baking powder
230 g butter	¼ teaspoon salt
170 g dark brown sugar	

Put the raisins, sultanas, currants and chopped dates into a bowl and pour in the dry ginger ale. Stir to thoroughly moisten the fruit. Cover the bowl and leave to stand overnight.

Prepare a 20 cm-square or 23 cm-round cake pan by lining the base and sides with a double layer of brown paper followed by a single layer of baking paper.

Preheat the oven to 150°C with a shelf in the middle position.

Soften the butter in a large bowl and cream with the sugar until light and fluffy. Add the eggs one at a time, beating well between additions. If necessary, add a spoonful or two of the weighed flour to help prevent curdling. Beat in the essences.

Sift the flour, baking powder and salt. Fold portions of the flour and fruit mixtures alternately into the creamed ingredients. Fold gently until thoroughly mixed.

Spoon evenly in to the cake pan. Smooth the surface with a spoon. Bake for 2–2 ½ hours. (How to test when a cake is cooked is explained on page 168.) Cover with a tea towel and leave in the cake pan to cool. Turn out on to a rack. Wrap in greaseproof paper and store in an airtight cake container or wrap in foil.

The cake is covered with a layer of almond paste, followed with royal icing. The top is then simply decorated with purchased glacé strawberries and home-dried and glazed kiwifruit slices.

beginning of the twentieth century for its ability to absorb moisture from the air.[102] In cakes, it slowed down the staling process. Its inclusion in this cake might suggest that the idea came from a professional baker.

Soon after World War II began, the recipe reached New Zealand. Precisely when depends on the date of publication of *Aunt Daisy's Cookery Book ... No. 5,* where the recipe appeared as 'Ginger Ale Christmas Cake'.[103] We have a copy gifted by Noeline Thomson to her mother in March 1943,[104] and we know that at Christmas in 1940 the publisher Whitcombe and Tombs was advertising for sale only Aunt Daisy's previous book, her fourth.[105] The recipe looks different from the Australian examples – but only because it has been doubled:

GINGER ALE CHRISTMAS CAKE

1 ¼ lb. butter, 1 ½ lb. flour, 1 lb. currants, 1 lb. sultanas, 4 oz. cherries, 2 tablespoons glycerine, 1 grated nutmeg, pinch salt, 1 lb. sugar, 12 eggs, 1 lb. raisins, ½ lb. peel, 4 oz. ground almonds, 2 tablespoons brandy, 1 teaspoon cinnamon, 1 bottle ginger ale. Cut up fruit very fine, and soak all night in ginger ale (a 6d. bottle will do). Cream the butter and sugar, add eggs well beaten, little by little, not to have the mixture curdle, and beat well. Then add flour and spices, fruit and lastly the glycerine and brandy. Cooking: About 4 ½ hours. Electric oven, put it at 400°, bottom element low; when temperature comes to 300° put top element on for a while. For gas oven, same time for cooking, shelf 3 ledges from the top all the time, regulo at 4 for an hour, then down to 2 for the remainder of the time.[106]

From the quantities, we think this recipe must have been submitted to (or acquired by) Aunt Daisy before rationing began. The precise cooking instructions seem too detailed for a recipe sent in by a home cook – they may have been added by Aunt Daisy herself, because of her affiliations with stove retailers.

This doubled version was given the title 'Christmas Cake (Excellent)' in the League of Mothers' twenty-fifth anniversary cookbook published in 1951 and reprinted in 1952. The wording was almost the same as in the Aunt Daisy recipe, except that the price of the bottle of ginger ale had risen to 8d. The submitter from Dunedin also reduced the cooking time to four hours.[107] We recorded five more examples of this version, including one from 1985 that was appropriately called 'Big Christmas Cake'.[108]

It is clear that although the idea of the ginger ale cake was appealing, not all New Zealand cooks wanted such a large cake, especially given the high price of eggs in the 1950s. By 1954, a more economical version had surfaced. In most quantities it is Aunt Daisy's c. 1943 version halved. Could it be derived from the original Australian recipe? We think this is unlikely because the butter has been reduced to just 8 oz, compared to the Australian 10 oz, and there were now four eggs instead of six. There were other cost-saving changes in this version: replacement of cherries by dates and alcohol by essences, addition of baking powder, and deletion of glycerine. In twelve examples of this version ranging from 1954 to 1990, seven recipes opted for pre-mixed fruit (2 lb or 1 kg). The recipe we have chosen to represent this type is a streamlined version from the Wanaka Improvement Society's *Souvenir Recipe Book* (1972):

GINGER ALE CHRISTMAS CAKE
Soak overnight in one large cup of ginger ale:

½ lb raisins	½ lb currants
½ lb sultanas	½ lb chopped dates

Next day cream ½ lb butter, 6 oz sugar; add 4 eggs, any essences, salt, then add soaked fruit and sift in 12 oz flour, 1 teaspoon baking powder. Cook 2 ½ hours in moderate oven.

Mrs O. J. Frater.[109]

One more version of the ginger ale cake emerged in 1974, submitted to *The New Zealand Radio and Television Cookbook*.[110] The quantity of butter was halved to 4 oz instead of 8 oz, and some golden syrup was added, along with some extra fruit. Recent examples of this recipe have been described as 'quick' and 'easy'.[111]

New Zealand cooks borrowed the original version of the 'Ginger Ale Cake' from the Australians, possibly from the recipes published in the *Australian Women's Weekly* in 1940, but they immediately altered the size of the cake and elevated it to the status of a Christmas cake. With a dozen eggs in the recipe, the 1940s was not the right decade for the introduction of such a large cake, and so the smaller form became the more popular version, giving rise in turn to a fruitier but less buttery version in the 1970s. Nevertheless, all the variants of this cake have their supporters and many are made to the present day.

Breaking with tradition – the pineapple Christmas cake

For hundreds of years the suite of fruits in rich cakes was restricted to dried currants and raisins, and candied cherries, ginger and citrus peel. Dried prunes, dates and figs were used occasionally, joined by dried apricots and candied pineapple early in the twentieth century. Cooks became used to these additions and their dried or candied state meant that traditional recipes needed no alteration in methods to accommodate them. However, the idea of opening a tin of canned fruit and adding the fruit, and sometimes the juice, to a Christmas cake represented a major break with tradition. Incorporating fresh fruits or vegetables like grated apple or carrot was even more radical, and the few examples we recorded seem to be a product of 1940s' rationing. Too much fresh fruit in the traditional Christmas cake would have compromised its keeping qualities; these 'alternative' recipes have never become common. As for canned pineapple, the high sugar content of the fruit and juice made for a Christmas cake that was moist and kept well. Not surprisingly, pineapple Christmas cakes gained nation-wide popularity.

Within New Zealand, we traced the germ of the idea of using pineapple back to this recipe from Aunt Daisy's third book, published in 1935:

DELICIOUS UNCOMMON CHRISTMAS CAKE.

1 cup butter.
1 cup fruit juice. (pineapple is nice)
1 ½ cups candied cherries.
1 ½ cups chopped figs.
1 cup raisins.
1 ½ cups brown sugar.
4 eggs.
2 cups chopped nuts.

½ cup shredded peel.
2 small teaspoons salt.
1 teaspoon baking powder.
2 teaspoons ground cinnamon.
2 teaspoons allspice.
1 teaspoon ground cloves.
3 cups flour.

Mix butter, sugar, and egg yolks, and beat for 2 minutes. Sift 2 cups flour, spices, salt, baking powder, and add alternately with the fruit-juice to the first mixture. Then add fruits and nuts, previously mixed with the other cup of flour. Fold in the stiffly-beaten whites of eggs, put into well-greased, papered tin and bake in a very slow oven for 3 to 4 hours. These quantities make a very large and deliciously flavoured cake which keeps moist for a long time.[112]

This third book is the most elusive of all of Aunt Daisy's recipe collections – to check its cake recipes, we had to interloan the relevant pages from Sydney. The book title hints at the nature of the problem of sourcing this particular recipe: *Aunt Daisy's Book of Selected Special Recipes From California, Canada, France, Australia and New Zealand*. Published late in 1935, it includes a foreword describing her trip to the west coast of the United States and Canada in February and March that year. The 'Delicious Uncommon Christmas Cake' was not in any of the sections identified as to nation, but in a 'Christmas Cookery Section'. We wondered if she had collected the recipe from a New Zealand contributor, the method she used for her first two books. The earlier books were published in early and late 1934 respectively.[113] Most of the recipes were sent in by listeners to her Auckland 1ZR and 1ZB radio shows, and by readers of her cookery pages in the *New Zealand Woman's Weekly* (4 January to 26 April 1934) and *The Weekly News* (from 13 June 1934).[114] However, there was one clue that suggested an American origin. In a recent conversation about tracking recipe sources, the eminent New Zealand food-writer Tui Flower pointed out to us the significance of recipes that express quantities in cups. That is an American food-writing style, she said, and her observation was readily confirmed in our book collections.

Online searching has now provided a possible prototype for Aunt Daisy's uncommon cake. It was a promotional recipe for a 'Fruit Cake' published in the American magazine *Good Housekeeping* in January 1927 and subsequently repeated.[115] We had expected the advertiser to be a pineapple canning company, but much to our surprise it was the Wesson Oil company, manufacturer of food-grade cottonseed oil from the early twentieth century. Instead of using butter, this recipe instructed the cook to beat oil, sugar and egg yolks together for two minutes. As well as some differences in quantities of fruits and nuts, the original recipe included a cup of candied pineapple, missing from Aunt Daisy's version. Further searching revealed that the Wesson Oil recipe was circulating in Australia by 1929, and it was in the Tasmanian newspaper *The Mercury* in 1934 that it acquired the title 'Pineapple Christmas Cake'.[116] But it was not this version that influenced Aunt Daisy, but the recipe called 'Delicious and Uncommon Christmas Cake', submitted to the *Australian Women's Weekly* in November 1934 as an entry in their 'Special Pineapple Contest'.[117] Aunt Daisy copied this recipe almost word for word, including the comment at the end about the cake's size and good keeping qualities. However, one important ingredient was omitted: '1 ½ cups of chopped pineapple (or candied pineapple if preferred)'. Since she provided no substitute, we think she left it out by mistake!

This deficient 'Delicious Uncommon Christmas Cake' was reprinted, along with most of the other 1935 Christmas cakes, in *Aunt Daisy's Cookery Book of Selected Recipes*, described on the cover as *Aunt Daisy's Radio Cookery Book No. 4*.[118] We know that it was on sale in Wellington by December 1940,[119] and it remained in print until the 1950s. *The Australian Women's Weekly* was the source of the next version of this recipe, 'Uncommon Christmas Cake (Delicious)' contributed by Mrs Taylor to *Further Reliable Tested Recipes Book 2*, raising money for the Hora Hora Free Kindergarten Association in Whangarei in 1958.[120] Her recipe specified both pineapple juice and the one and a half cups of 'chopped pineapple (preserved)' missed out by Aunt Daisy. By 1964, the recipe called for a small tin of crushed pineapple.[121] Crushed pineapple was specified in subsequent recipes. The last appearance that we have recorded of this distinctive recipe is from 1978,[122] when cooks were given the option of replacing the pineapple juice with a cup of brandy!

From the mid-1950s, there was another pineapple cake in circulation. It had six instead of four eggs, and the cook was not required to beat the yolks and whites separately. Because brandy was included, there was no need for the pineapple juice. The cake contained drained, cut or crushed pineapple, as well as cherries, ginger and sometimes dates. A third or half teaspoon each of vanilla, lemon and almond essences were also included. We found four examples of this recipe, all in fund-raising cookbooks between 1955 and 1969, spread between Takanini and Gore.[123]

Some of the features of this six-egg cake are shared with the most popular pineapple Christmas cake recipe in New Zealand, developed by Alison Holst. Our earliest record of this is from the first volume of *Alison Holst's Kitchen Diary: A Book of Seasonal Recipes*, published in 1978.[124] The quantities in this recipe have always been given in metric measurements. Compared to the earlier six-egg cake, it has comparable amounts of butter, a little more flour but less sugar, the same number of eggs, and a similar quantity of fruit. The preserved ginger of the earlier recipe has been replaced by ground ginger, while the essences vary between the original three and just two (vanilla and lemon). Brandy is included in both and the pineapple is in all but one case drained before being added. In keeping with her qualifications and subsequent teaching position in the School of Home Science at Otago, Alison Holst provides much more detail in her recipes than is found in those from the 1950s and 1960s, especially relating to the preparation of the tin, and the cooking times and temperatures. She recognises that fruit cakes are best cooked with a falling oven temperature. This reflects their evolutionary origins – being cooked in wood-fired bread ovens after the bread had been removed.

We have recorded eight examples of Alison Holst's recipe in her books from 1978 to 1995, nearly all with small differences as she improves and adapts the recipe. They are unquestionably more useful to today's cooks than the old pineapple cake recipes that assumed that a housewife knew how to prepare a tin, what size it should be, and how to manage her oven. Needless to say, Alison's recipes have also been copied out and later contributed by others to fund-raising cookbooks – we noted eight, and it is probably significant that most are associated with high schools where students require clear and precise details in a recipe.

One other version of the pineapple Christmas cake overlapped with Alison Holst's – we have found five examples from 1968 to 1984. Like the other versions it required about 8 oz (250 g) each of butter and sugar, a little less flour than the others, but about the same weight of fruit. The quantity of pineapple was reduced to just a half cup of 'crushed pineapple including juice', perhaps because this cake also contained a half cup of orange juice and another half cup of dark-coloured jam. The name of the cake reflected its characteristic feature – Dark Christmas Cake – achieved with the help of cocoa as well as the jam. Because it is less well known than Alison Holst's cake, but has a significant lineage, we chose it as the representative of the many versions of pineapple-based Christmas cake:

DARK CHRISTMAS CAKE

1 lb currants
1 lb raisins
8 oz sultanas
4 oz dates
4 oz crystallized ginger
4 oz crystallized cherries
4 oz crystallized peel
4 oz blanched almonds
½ cup orange juice
1 tablespoon grated orange rind
½ cup dark coloured jam
½ cup crushed pineapple including juice

¼ teaspoon almond essence
¼ tsp lemon essence
½ teaspoon vanilla essence
2 ½ cups flour
1 tablespoon cocoa
½ teaspoon baking soda
½ teaspoon cinnamon
½ teaspoon nutmeg
8 ounces butter
8 ounces brown sugar
5 eggs

Select a 9 to 10in round or square cake tin. Line sides and bottom with several layers of paper, the inside one being greased.
Mix the fruits and nuts together, cutting the dates, ginger, cherries, peel and almonds to even sizes.
Mix the orange juice, rind, jam, pineapple and essences together.
Sift the flour, cocoa, soda and spices. Take about a cup of this sifted dry mixture and dust through the fruit with it.
Cream the butter and sugar until light and fluffy.
Add the eggs one at a time, and beat thoroughly after each addition.
Mix in the liquid jam mixture.
Add the fruit and flour alternately until the cake batter is even in texture.
Turn into the prepared tin.
Bake at 250 degrees for five hours.
Weight 6 ¼ lb[125]

This recipe was one of several prepared by Tui Flower in the test kitchen of the *New Zealand Woman's Weekly* for the 1968 article, 'Close-up on Christmas Cakes'. In charge of the test kitchen from 1965 until 1984, Tui Flower brought a degree in Home Science from the University of Otago, together with professional training

9

DARK CHRISTMAS CAKE

Adapted from 'Dark Christmas Cake', first published in the *New Zealand Woman's Weekly* in 1968 in Tui Flower's column, 'Close-up on Christmas Cakes'.

Mary first made Tui's Christmas cake in 1971, not long after purchasing the first edition of *The New Zealand Woman's Weekly Cookbook,* where the recipe was reprinted. Testimony to the success of this book is that it still has a place on a kitchen shelf, amongst Mary's most-used recipe books. Needless to say, the recipe for the Christmas cake is well written, reliable and produces an excellent result. The only updating needed was a conversion to convenient metric measures.

450 g currants	115 g crystallized ginger, chopped
450 g raisins	115 g glacé cherries
230 g sultanas	115 g glacé peel
115 g dates, chopped	115 g whole almonds (blanching optional)
zest of one orange	½ cup crushed pineapple, juice included
½ cup freshly squeezed orange juice (about 2 oranges)	¼ teaspoon almond essence
	¼ teaspoon lemon essence
½ cup of dark-coloured jam	½ teaspoon vanilla essence
320 g bread flour	½ teaspoon ground cinnamon
1 tablespoon cocoa	½ teaspoon freshly grated nutmeg
½ teaspoon baking soda	
230 g butter	5 eggs
230 g dark brown sugar	

whole blanched almonds (optional decoration instead of icing)

Prepare a 25 cm-round or 22 cm-square cake pan by lining with a double layer of brown paper and a single layer of baking paper. Heat the oven to 130°C with a shelf in the middle position.

In a large bowl combine the fruits and almonds.

In a small bowl or jug combine the orange zest, orange juice, jam, crushed pineapple, and essences.

Sift the flour, cocoa, baking soda, cinnamon, and nutmeg. Use a cup of the sifted mixture to stir through the fruit and nuts. Use your fingers to break up any clumps of fruit.

Soften the butter in a large bowl and cream with the sugar until light and fluffy. Add the eggs one at a time, beating well between each addition. If necessary, add a spoonful or two of the flour mixture to help prevent curdling.

Stir in the juice mixture. Add the fruit and flour mixtures alternately until the cake batter is even in texture. Spoon into the prepared cake pan and spread the mixture evenly. Use the back of a spoon to smooth the surface.

The original recipe does not specify icing. Instead Mary often decorates with whole blanched almonds, arranged symmetrically or randomly on top of the uncooked cake. (When serving, a ribbon and seasonal flowers may be added to create a simple but festive effect.)

Place in the preheated oven and bake for 4 ¼–4 ¾ hours. (How to test when a cake is cooked is explained on page 168.) Cover with a tea towel and leave the cake in the pan until cool. Turn out on to a cake rack. Wrap with greaseproof paper and store in an airtight cake container or wrap in foil.

The pineapple cake cuts beautifully.

in France, international experience and contacts to this position.[126] The 1960s saw New Zealand cooks embracing international cuisine, especially when entertaining guests, and Tui Flower translated 'foreign' recipes into dishes that were feasible for a New Zealand kitchen and acceptable to local tastes. This 'Dark Christmas Cake' recipe is an excellent example of food-writing, taking readers methodically through the mixing steps in the face of a very long list of ingredients.

Tui Flower reproduced the recipe for the 'Dark Christmas Cake' under the title 'Christmas Cake' in the first *New Zealand Woman's Weekly Cookbook*, published in 1971.[127] It found its way into at least one fund-raising cookbook, from the Wairarapa in 1977,[128] and then appeared in Eleanor Gray's *Basic New Zealand Cookbook* in 1978. Because New Zealand had adopted metric measures in 1974, most of the quantities from the original 1968 recipe were converted into metric cups. Unfortunately Eleanor Gray, who formerly headed the Foods Department at the School of Home Science (University of Otago), followed a classificatory approach to recipes, presenting the basic version and then the variations on that theme. Her pineapple Christmas cake recipe became a variation of her 'Rich Butter Cake', requiring the cook to make substitutions in the basic recipe, and to correctly interpret the instruction at the start of the 'Christmas Cake' variation to 'Make twice the recipe'.[129] We still don't know whether she meant us to double the quantities of the basic recipe, or the variation, or both. When compared to Alison Holst's pineapple Christmas cake recipe, also published in 1978, Eleanor Gray's version was too complicated to follow.

The origins of pineapple Christmas cakes have proved complex and intriguing. From a 1927 American fruit cake made with oil, Australian cooks developed a butter version with enhanced pineapple flavour, and this inspired other adaptations in turn. The canning industry was increasingly active in persuading cooks to add pineapple to their cakes. Hawaiian pineapple production grew rapidly when James Dole launched the Hawaiian Pineapple Company – by 1927, fifteen pineapple canneries were operating in Honolulu alone.[130] Crushed pineapple was always part of their output, since it was an effective way of using the sections of the fruit unsuited to canning as slices or chunks. The Australian industry was slower to be established, but was actively promoting its product from the late 1920s. At first it was chopped canned pineapple and juice that was incorporated in fruit cakes, as in the 1934 'Delicious and Uncommon Christmas Cake'. Gradually crushed pineapple became accepted as a cake ingredient after several decades as a fashionable addition to desserts or summer drinks. The first Australian cake recipes to include crushed pineapple appeared in newspapers and magazines in the late 1930s, but the cakes were butter sponges, not fruit cakes.[131] It was not until the 1950s that Australian cooks began to submit crushed pineapple fruit cake recipes to the competitions in their favourite magazines.

As we make our pineapple Christmas cakes today, we can thank an American oil company and Australian magazines for getting us started on our own popular versions.

One challenge and four solutions

As children, we were often tempted to slip into the pantry, spoon in hand, and take just a little from an opened tin of sweetened condensed milk left in the safe after the salad dressing had been made. The Highlander label with its distinctive kilt-wearing piper has lured New Zealand children into condensed milk raids since 1901,[132] though on some of today's tins the piper has shrunk to a tiny figure mounted on top a giant pile of Chocolate Caramel Slice. Locally produced condensed milk was in New Zealand homes for over a century, and was made in Australia from the 1880s. It was a very common import to New Zealand from 1865, so ours was not the only generation led into temptation. Of course, Christmas cakes are an equally delicious treat and in theory combining sweetened condensed milk with a rich fruit cake seems an excellent idea. The challenge was surprisingly slow to be taken up.

Condensed milk's long history started with Nicolas Appert's experiments in France in 1820, then commercial production in America in the 1850s by the inventor Gail Borden. The objective was to preserve milk in a safe form without refrigeration. The ingredients listed on today's tin are the same as they have been since Gail Borden's 'Eagle' brand was first launched: milk and sugar. In the factory, some water is extracted from the milk and replaced by sugar in sufficient quantity that micro-organisms cannot grow. Sugars make up nearly 56 per cent of the thick condensed milk. Their inherent sweetness, together with the subtle changes in the milk components during processing, make the product irresistible. Evaporated milk is sometimes confused with condensed milk, but evaporated milk's old name makes the difference plain: it was called 'unsweetened condensed milk'. About 60 per cent of the water is evaporated, and the subsequent canning involves sterilisation. This heating gives evaporated milk its distinctive colour.

For the first few decades of the twentieth century, sweetened condensed milk was used by consumers as a safe form of milk. They reconstituted it with water in order to avoid the perils of fresh unpasteurised milk, every drop of which contained 'hundred of thousands of bacteria', according to the makers of Highlander Milk.[133] Hopefully, their water supplies were as uncontaminated as the tinned milk. The earliest usage of sweetened condensed milk in other food items seems to have been in confectionery. A popular home-made sweet in New Zealand during World War I was Belgium Fudge, made with a tin of Highlander condensed milk.[134] However, *The Highlander Economical Cookery Book* contained only six baked items that used the sweetened condensed milk undiluted, and then only in very small quantities. The one fruit cake recipe, Block Cake, which called for a whole tin, specified 'Unsweetened Highlander milk, undiluted', in other words evaporated milk.[135] We have looked at a wide selection of international cookbooks, and searched many on-line databases, but failed to find any recipe for a fruit cake using a tin of sweetened condensed milk until 1952.

It is appropriate that we found the first such recipe in *Borden's Eagle Brand 70 Magic Recipes*, published in the United States in 1952, and included in an advertisement placed in the widely read *Life* magazine the following year.[136] Readers of *Life* were invited to write in for two recipe booklets, one of which contained the original recipe. Using a can of condensed milk and a packet of Borden's mincemeat, the 'loaf-cake' took only fifteen minutes to prepare. Walnuts and a cup of mixed candied fruit were included, and even though this 'Magic Fruit Surprise Cake' used just one egg, it was photographed with a festive topping of glacé cherries and split almonds. We don't know when the recipe reached New Zealand, but it featured in Tui Flower's selection of Christmas cakes published in the *New Zealand Woman's Weekly* in December 1968. It was the first of four different fruit cake recipes containing sweetened condensed milk to become popular in New Zealand.

EASY MIX CAKE

1 lb ready mixed dried fruit
½ cup water
1 cup coarsely chopped nuts
14 oz tin sweetened condensed milk
1 egg
¾ cup flour
½ teaspoon baking soda

Put the fruit and water in a saucepan and bring to boil.
Boil one minute, taking care not to let fruit catch.
Set aside to cool.
Mix in the nuts and condensed milk, then the well beaten egg.
Sift in the flour and soda.
Turn the mixture into a lined and greased 9 inch loaf tin.
Bake at 350 degrees for 2 hours or until set.
Allow to cool before taking from tin.
Weighs about 2lbs.[137]

The only significant difference between Borden's and Tui Flower's recipes was an increase in cooking time from one and a half to two hours, after the recipe was trialled in the test kitchen. We found three more occurrences of this recipe, not based on the *New Zealand Woman's Weekly* version, but reflecting Rosemary Dempsey's 'Last-Minute Fruit Cake' from *1,001 Ways With Food*, a compilation from the *New Zealand Herald* and *New Zealand Weekly News*.[138] Her recipe may have come from Borden's booklet directly. In 1974, a simplified version of this recipe was submitted to the *Australian Women's Weekly* by a New Zealand reader, eliciting a comment from the editor that it was 'an unusual, good-tasting fruit cake'.[139] That implies that condensed milk cakes were not yet common in Australia.

Borden's cake was quick and easy to mix, contained no butter, no extra sugar (beyond what was in the tin of sweetened condensed milk), and just one egg. Its success may have stimulated further experiments. Within a year of testing the American cake, the *New Zealand Woman's Weekly* published a reader's recipe for a second, quite different variant, which was egg-free, contained no extra sugar, but included a generous amount of butter:

MOST MARVELLOUS CHRISTMAS CAKE

8 oz currants
8 oz sultanas
4 oz raisins
4 oz mixed peel
4 oz glace cherries
2 oz blanched almonds
½ teaspoon vanilla essence

1 tin condensed milk
10 oz butter
1 ¼ cups cold water
1 tablespoon marmalade
¾ teaspoon baking soda
2 ½ cups flour
2 tablespoons brandy

Place all ingredients in a large saucepan – except soda, flour and brandy.
Stir well and bring to the boil. Simmer for 5 minutes, remove pan from heat and allow to cool, stirring once or twice.
Sift soda into cooled mixture and stir well.
Stir in sifted flour.
Place mixture in paper-lined 8 in square tin.
Bake at 325 degrees for 2 to 2 ½ hours.
When almost cold, make several skewer holes on top of the cake and pour over the brandy.
– *Bran, Auckland*[140]

Was this recipe developed in a New Zealand home kitchen? We suspect not, because the second volume of *Catering Recipes*, issued by Nestlé's Catering Service between 1967 (when the word tamarillo was officially adopted) and 1974 (when

SWEETENED CONDENSED MILK CHRISTMAS CAKE

Adapted from the 'Sweetened Condensed Milk Christmas Cake', contributed by Mary Browne to New Zealand Guild of Food Writers' *The Cookbook* (2000). This recipe was an updated and metricated version of a popular Christmas cake of the early 1970s. Mary revised it from a hand-written version, found in a coverless cookbook from Oamaru, to satisfy the many requests for the recipe from family and friends who appreciated the 'quick-mix' method and the cake's excellent flavour and moist texture.

Mary's youngest daughter makes at least three before Christmas each year because her husband loves rich fruitcakes and each one disappears before the official celebrations begin. As a result, time runs out for icing and decorations.

125 g butter
2 tablespoons golden syrup
1 x 400 g can sweetened condensed milk
4 eggs
½ teaspoon vanilla essence
½ teaspoon lemon essence
½ teaspoon almond essence

1.2 kg mixed dried fruit
¼ cup rum, sherry or port, plus extra 2 tablespoons to pour over cake when cooked
½ teaspoon baking soda
¼ cup milk
350 g bread flour

Line the base and sides of a 20 cm-square or 22 cm-round cake pan with a layer of brown paper followed by a layer of non-stick baking paper. Preheat the oven to 130°C with a shelf in the middle or just below.

Choose a large-enough saucepan to hold all the ingredients for the final mixing. In it, melt the butter, golden syrup and sweetened condensed milk over gentle heat, stirring constantly until the butter has melted. Remove from the heat.

Beat the eggs with the essences until light-coloured and thick.

Place the dried fruit in a bowl and add the ¼ cup of rum, sherry or port. Stir to mix thoroughly. Dissolve the baking soda in the milk. Sift the flour.

Fold the eggs and essences into the mixture in the saucepan. Add half the fruit and half the flour. Mix gently. Add the remaining fruit and flour. Add the milk mixture.

Stir gently until thoroughly combined.

Spoon into the prepared cake pan and spread evenly. Bake at 130°C for 3–3 ½ hours.

After baking, sprinkle with the extra measure of rum, sherry or port. Cover loosely with foil and leave to cool completely before turning out. Wrap in greaseproof paper and store in an airtight cake container or wrap in foil.

A piece of Sweetened Condensed Milk Christmas Cake is left on the mantelpiece with a glass of port wine to thank Santa Claus.

metric measurements came into force) contains the same recipe under the name 'Fruit Cake', in quantities suitable for 25, 50 and 100 portions.[141] The dried and candied fruits were not specified, and there was no marmalade. Mixed spice provided flavour in the absence of the brandy. Why do we think the Nestlé recipe came first? Several of the quantities in 'Most Marvellous Christmas Cake' include small, hard-to-measure fractions, such as '¾ teaspoon', suggesting that the recipe has been cut down from a larger prototype. Nestlé's home economists issued several publications in the 1960s and this recipe may have originated in their test kitchen. They published it later in metric form in the booklet *Highlander Quick 'n' Easy Cookbook* and with small changes in *Baking At Its Best*.[142] However, it was the *New Zealand Woman's Weekly* version, where the fruit was simmered for five minutes, which circulated throughout the country in the 1970s and 1980s, in most cases still called 'Most Marvellous Christmas Cake'. In contrast, the Nestlé recipe stipulated only three minutes' simmering. Several different variants emerged after 1974, depending on the metric conversion factors used by home cooks or editors when the recipes were included in fund-raising cookbooks.

Much of the appeal of Borden's and Nestlé's condensed milk cakes came from their easy-mix method, which accomplished the whole process in a large saucepan. The fruit swelled up nicely and with the condensed milk contributed to a moist, long-keeping cake. You might expect that these two versions would satisfy New Zealand cooks, but a third, apparently unrelated recipe was published as 'Fruit Cake (No Eggs)' in the *New Zealand Woman's Weekly* early in 1969.[143] It contained just half a tin of sweetened condensed milk and half a pound of mixed fruit. Not surprisingly, about three years later the recipe was submitted to the same magazine in a more convenient doubled form.[144] Instead of the 10 oz of butter in Nestlé's cake, this had 8 oz or ½ lb. The quantity of flour was similarly reduced, from two and a half cups to two. Baking powder was added to the baking soda, spices were included, along with a tablespoon of vinegar. We recorded ten examples of this version, referred to as 'Christmas Cake', or 'Eggless Christmas Cake' from the late 1970s to 1990.

The fourth version of the condensed milk cake has been in circulation from about 1970 to the present day. We have found printed examples with imperial measurements from the Bay of Plenty to Invercargill, and a hand-written copy tucked inside a coverless cookbook obtained in Oamaru. We have been making this recipe for several years, but in view of its unknown origins and date we have decided to print here an almost identical recipe from a published source. It appeared in *Recipe Rendezvous*, a fund-raiser compiled by the Gladstone Scout Mothers' Committee in Invercargill around 1970:

CHRISTMAS CAKE
(Economical and Delicious)

Mix together in a saucepan:
2 tablespoons golden syrup
¼ lb. butter
1 tin sweetened condensed milk

Add 4 well-beaten eggs and essences of vanilla, lemon and almond. Fold in 12 ozs. sifted flour, then add 2 ½ lb. mixed fruit. Lastly add ½ teaspoon of baking soda dissolved in ½ cup of milk. Pour into an 8-inch square tin. Bake for 3 hours at 250 degrees.

B.McC.[145]

The only difference between the Invercargill recipe and the hand-written recipe from Oamaru was the replacement of half of the milk with port wine.

A very similar recipe was submitted as 'Christmas Cake' to *Our Favourite Recipes*, a fund-raiser for seven Plunket Mothers' Clubs in the Bay of Plenty, around 1972.[146] Given the distance between Southland and the Bay of Plenty, it is unlikely that one book influenced the other – both recipes were probably taken from the cookery column of a national magazine or newspaper. Of the four condensed milk cakes we have described, this version had the most eggs and the most fruit, while at the same time a modest quantity of butter. It was more like a traditional Christmas cake, yet was quickly mixed in the saucepan like the others. It should have persisted in its original simple and useful form, but for a remarkable instance of hybridisation. This may seem an unusual claim in a book about recipes. However, hybridisation can play an important role in evolution, both biological and cultural.

What happened to the four-egg condensed milk Christmas cake was that a cook or food editor who happened to like the pineapple Christmas cake, but not its traditional method of mixing, decided to add drained crushed pineapple to the condensed milk cake instead. The extra liquid made the cake fairly moist so as this variant spread through the country in the 1980s, cooks passing on the recipe stipulated '2 good cups' of flour, then '2 large cups', then '2 heaped cups'.[147] But it wasn't just pineapple that enriched this once simple cake, but an array of essences and unexpected spices:

CHRISTMAS CAKE
Jill Young

1 can condensed milk
125g butter
2T golden syrup
4 eggs
1t each, vanilla, lemon, almond, whiskey, rum and brandy essences
2 heaped c flour
3 pkt mixed fruit
¼t nutmeg
¼t curry powder
1t mixed spice
¼t salt
1t baking soda
Shake of pepper
¼c milk
1 small can drained pineapple

Melt and blend condensed milk, butter and syrup over hot water. Beat in eggs then essences. Sift flour over fruit. Coat fruit with flour then [add] spices, baking soda dissolved in milk, pineapple and egg mixture. Mix well then pour into 9"[inch] cake tin. Bake 1hr at 120°C then 2 ½–3 hrs at 100°C. Turn oven off and leave for 1 hour before removing from oven.[148]

Curry powder had been an ingredient in one of the custard Christmas cakes before it was included in boil-and-bake cakes such as this condensed milk-pineapple hybrid. A few contributors felt the need to justify its presence. The submitter of a Wholemeal Christmas Cake recipe to *Aunt Daisy's New Cookery No. 6* stated that curry powder 'has the same effect as brandy and improves the flavour'.[149] The use of multiple essences was another 'throw-back' – it was the distinguishing feature of a war-time half-pound cake popularised by Aunt Daisy and included in her columns until 1961.[150] The maximum number of essences we recorded was seven, in Aunt Daisy's often-reprinted '1ZR Special Christmas Cake'.[151]

We have highlighted the four main recipe versions that successfully replaced sugar in a Christmas cake with sweetened condensed milk. In doing so, they encouraged the adoption of a quick and easy method of mixing, and provided an opportunity to economise on eggs and in one version on butter. All four can be traced back in New Zealand to the period 1967–74. During that time, the country entered a period of rapid uncontrolled inflation and economic pressure. Even the Nestlé Maggi Recipe Club was forced to close down in December 1970 as the company made economies.[152] Although the condensed milk Christmas cake represented the fusion of two delicious foods – fruit cake and sweetened condensed milk – we suspect that the chance to indulge our sweet tooth while making a saving on costs provided a strong incentive for home cooks to try it.

One Christmas cake, ten names

Before we can tell the story of this cake, we have to settle on a generic name for it. About 1970 Rosemary Dempsey called her version 'Christmas Cake (Brazil Nut Date Cake)', and the part in parentheses sums up two key ingredients in this cake – whole brazil nuts and dates.[153] We have recorded fourteen New Zealand recipes for this cake, all of which have brazil nuts, while ten include dates. For convenience, then, we call it the brazil nut date cake. Most cooks know this cake today as the 'Christmas Jewel Cake',[154] or the 'Cathedral Window Cake' or simply 'Cathedral Cake',[155] because in a thin slice light can shine through the multi-coloured glacé fruits. However, these evocative names have only been in use since the late 1980s, and the brazil nut date cake as a concept has been around since the early 1950s.

Like many fruit cakes that emerged after World War II, this was a significant departure from the classic pound cake with its two-hundred year-old pedigree. Rich fruit cakes in that tradition restricted nut use to almonds. In the seventeenth century these were invariably pounded to a paste, but in the eighteenth and nineteenth centuries they might be slivered or chopped, as well as ground. The first rich fruit cakes to include other types of nuts appear in American cookbooks from the southern states in the second half of the nineteenth century. Since that time, the native pecans of south and central North America have been used as an alternative to English walnuts, and are included in many southern dishes, including cakes. Brazil nuts were less common, perhaps because they are a product of a vulnerable tree species growing in the Amazon rainforests, and have never been successfully cropped in plantations. The emergence of a cake full of large un-chopped nuts is remarkable in itself, but when those nuts have been gathered from the wilds of Bolivia or Brazil, the result looks exotic and 'rich', drawing attention to the individual components.

In New Zealand, locally grown walnuts were added to Christmas cakes to supplement imported almonds during the Depression and World War II. Exotic nuts such as cashew or brazil nuts did not feature in the cake recipes until the 1960s. Both of these nuts were available in the grocers' shops from the 1930s, and brazil nuts had been imported to New Zealand as early as the 1860s. However, Christmas custom was to serve whole nuts at the table at the end of Christmas dinner – including brazil nuts, 'eating' almonds, walnuts, cashews and 'Barcelonas' (a type of hazelnut) – along with muscatel raisins and figs. Advertisements show that in the 1930s brazil nuts were a little less expensive than the best quality 'eating' almonds.[156]

In fact, brazil nuts were not the most expensive ingredients in the brazil nut date cake. Cherries were nearly twice the price of brazil nuts, and most of the recipes call for a cup of cherries, preferably equal quantities of red and green. Some of the earlier recipes specified Maraschino cherries – these are made by bleaching stoned cherries, then putting them into almond-flavoured syrup, with either red or green colouring.[157] Candied cherries sold in packets as glacé cherries also have their colour restored with synthetic food dyes. Their shelf life is secured with the preservative, sulphur dioxide.

Glacé peel was another ingredient that cost more than the equivalent quantity of dried fruit. To make this product, pieces of citrus fruit skin go through a similar candying process to the cherries, with the replacement of water within the cells by sugar. Candied citron is probably the oldest of the peels and is now hard to obtain. Today most packets of mixed peel contain mixtures of candied lemon and orange peel. All told, the brazil nut date cake increased the amount of all the more expensive components of the traditional Christmas cake: cherries, nuts, candied fruits and peel. Some saving would have been made in eggs – it usually has only three – and there was no butter at all.

The earliest recipe we have found for the brazil nut date cake in New Zealand was submitted by Elsie Bartosh (née Barber) to *What's Cooking? 300 Favourite Recipes of Queen Margaret College Old Girls*, issued about 1965.[158] In the light of the ingredients, its name was quite appropriate: 'Christmas Loaf (Very rich.)'. The quantities and wording closely match those of the following recipe published in the *Australian Women's Weekly* for the first time in 1954, then repeated in 1958, 1961, 1962 and 1963.

NEW STYLE CHRISTMAS CAKE

1 ½ c shelled whole Brazil nuts
1 ½ c walnut halves
½ lb. stoned dates
⅔ c chopped candied peel
½ c red maraschino cherries
½ c green maraschino cherries
(both drained free of syrup)

½ c seeded raisins
¾ c flour
½ tsp baking powder
½ tsp salt
¾ c sugar
3 eggs
1 tsp vanilla

Grease sides and base of large loaf-tin (8 in x 5 in) and line with 1 layer of greased paper. Place unchopped Brazil nuts, walnuts, dates, peel, cherries, and raisins into a large basin. Sift flour, baking powder, and salt together 2 or 3 times, then mix with sugar. Add to nuts and fruits and mix thoroughly. Make into a stiff mixture with beaten eggs and vanilla. Spoon into prepared tin, pressing and flattening with the back of a spoon. Bake in slow oven 2 to 2 ½ hours. Leave in tin 10 minutes, loosen around edges and turn on to cake-cooler, then remove paper. When completely cold, wrap in food-wrapping plastic and store in refrigerator.[159]

The 'Food and Cookery Experts' at the *Australian Women's Weekly* could not agree on its name, for when the recipe was reprinted in 1958 it was 'New Style Festive Cake', and in 1961 simply 'Fruit and Nut Cake'. In 1962, it had reverted to 'New-Style Christmas Cake' and when it appeared in their booklet commemorating thirty years of favourite recipes in 1963, it was 'New Style Festive Cake' again.[160] Those titles seemingly did not appeal to New Zealanders, who took up the recipe with as much enthusiasm as the Australians, but under a new name.

Before its first publication in the *New Zealand Woman's Weekly*, under the new title 'Continental Christmas Cake', the recipe had undergone some modifications. The flour and raisins were each increased to one cup, and a half-cup each of prunes, apricots and ginger were added. Instead of a loaf tin, a square cake tin was employed.[161] This recipe was reprinted two years later in the *New Zealand Woman's Weekly Cookbook*.[162]

A decade later, New Zealand food-writers adopted the brazil nut date cake and made more substantial changes. Alison Holst dropped the dates, reduced the quantity of sugar and eggs, replaced the walnuts by almonds and cashews, and cooked this new version, which she called a 'Rich Fruit Wreath', in an eight-inch ring tin.[163] In 1991 she published a doubled version, with two cups of nuts and three of candied fruits – she suggested pineapple, mango, peach and apricot. With even more potential for translucency due to the extra candied fruit, this recipe was named 'Cathedral Window Cake'.[164] When the smaller 'Rich Fruit Wreath' recipe was re-issued in 1995, it became the very popular 'Cathedral Cake'.[165] There have been other 'Cathedral Cakes' in culinary history – usually iced wedding cakes complete with decorated portals and spires – but this unique New Zealand naming is far more descriptive of the brazil nut date cake than of any of its earlier titles.

The recipe we have selected to represent this cake of multiple aliases also has an appealing title. Food-writer Joan Bishop worked on this cake for her 'Simply Entertaining' column in the *Otago Daily Times*. It was published first in 1987, and again in 1991. In quantities and ingredients it is closer to the original Australian recipe, but Joan has measured out all the dry ingredients by weight instead of in cups:

CHRISTMAS JEWEL CAKE
Crammed full of glistening fruit and whole nuts, this colourful cake will keep for several months wrapped in foil in the fridge.

I have seen several variations of this recipe, but I prefer this particular combination of ingredients. The more traditional Christmas Cake needs a few weeks to mature. This one however is ready to eat in 24 hours. If you haven't made your cake yet, this could be the answer.

200g stoned dates
150g mixed peel
100g red glacé cherries
100g green glacé cherries
100g raisins
200g walnut halves

250g brazil nuts
100g flour
½ teaspoon baking powder
170g sugar
3 eggs

Line a six-cup capacity loaf tin with three layers of paper finishing with grease proof paper. Take the paper about 5cm higher than the sides of the tin.

Combine the fruit and nuts in a large bowl. Sift flour and baking powder together and add the sugar. Tip the dry ingredients into the bowl and mix well.

Beat the eggs until thick and creamy and pour into the fruit and nut mixture. Stir to combine thoroughly.

Spoon into the prepared tin and spread evenly.

Bake for about 2 ¼ hours at 150deg. C.[166]

A thin slice of Christmas Jewel Cake reminds us of the beautiful stained glass windows found in many churches.

CHRISTMAS JEWEL CAKE

Adapted from Joan Bishop's 'Christmas Jewel Cake', published in her food column in the *Otago Daily Times*, 8 December 1987.

The fruits and nuts are deliberately left whole so that when the cake is cut into thin slices and held up to the light one is reminded of the beautiful colours of a stained glass window.

200 g pitted dates
150 g crystallised mixed peel (include glacé citron or orange pieces if available, in pieces similar in size)
100 g red glacé cherries
100 g green glacé cherries
100 g raisins

200 g walnut halves (freshly shelled for the best flavour)
250 g brazil nuts
100 g plain flour
½ teaspoon baking powder
170 g sugar
3 eggs (size 7)

Preheat the oven to 150°C, with a shelf in the middle position.

Prepare a 6-cup capacity loaf pan by lining the base and sides with a double layer of brown paper and a single layer of baking paper. The paper should extend about 5 cm above the sides.

Combine the fruit and nuts in a large bowl. Sift the flour and baking powder into a small bowl and stir in the sugar. Tip the dry ingredients into the fruit and nuts and mix well, breaking up any clumps of fruit.

Beat the eggs until thick and creamy and pour into the fruit mixture. Stir to combine thoroughly, with no loose flour visible.

Spoon into the prepared loaf pan, pressing well into the corners and spreading evenly. Bake for 2–2 ½ hours. The surface should be golden brown and when the centre is pressed it should feel firm. It is difficult to test with a skewer as the large pieces of fruit tend to stick to the surface. If the top starts to brown too much, cover the surface with a double layer of baking paper.

Remove from the oven and place on a rack. Cover with a tea towel or a piece of foil and leave until cool. Remove from the pan and wrap in greaseproof paper and store in an airtight cake container or wrap in foil.

One other food-writer, Tui Flower, gave weights as an alternative to cup measures when she edited an earlier version of the recipe for the 1971 *New Zealand Woman's Weekly Cookbook*.[167] When we outlined the history of the ginger ale Christmas cake earlier, we noted her observation that American recipes usually give quantities in cups rather than weights. In contrast, cup measures are uncommon in Australian recipes. The page of the *Australian Women's Weekly* where the 'New Style Christmas Cake' first appeared contained two other fruit cake recipes and two Christmas pudding recipes. All four used pounds and ounces – only our brazil nut date cake's measurements were expressed as cups. So is this cake of American origin?

We have found it under the name 'Brandy Yule Cake' in a 1967 issue of the American *Woman's Day* magazine.[168] The recipe matches the 1954 Australian one very closely, though the brazil nuts have been replaced by an equal quantity of almonds. When Digby Law published a small version of the recipe in *Cuisine* in 1987, under the title 'Nutty As A Fruit Cake', he wrote that he had first encountered the cake in Arizona, where it had been made as Christmas gifts.[169] Our most significant discovery, however, is the recipe for a Yule Cake published in the New England Dairies' *United Farmers News* in December 1953.[170] Submitted by Mrs Roger Cote, of Morrisville, Vermont, it is almost identical to the 1954 recipe from the *Australian Women's Weekly*. The increasing number of similar recipes from American sources is a strong argument that the brazil nut date cake began in the United States and spread to Australia in 1954. From there it came to New Zealand, where it has finally achieved distinctive and memorable names.

Making 'healthy' Christmas cakes

If you compare Eliza Acton's innocuous introduction to 'Cakes' in her first edition of *Modern Cookery*, issued in 1845, with the revised edition of 1855, you will find that she added an extraordinary attack on the classic rich cakes of Britain. She began the revised section with these words:

> We have inserted here but a comparatively limited number of receipts for these '*sweet poisons*', as they have been emphatically called …. more illness is caused by habitual indulgence in the richer and heavier kinds of cakes than could easily be credited by persons who have given no attention to the subject.

> Amongst those which have the worst effects are almond, and plum *pound* cakes, as they are called; all varieties of the *brioche* and such others as contain a large quantity of butter and eggs.[171]

We don't know what inspired such an outburst, but she wasn't the only person to damn the pound cake, the category to which most traditional Christmas cakes belong. In 1870, an American physician writing about the benefits of sugar for treating the indigestion caused by 'greasy articles of diet', declared that it had to be taken in pure form, not 'cooked, nor intimately mixed with the other substances; an example of this we see in pound-cake, a poison which should never be seen on a physician's table'.[172] Did the nineteenth-century proponents of this view offer any alternatives? Ella Eaton Kellogg, wife of John Harvey Kellogg who ran the Battle Creek Sanitarium, included just one 'Fruit Cake' in her influential book, *Science in the Kitchen* (1893). Because she was opposed to chemical raising agents, this cake was raised by yeast, with the ingredients similar in proportion to seventeenth-century fruit cakes.[173] Her cake used no butter but did incorporate some cream.

Early editions of Mrs Beeton's *The Book of Household Management* were more concerned with economy than with the dangers of rich cakes. Rather than reduce the fat content of 'common' or 'plain' fruit cakes, the recipes supplemented the butter or replaced it with 'good beef dripping'.[174] Mrs Beeton's 'Christmas Cake' recipe had less fat than most of the cakes in her book – but, as we have shown, this relates more to its origins as a soft gingerbread than as a true fruit cake. In the introduction to the chapter on breads, biscuits and cakes, Mrs Beeton showed no concern with excessive fat but dwelt on the drawbacks of white bread, noting that 'In many parts of Germany the entire meal [wholemeal] is used; and in no part of the world are the digestive organs of the people in a better condition'.[175] She did not, however, include a single cake recipe calling for wholemeal flour.

New Zealand newspapers introduced wholemeal scones and biscuits in their recipe columns at the end of the nineteenth century, but we could not find a wholemeal fruit cake until 1927.[176] It was supplied by Mrs Wetherell, whose recipes appeared in cookery columns for Wellington's *Evening Post* in the 1920s. There was a steady increase in wholemeal recipes and advice during the 1930s, and eventually a wholemeal Christmas cake was printed in Aunt Daisy's fourth book in 1940. It is clearly a pound cake, with the reduced quantity of eggs compensated for by the baking soda. As such, it remains a rich cake.

CHRISTMAS CAKE (Wholemeal)

1 lb. butter.
1 lb. sugar (raw if possible).
1 lb. currants
1 lb. sultanas.
¼ lb. peel.
Pinch salt.
½ lb. minced walnuts if desired.
4 eggs.
5 breakfastcups wholemeal.
1 heaped teaspoon soda.
1 pint hot milk.

Method: Beat butter, and sugar. Add beaten eggs. Put soda in hot milk, then add a little to mixture, then little wholemeal alternately until all is well beaten in. If baked in flat tin, will take 3 hours, but requires longer in round tin.[177]

We recorded eight Christmas cake recipes containing wholemeal from the 1940s and half of these also contained some white flour. Six could be described as pound cakes halved. None appear to have survived the end of rationing.

One recipe submitted to the *New Zealand Woman's Weekly* in 1962 stands out as quite different in concept from the wartime wholemeal cakes. In its high proportion of fruits and nuts, it reminds us of the brazil nut date cake:

WHOLEMEAL XMAS CAKE

Mix
Quarter cup candied orange strips
Half pound raisins
Half pound currants
Quarter cup cut up prunes
Quarter cup chopped apricots
Half pound chopped figs
One cup honey

Pour honey over the fruit and let stand overnight.

One cup butter
Three eggs
One cup all-bran
Half teaspoon salt
Quarter teaspoon spice
Quarter teaspoon ground cloves
Six ounces brown sugar
Six ounces wholemeal flour
Quarter teaspoon cinnamon
One cup chopped nuts

Cream butter and sugar, add beaten eggs gradually. Sift all dry ingredients together, then add chopped nuts. Add the sifted dry ingredients gradually to the creamed mixture, alternating with the honeyed fruit. Line a large tin thickly with greased paper and bake slowly for three hours in slow oven. Will keep well for months if stored in an air-tight tin wrapped in several thicknesses of greaseproof papers – "Hoki."[178]

The rising interest in 'healthy food' seems to have by-passed Christmas cakes in the final decades of the twentieth century. From the decade 1980–89 we recorded just two recipes with wholemeal, one a ginger-ale cake, and the other a large boil-and-bake cake with a pound of butter.[179] Three out of four recipes with wholemeal from the 1990s had been developed for diabetics, and the fourth was a microwaved Christmas cake.[180]

Perhaps we should not expect a once-a-year treat to conform to notions of what is good for us. Cooks were forced to adjust to rationing in the 1940s and as soon as that finished they returned to making the rich Christmas cakes of more affluent decades, though these were generally reduced in size. However, a change in attitude may now be underway. To many of us, the pleasure imparted by a dish is affected not just by its taste and appearance, but also by its ethical standing. If it contains an ingredient of animal origin, then that creature must have been humanely treated both in life and at the time of its death. If plant products are included, they should be from a sustainable agricultural or horticultural system. Nutritional awareness is greater than at any previous time, and has driven the regulations for identification of additives and the provision of nutritional tables on food containers. Country-of-origin labelling is also sought, especially by consumers concerned with 'food miles'. We cannot expect Christmas cakes to be exempt from this level of scrutiny.

The core ingredients of the Christmas cake are the same as in most cakes – flour, sugar, butter and eggs – and they should be assessed in just the same way. Cooks opposed to the caging of laying hens will already be buying free-range eggs. Those who want to increase the fibre and wheat germ content of their flour can source wholemeal or blend their own wheatmeal. Sugar of any type will always pose a problem. Those who have tried to devise diabetic cakes know how difficult it is to remove sugar without affecting the quality of the cake. However, there is no need to stick to the traditional pound-cake ratio of equal weights of sugar, butter, flour and eggs. Several of the cakes we have selected already have reductions in sugar and butter. In the case of the condensed milk cake, this was achieved by a radical departure from the traditional method of mixing a pound cake, and in that of the brazil nut date cake by the loss of long-keeping qualities.

Our final recipe selection demonstrates that the traditional cake can be reformed without the loss of any of the assets of the old-fashioned Christmas cake. In 2002, Dunedin food-writer Joan Bishop decided to make an extremely low-fat cake without compromising the rich taste, dark colour, moistness, and long-life of the best traditional cakes. Over several months she made six versions, until she was satisfied that the result would be just as acceptable to those who were working hard to lower their cholesterol

FESTIVE FRUIT CAKE

Adapted from 'Christmas Cake', in Joan Bishop's food column, *Otago Daily Times*, 4 December 2002.

A dark, moist cake full of fruit but minus the fat! Traditional fruit cakes contain large quantities of butter that many of us are better to limit. Joan's version tastes so 'rich' that fruit-cake lovers don't notice the omission. We not only make this cake for Christmas but also to take on holiday as a special treat when tramping is on the itinerary.

Mary and Helen made this cake for the first series of *Kiwi Kitchen*, presented by Richard Till. We decorated it with dried fruits and nuts instead of the icings suggested in Joan's column.

Recipes for both icings are on pages 163–4. They are quick and simple to prepare – once you have tasted the homemade versions the commercial products do not measure up.

For its television debut, we served the cake with a single malt whisky and wedges of farmhouse-style cheese – a particularly successful combination.

1 kg mixed dried fruit	150 ml whisky, brandy or dry sherry
100 g crystallised ginger, chopped	(plus 4 tablespoons extra to drizzle on
100 g dried apricots (preferably from Central Otago), chopped	the cooked cake)
90 g dates, chopped	200 ml freshly squeezed orange juice
90 g pitted prunes, chopped	(3 or 4 oranges)
zest of one orange	
2 eggs, size 7	2 tablespoons treacle, warmed
150 g dark brown sugar	
300 g bread flour	1 teaspoon ground cinnamon
½ teaspoon baking powder	1 teaspoon ground mixed spice

200 g whole unskinned almonds or Brazil nuts, cut into halves or quarters

Suggestions for topping decorations –
blanched whole almonds or Brazil nuts cut into halves or quarters or walnut halves; glacé cherries, sliced in half; slices of other crystallised fruits, such as citron, orange, pineapple

Place the dried fruit, ginger and apricots in a non-metallic bowl. Pour the alcohol over the fruit and mix well. Cover and leave to soak overnight.

For a cake to be decorated with nuts and fruits, position a wide, double layer of brown paper to form a strap. Make it long enough to extend well above the top of the pan. This will enable the cooked cake to be lifted from its pan without having to invert it and possibly damaging the topping. Lay the strap inside the pan before lining the base and sides of a 22 cm-round or 20 cm-square cake pan with a double layer of brown paper and then a layer of baking paper.

Place the dates, prunes, zest and orange juice into a small saucepan, bring to the boil, cover with a lid and simmer gently for 10 minutes. Mash the fruit until the mixture is a thick purée. Set aside to cool.

Preheat the oven to 150°C with a shelf in the middle position.

Beat the eggs and sugar until light coloured and creamy. Add the warm treacle and beat again. Stir in the puréed fruit and mix well. Pour this into the soaked dried fruit and stir to combine.

Into a large bowl, sift the flour, baking powder, cinnamon and mixed spice. Add the fruit mixture and the nuts. Mix thoroughly. Spoon evenly into the prepared cake pan, level and smooth the surface. Arrange the topping ingredients in an attractive pattern on top.

Bake for 2 ¼–2 ½ hours. (How to test when a cake is cooked is explained on page 168.) Remove from the oven and drizzle the extra whisky, brandy or sherry over the surface. Cover with a tea towel and leave to cool in the cake pan. Turn out carefully and wrap with greaseproof paper and store in an airtight cake container or wrap in foil.

or body weight, as to family and friends who liked traditional cakes. She was able to eliminate butter, and reduce the number of eggs to just two, by making a prune, date and orange juice purée that is added to a well-beaten mixture of eggs and sugar instead of the usual creamed mixture of sugar and butter:

Delicious low-fat cake perfect for Christmas …
Christmas Cake

Rich fruitcakes usually improve with keeping. If however, despite your very best intentions, the cake is not baked until a day or so before Christmas, it will still taste wonderful. I cut into this cake within 12 hours of taking it from the oven and it was very good. Half of the cake was wrapped in greaseproof paper and stored for two weeks. It is maturing beautifully.

1kg mixed dried fruit
100g crystallized ginger, chopped
100g dried apricots, chopped
150ml brandy
90g dates, chopped
90g pitted prunes, chopped
200ml orange juice
300g plain flour

½ teaspoon baking powder
1 teaspoon ground cinnamon
1 teaspoon mixed spice
2 eggs (size 7)
150g brown sugar
2 Tbsp treacle, warmed
200g brazil nuts, halved
¼ cup of brandy, second measure

Prepare the fruit, which requires soaking the night before baking. Place 1kg dried fruit, the ginger and apricots in a large bowl. Pour the brandy over the fruit and mix well. Cover and leave overnight.

Grease and line a deep 20cm square cake tin, first with brown paper and then with nonstick baking paper.

Place the dates, prunes and orange juice into a small saucepan, bring to the boil, cover with lid and simmer gently for 10 minutes. Mash until fruit is well pulped and the mixture is a thick puree. Cool.

Preheat oven to 150degC.

Sift the flour, baking powder, cinnamon and spice into a large bowl.

Beat the eggs and sugar well. Add the treacle and the pureed prunes and dates and beat to combine. Pour this into the dried fruit and stir. Tip the fruit mixture into the bowl containing the dry ingredients, add the brazil nuts and mix well.

Spoon into the prepared tin and smooth the surface of the cake. Place in the preheated oven and bake for 2 ¼–2 ½ hours or until a skewer comes out clean when inserted in the centre.

Loosely cover the top of the cake with baking paper if it starts to darken too much during cooking.

Sprinkle ¼ cup of brandy over the cake. Leave cake to cool in the tin.

When completely cold, wrap the cake in greaseproof paper and store in an airtight tin until required.[181]

We used an artificial Pohutukawa flower (*Metrosideros excelsa*) – the New Zealand Christmas tree – to decorate our mid-winter Festive Fruit Cake (p. 156–7).

Joan Bishop has given us a well-tested alternative to a butter-rich cake. The next step for cooks might be to rethink the dried and candied fruits. They are the most expensive component but have been an integral part since the seventeenth century at least – they put Christmas into the cake. Because they could not be grown in Britain, and had been subject to a range of processes, from drying to candying, these fruits were collectively too costly to be everyday items. That situation still applies to many of our dried fruits and sweetmeats. Our evaluation should include the preservatives or synthetic colours used in the processing, as well as the distance the products have travelled. Cooks may be prepared to pay a premium for sun-dried fruits and to accept dark rather than dyed cherries. New Zealand is fortunate in that the important dried fruit and ginger production areas of Australia are much closer than the sources that supply Britain. Alternatively, some of us might wish to candy our own fruit, as in seventeenth-century British households. Using marmalade as a substitute for candied peel is already recommended in some recipes.

Nuts are not so vital a component of the Christmas Cake as the fruit, and some cooks will omit them if a family member has a strong dislike or allergy. However they are nutritionally valuable, provided they are fresh. That was not always the case in the past, and rancid almonds must have spoiled many Christmas cakes. New Zealand now produces excellent walnuts and hazelnuts, and should be capable of growing almonds, pecans and pistachio nuts commercially. Australians can source their own organically grown pistachios and almonds. Until the brazil nut date cake appeared, most Christmas cakes contained just almonds, or in hard times, walnuts. This blinkered approach to nuts – almonds or nothing – is hard to explain without recourse to history. In the days before essences, almond flavouring was imparted by ground almonds, and so they served both as a source of nutmeat and a desirable taste. No other nut could be substituted. Once almond essence was available, however, other nuts could have been introduced into the Christmas cake. It took over sixty years for a nut-rich cake to become acceptable and then it featured a wild-sourced nut with major questions concerning its sustainability. We believe that in the twenty-first century there is great scope for increasing nut variety and amounts in Christmas cakes.

7
So what Christmas cake will we make this year?

While working on this book we have become familiar with over a thousand recipes for festive cakes from Britain, America, Australia and New Zealand. Some recipes have survived from the mid-seventeenth century, while others first appeared in print just a few years ago. We have taken the view that old recipes are not necessarily out-of-date, and so we will make our choice of recipe from the full set. The oldest contenders pose some extra challenges for today's cooks, but as we have shown with the yeast-raised 'Excellent Cake' (1669), quantities can be scaled down. Finding modern equivalents of seventeenth-century ingredients is a fascinating quest, which has been made easier by online search engines. We may make this 'Excellent Cake' for a family get-together – as a bread, it is best eaten soon after baking. It is also a 'healthier' cake compared to many later types.

If we decide to give guests a taste of the eighteenth century, then Hannah Glasse's 'Rich Cake' (1747) is truly representative of a festive cake that spared no expense. Connoisseurs of Christmas cakes will recognise in this the flavour of the cakes they enjoyed as children, for this recipe is an ancestor of many that were made in the first half of the twentieth century. In contrast, Isabella Beeton's 'Christmas Cake' (1861) came from another lineage of cakes, that of the gingerbreads. If the Victorians had known it was an American recipe, would they have accepted it so readily? There will be some explaining to do when we bring it to the table …

Edmonds' 'Christmas Cake' (1908–) is a classic pound cake of eighteenth-century origin. Like all pound cakes, it mellows with keeping. We have two illustrations of this cake (pp. 96 and 162), and we know it was iced with the delectable combination of almond paste and royal icing. Another cake from Edwardian Christchurch, Mrs Harman and Mrs Gard'ner's 'Christmas Cake or Bride Cake' (1904–), comes from a long American line of wedding cakes. These two cookery teachers were not the first, nor the last, New Zealand food-writers to change the names and roles of cakes in their search for a good Christmas cake.

Edmonds' Christmas cake, one of the long line of pound cakes, was made throughout the twentieth century. This illustration is from the sixth edition of *The "Sure to Rise" Cookery Book* (opp. p. 20) published in 1936. H. Leach Collection.

RECIPES FOR ICINGS

The following recipes have been adapted from Joan Bishop's column, *Otago Daily Times*, 4 December 2002.

A Christmas cake stores best without icing, so leave this task until just a few days before the festivities start. A glaze is applied first, followed immediately with a layer of almond paste. This is left for 24 hours to dry before a top layer of royal icing is applied.

Almond Paste

Makes sufficient to cover the top of a 20 cm-square cake. Double the recipe to cover the sides as well, or to cover the top of a larger cake. To ensure your icing has the best flavour, buy ground almonds from a shop with a high turnover. Check expiry dates on packets.

180 g ground almonds
180 g icing sugar
1 egg white (size 6)
2–3 teaspoons lemon juice

Place the ground almonds, icing sugar and egg white into the bowl of a food processor with the metal chopping blade in place. Add 2 teaspoons of the lemon juice and process for about 40 seconds until the almond paste forms a ball around the blade. Add a little more lemon juice if necessary.

Icing the cake – first layer

Make a glaze with 2 tablespoons of sieved apricot jam or marmalade and 1 tablespoon of water. Heat in a small saucepan until boiling. While still hot, brush the surface of the cake just before applying the almond paste. This will help the almond paste adhere to the cake.

Roll out the almond paste between two large pieces of cling-wrap film dusted lightly with icing sugar. Using the cling-wrap to help provide support, lift the paste and position it over the glazed cake, gently pressing it on with a rolling pin. Use a knife to cut away any surplus. Leave to dry for 24 hours before applying the royal icing.

Royal Icing

Makes sufficient to cover the top and sides of a 20 cm-square cake. Double or treble the recipe for larger cakes. The glycerine (also called glycerol) keeps the icing from hardening too much.

    350 g icing sugar (sift if lumpy)
    1 egg white (size 6)
    3–4 teaspoons of lemon juice (strained)
    ½ teaspoon glycerine (optional)

Place the icing sugar, egg white, 3 teaspoons of the lemon juice and the glycerine into a bowl and beat until soft and smooth. Add the extra lemon juice if the mixture is too stiff.

Spread the royal icing evenly over the cake. Use a spatula dipped in hot water to either smooth the surface, or roughen the icing to resemble snow. Leave the iced cake in the air for an hour or two to dry before storing in an airtight cake container.

An electric beater makes an easy job of mixing royal icing.

For a cake that evokes the tastes and smells of a country kitchen, we may choose the 'Howick Christmas Cake' (1935–). With its 'mystery' ingredient, blackcurrant jam, and combination of walnuts and almonds, it shows that the Christmas cake could adapt to economic depression without loss of quality. Wartime and post-war rationing made it even harder to produce a rich-tasting Christmas cake. We may make the '2-Egg Custard Christmas Cake' (1948–) in memory of our mothers' generation, who accepted the challenge of keeping up Christmas traditions for their families.

Although it had reached New Zealand from Australia by 1943, the 'Ginger Ale Christmas Cake' did not circulate widely until the 1950s. Once its size and costs had been adjusted, it offered a quickly made, moist cake, with an unusual ingredient and a novel method of preparing the fruit. It still has many supporters, though probably not as many as those who swear by pineapple Christmas cakes. These pineapple cakes reflect American and Australian influences in the 1930s, then the development of four different New Zealand versions from the 1950s to the present day. Pineapple Christmas cakes don't need to be iced, and we make Tui Flower's 'Dark Christmas Cake' (1968) when we want a long-lasting, moist cake with tropical hints.

For a simple Christmas cake, quickly made in a saucepan, we often choose a condensed milk cake recipe from 1970. The flavours imparted by the golden syrup and condensed milk take us back to our childhood, and we know that this cake appeals to our grandchildren just as much as it does to us. Of course, if we feel like showing off a little, we may bake a 'Cathedral Cake' or 'Jewel Cake', noting of course that although this cake may have been fashionable in the 1990s, it was not new. It can be traced back to America in the early 1950s.

For a guilt-free Christmas we will make Joan Bishop's low-fat Christmas cake, and marvel that it tastes as good, and lasts as long as the rich cakes of the past, despite a significant change in the ingredients. It is an excellent example of how Christmas cakes can be adapted to suit the times. In wartime, home cooks found ingenious ways of making an acceptable Christmas cake, despite rationing and shortages. The challenge for an increasing number of cooks in the twenty-first century is to produce a cake that is nutritionally and ethically acceptable.

The type of study we have undertaken relies on a fundamental property of virtually all recipes – that they are passed from one cook to another, and are subject to change each time they are written down or published. In this sense, all recipes are heirlooms, even those presented as new. All draw on elements of pre-existing recipes. Unlike most heirlooms that depend on family memories or records for their status, recipes carry their heritage encoded within them. It may take the form of a distinctive set of ingredients, a unique combination of quantities, or a characteristic method. We have provided examples where several steps in the evolution of the recipe have been uncovered. Our greatest surprise was that five of our twelve selected cakes could be traced back to America.

Before our first study of Christmas cakes, published in 2003, we thought this type of cake would prove to be very conservative, persisting over hundreds of years with little change. We should have known better, for our 'working' recipe books (the ones in the kitchen) are full of pineapple Christmas cakes and condensed milk Christmas cakes, and close-up colour pictures of cathedral cakes, all of which emerged as popular varieties in our lifetimes. The lesson we have learned is to question any claims that a type of cake or recipe is 'traditional'. You might reply that the recipe for the rich fruit cake that your mother or grandmother used to make has been handed down through your family for 200 years or longer – doesn't this fact make it 'traditional'? Not if it contains sultanas or baking powder or essences. What we have found is that each generation modifies its recipes to suit the times. Your family cake has been evolving.

As a category of festive cake, the 'excellent' cakes of the seventeenth century, which were yeast-raised, fruited breads, underwent a dramatic change during the eighteenth century to 'rich' cakes with high proportions of butter, and increasing amounts of sugar. A revolutionary new way of mixing accompanied this change – it began with creaming or beating the butter. By the start of the nineteenth century, most rich fruit cakes followed pound-cake principles. During the nineteenth century, the extra-large specimens of fruit cakes that had served as twelfth cakes declined to extinction, as cooks and housewives sought a general-purpose Christmas cake. We found that they co-opted plum cakes, bride or wedding cakes, and even American gingerbread for this new role. These became the ancestors of many twentieth-century Christmas cakes. Because bride cakes had been iced with both almond and royal icing since 1769, it was not surprising that their Christmas-cake descendants took over this special topping. The second half of the twentieth century brought more revolutionary changes in both method and ingredients. All told, there has never been a period when festive cakes could be described as conservative.

For the future, we should accept change as normal. If historians are right that Twelfth Night evolved out of the Roman festival of Saturnalia, then it is possible that centuries (or millennia) from now the Christmas cake could be attached to another festive occasion, or another religion. The cake may not keep the name, but the chains of recipes will continue to unroll. The key feature of the Christmas cake

HINTS FOR MAKING RICH FRUIT CAKES

1. As rich fruitcakes are in the oven for an extended time, it is wise to line cake pans to prevent excessive browning on the base and sides. We use a double layer of brown paper followed by a single layer of baking paper. There is no need to grease either the pan or the baking paper. We have inherited several of our mother's dark-coloured, heavy-grade pans that are a delight to use but it is very important to line these to prevent over-browning. The corners of cakes cooked in square pans are particularly vulnerable. In the past, some recipes suggested standing the cake on a thick layer of newspaper. This is not an option today, as the ink used for modern printing tends to emit a pungent smell when hot.

2. We suggest positioning rich fruit cakes on a middle shelf, or slightly below, and setting the oven function to BAKE. Check the manual for advice on your particular oven. Large cakes are usually baked at a lower temperature than small ones. Oven thermostats may vary with actual temperatures ranging from 10°C below to 10°C above the marked temperature. Home cooks become familiar with their particular oven and know to either bake a cake for a longer or shorter time or to increase or decrease the temperature setting. If in doubt, buy a good quality oven thermometer to check the accuracy of the thermostat. An older thermostat may lose accuracy with age.

3. Older recipes often specify just one cake pan size for both square and round pans. This would result in a deeper cake if made in a round pan, due to the larger surface area of the square pan. For example, if a 20 cm-round pan is suggested, to achieve approximately the same cake depth in a square one you would need to use an 18 cm x 18 cm pan.

4. Bread flour is better than plain or standard flour, due to its higher protein content. Packets of flour are often labelled as 'High Grade' for bread, fruit cakes, etc. or 'Plain' or 'Standard Flour' for sponge cakes, biscuits, pikelets, etc. Check labels on flour packs for suggested uses.

5. If using ordinary salted butter, there is no need to add extra salt. With unsalted butter, it is optional to add a small quantity of iodised salt (½ teaspoon for a medium-sized cake).

6. Ground spices should be fresh. Check use-by dates when purchasing, and discard old packets lurking at the back of a cupboard. All spices, whole or ground, should be kept in airtight glass containers and stored in a cool place away from light. Whole spices retain their fresh flavours for a much longer period and for that reason we often grind our own.

7. Remove the correct number of eggs from the fridge about an hour ahead of using them – they will beat more easily at room temperature and produce a greater volume.

8. Essences are used in many cakes to add flavour. Buy natural essences rather than the cheaper, synthetic versions.

9. When creaming butter and sugar, ensure that your bowl is warm and the butter soft but not melted. If using a metal or pyrex bowl, add the butter and sugar and place in the oven as it is preheating. Set a timer for one minute to ensure it is not forgotten. This may have to be repeated depending on how cold the butter is. A microwave oven can also be used with a glass bowl. Creaming is most easily done with an electric cake mixer. Scrape the sides of the bowl down from time to time and keep beating until the mixture is pale coloured and creamy. This will take several minutes and even longer if beaten by hand. At this stage, the eggs are added. Break one egg at a time into a cup and then tip into the creamed mixture. Continue beating for several minutes. Repeat with each remaining egg. The mixture may show a tendency to curdle. If so, add a spoonful of the weighed flour with each egg addition. Don't worry if the curdling continues, as it does not seem to affect the finished cake.

10. We recommend sifting flour with other dry ingredients, such as baking powder and spices. It is a good way of incorporating air and making sure the raising agent is distributed evenly.

11. A domestic electric cake mixer may not be large enough for mixing big cakes. If this is the case, use the mixer for creaming butter and sugar and adding eggs, then transfer the mixture to a larger bowl or preserving pan for the final combining with the dry ingredients and fruit. This is the time to enlist the help of family members to take turns with the stirring. Our mother told us that one could make a wish while stirring – this ensured a queue of eager assistants.

12. Check that the surface of the cake is not browning too much and if so cover with a double piece of baking paper. Bake the cake for the shorter time specified in the recipe and test for doneness. When cooked, a cake will have shrunk slightly from the sides of the cake pan, the middle will be firm when gently pushed at the centre and the colour will have darkened. If these criteria are met, then use a warm skewer or wire cake tester to insert into the middle of the cake. It should come out with no uncooked mixture adhering to it. If necessary, continue to bake for another 10–15 minutes and test again.

13. Remove the cooked cake from the oven and stand on a cake rack. Leave in the pan until it has cooled to room temperature. This may take overnight. Cover with a tea towel or a piece of foil to ensure that the surface stays soft. Once at room temperature, carefully invert on to a rack and gently remove the pan. Remove the paper before wrapping the cake with greaseproof paper and storing in an airtight cake container; if too large, wrap in a double layer of foil. Store in a cool pantry or if temperatures and humidity are too high, keep for a week or two in a fridge or freeze for up to 6 months.

14. Many cakes improve with storage of up to several weeks. They become less dry and crumbly as moisture moves from the fruit into the surrounding crumb. The flavour will mellow and improve with time.

is a mixture of ingredients that are of exotic origin and therefore expensive. Our ancestors did not always know the country of origin of mace, or dates, or almonds, but they knew that it lay to the east and was warm. These ingredients brought romance and mystique to the Christmas cake. Steps to reduce 'food miles' and identify place-of-origin undermine those exotic values. In their place, however, we may see the products of small-scale organic suppliers become the expensive (and therefore exclusive) ingredients in some future cakes. But as we found in the case of the 'Howick Christmas Cake', home-grown produce can also give high-quality results. Cooks who make chunky marmalades can use these as substitutes for peel, while home-made jams such as blackcurrant, apricot or plum contribute both flavour and colour. Locally sourced walnuts and hazelnuts can provide an excuse for a pre-Christmas nut-cracking party.

To survive, Christmas cakes must evolve with the times. Provided they remain a special, festive treat shared with family and friends, their recipes will be handed down for many generations to come. Merry Christmas!

Notes

Chapter 1

1. Holst 1978:64
2. Leach 2008a
3. Piperno et al. 2004
4. Willcox 2002
5. Evershed et al. 2008
6. Copley et al. 2005
7. Terral et al. 2010
8. McGovern et al. 1996, McGovern 2003
9. Miller 2008
10. Cartwright 2003
11. Miller 2008
12. Ladizinsky 1999:143
13. Ladizinsky 1999; Browicz and Zohary 1996
14. Zohary and Hopf 1994:176
15. Liu et al. 2006
16. Serjeantson 2009:270
17. Thompson 199-?:188
18. Hooper 1934:471, 473
19. Roose and Close 2008
20. Wilkins et al. 1995:3
21. Flower and Rosenbaum 1958:53
22. Faas 2007:19
23. Faas 2007:163–5
24. Dalby 1998:181
25. Dalby and Grainger 1996:109
26. Faas 2003:189–90
27. Donahue 2004:17–18
28. Donahue 2004:16
29. Cosman and Jones 2008:766
30. Van der Veen et al. 2008; Bakels and Jacomet 2003; Kuijper and Turner 1992
31. Thomas and Stallibrass 2008
32. Wilson 1976:225
33. Scully 1995:9
34. Austin 1888
35. Cappellini et al. 2010; Dickson 1996; Moffett 2006:46
36. A. W. 1591
37. A. W. 1591
38. *Twelfth Night*, Act 2, scene 3; *King Henry the Eighth*, Act 5, scene 3
39. *Troilus and Cressida*, Act 1, scene 1
40. *The Taming of the Shrew*, Act 5, scene 1
41. Palmer 1972
42. Laroque 1993:148–54

Chapter 2

1. Herrick 1648:376–7
2. Jonson 1641:3, 6
3. W. J. 1653
4. David 1979
5. W.J. 1653:133–4
6. W.J. 1653:69–70
7. Knoppers 2007:466, 480 reviews the claim that 'W. M.' was Walter Montagu, one of the queen's favourites
8. W. M. 1655:255–6
9. Latham and Matthews 1970 I:10
10. Latham and Matthews 1970 II:7
11. Latham and Matthews 1972 VI:4
12. Latham and Matthews 1976 IX:13
13. Latham and Matthews 1970 IX:409
14. Thompson 1976 refers to eight reprints between 1655 and 1679
15. Driver and Berriedale-Johnson (1986:116) date this to 1664
16. Anon 1675:2
17. Beveridge 1939, Clark 2007
18. Sources for Table 2.1: 1 & 2. W. J., 1653 *A True Gentlewomans Delight*; 3. W. M., 1655 *The Queens Closet Opened*; 4 & 5. May, Robert, 2000 [1660], *The Accomplisht Cook*; 6. Anon, 1675 [1st ed. 1664?] *The Gentlewomans Cabinet Unlocked*; 7. Woolley, Hannah, 1664, *The Cook's Guide*.
19. Driver and Berriedale-Johnson 1986:13
20. Latham and Matthews 1971 V:283
21. Latham and Matthews 1972 VI:46
22. Latham and Matthews 1972 VII:125
23. Latham and Matthews 1972 VII:243
24. Clark 2007
25. Stevenson and Davidson 1997
26. Stevenson and Davidson 1997:183
27. Driver 1997
28. e.g. M. H. 1683
29. Daish 2005:131
30. Beveridge 1939, Clark 2007
31. W. M. 1655:9
32. Driver 1997:179, 188
33. Hess 1981:11, 28

Chapter 2 Icing box
1. OED 2011
2. e.g. Hess 1981:322–8
3. Plat 1602:Recipe 18
4. Plat 1602:Recipe 56
5. Davidson in Henisch 1984:204–7
6. Stevenson and Davidson 1997:182–3
7. May 2000:238
8. OED 2011
9. Driver 1997:159–60
10. Raffald 1769:243

Chapter 3
1. 'Cosmopolita' 1762:4
2. 'Tell-Truth' 1765?:13
3. 'Gambolio' 1774:4
4. Anon 1796
5. Anon 1773a:6
6. Henisch 1984:143, 150–51
7. Anon 1773b:3
8. Anon 1769:4
9. Anon 1775:27
10. Vaisey 1984
11. Beresford 1924 I:43
12. Beresford 1924 I:148
13. Beresford 1929 IV:94
14. Beresford 1929 IV:201
15. Beresford 1927 III:239
16. Beresford 1924 I:120
17. e.g. Glasse 1995 [1747]; E. Smith 1973 [1753]
18. E. Smith 1973 [1753]:170, 183–4
19. Lehmann 2003:200
20. e.g. Driver 1997:125, 126, 173
21. Salmon 1705:43
22. Davidson 1995:182
23. Driver 1997:124
24. Howard 1717:107–108
25. Lehmann 2003:96
26. Yost 1938:426
27. E. Smith 1728:137
28. Lehmann 2003:109–110
29. Stead 1995:iii
30. Stead 1995; Bain 1995
31. Leach 2010:29
32. Glasse 1995:138
33. Jenks 1768:246
34. Taylor 1769:252
35. Raffald 1769:249, 251

Chapter 3 Icing box
1. Jenks 1768:246–7
2. Holland 1843:342
3. Stead 1995:iii
4. Raffald 1769:243–4
5. Carter 1730:169–70
6. Anon 1733; Harrison 1738:109
7. Frazer 1791:216–7

Chapter 4
1. W. G____N 1820:3
2. Henisch 1984:148–9
3. Hone 1838 I:48–9
4. Anon 1843; Hassall 1855:620
5. Anon, 1851:27; Anon 1858:641
6. Anon 1858:641
7. Anon 1800:1
8. Briscoe 1876:5
9. Anon 1848a:3
10. Anon 1841:3
11. Anon 1847:3; Anon 1848b:1
12. Anon 1857a:2
13. Anon 1866:1
14. Anon 1869:1
15. Anon 1870:3
16. Anon 1882:2
17. Anon 1860a:9
18. Anon 1861:12
19. Dickens 1853:74
20. Anon 1857:7
21. Anon 1860b:8
22. Henisch 1984:127, 179
23. Henisch 1984:180–7
24. The recipe was printed in Davidson's appendix for Henisch (1984:209)
25. Carter 1749:132
26. Bradley 1762:149
27. Mollard 1802:286–7
28. Kitchiner's recipe was added in 1823 to the fifth edition of his 1817 book, *The Cook's Oracle* – it is reproduced in Henisch 1984:211
29. Parkinson 1849:116
30. Copley 1838:355
31. 'A Lady Resident' 1864:182
32. [Payne] [1878]:1023
33. Ellet 1857:479
34. Anon 1905a:3; Anon 1906:3
35. Garrett [1894]:673–4
36. Warren 1858:83
37. Beeton 1861:855
38. Hughes 2006:220, 225

39	Leach and Inglis 2003:147
40	Anon 1859:591
41	Stuart [1863–6]
42	MacInnes 1896:128
43	Anon 1899a:3
44	Anon 1929:23
45	Anon 1930:21
46	Anon [1969a]:78
47	Jewry 1869:134
48	Anon 1883:27; 'Rita' 1891:7; Anon 1892a:1
49	Davidson in Henisch 1984:210
50	[Abbot] 1970:120
51	Anon 1897:16
52	Payne 1882:124; 'Meta' 1891:7; Anon 1892:49
53	Anon 1892c:43; Anon 1894a:3; Anon 1902a:63; Anon 1874:162
54	[Rundell] 1808
55	Acton 1845:514
56	Beeton 1863

Chapter 4 Icing box

1	Davidson in Henisch 1984:212
2	Cox and Dannehl 2007
3	Davidson in Henisch 1984:212
4	Jarrin 1827:149
5	Roberts 1836:238
6	Massey and Massey 1866:34
7	Massey and Massey 1866:43
8	Henderson 1877:304
9	Parloa 1882:332
10	Gillette 1887:253
11	Beeton 1899:1103–4, 1127–8
12	Beeton 1899:1104
13	Anon 1885:26–7
14	Croly 1866:194–5
15	Anon 1895b:32

Chapter 5

1	Leach and Inglis 2003
2	Leach 2008a
3	Harris 1977:53; Pool et al. 2007:169, 190–1, 218, 248
4	Bailey and Earle 1999:167
5	Leach and Inglis 2003:156
6	Gilchrist 1948:858
7	Holst 1986:69
8	Bell 1960:112; Galloway [1946–9]:6
9	Browne, Leach and Tichborne 1996:18
10	Anon 1935:20
11	Anon 1938:1
12	Anon 1962b:134
13	Gilchrist 1948:856

Chapter 6

1	Anon 1908
2	Leach 2008b:28; Anon 1936a:65
3	Leach 2008b:28
4	Anon 1908:31
5	Anon [1931]:11
6	Anon 1964a:1
7	Teal 2010:91
8	Anon 1964a:20
9	Anon 1968a:20
10	Leach 2008a:125
11	Anon 1978:28
12	Cameron 1929:91
13	Anon 1939:142
14	Sherriff 1961:14
15	Chase 1886; Leach 2008b:36–7
16	Anon 1903; Brandon and Smith 1905
17	MacInnes 1896:144
18	Anon 1902b:11
19	Simmonds 1877:432, 436
20	Anon 1873:2
21	Anon 1900:2; Anon 1904a:2
22	Anon 1905b:66
23	Harman and Gard'ner 1904:162
24	Harman and Gard'ner 1904:162
25	Taylor 1996:169
26	Anon 1904b:11
27	'Ladies ...' 1873:112
28	Anon 1904c:3
29	Anon 1915a:96
30	Thomson 1927:58
31	Basham [1947]:181
32	Harvey 1933:51–2
33	Basham [1947]
34	Teal 2010:87
35	Anon [1951]:68
36	Sources for Table 6.1: Leslie 1832:50; Leslie 1840:338; Beecher 1850:168–9; Hale 1852:358; Ellet 1857:475; 'Ladies...' 1873:112; Harman & Gard'ner 1904:162; Anon 1904c:3; Thomson 1927:59; Anon 1915:96; Harvey [1933]:51–2; Basham [1947]:181; Anon [1951]:68; Anon [1952]:55; Anon 1988:131.
37	Anon 1892d:5
38	Charsley 1992:22
39	'Ladies ...' 1873:112
40	Anon 1890:3; Anon 1894b:3
41	Anon 1895a:4
42	Anon 1899b:4
43	Anon 1936b:81

44	'Tui' [1936]:3	95	Anon 1997:32
45	Veart 2008:194	96	Gye [1939]
46	'Tui' [1936]:3	97	Gye [1939]:195
47	Leach 2008:70, 73	98	Anon 1968:32
48	'Tui' [1933]:5	99	Anon 1940a:54S; 1940b:50
49	Basham [1935]:142–3	100	Anon 1940b:50
50	Vosburgh cited in Toynbee 1995:27	101	Anon 1925:14
51	Anon 1936c:1, 2	102	McGee 2004:802; Kirkland [1907]:274
52	'Tui' [1936]:188	103	Basham [1943]
53	Roxburgh 1996:127	104	Leach 2008:23–5
54	Anon 1939:142	105	Anon 1940c:8
55	Basham [1935]:142–3; [1940]:151; [1943]:123; 1959:176; 1961	106	Basham [1943]:124
		107	Anon 1951:104
56	Basham [1935]:142–3	108	Larkins 1985:14
57	Anon 1911:19	109	Scaife and Scurr 1972:80
58	Anon 1934b:54S	110	Holst 1974:337
59	Anon 1920:8	111	Rayne et al. 1985:88; Forbes 1991:117
60	Anon 1937a:25	112	Basham [1935]:140–141
61	Leach & Inglis 2003:155	113	Basham [1934a]; [1934b]
62	Leach 2008a:91	114	Inglis 2007:191–2; Downes 1998:36–7
63	Leach 2008a:90–2; Taylor 1986:825	115	Anon 1927a:120
64	'Housewife' [1944]:12	116	'Villette' 1934:6
65	'Housewife' [1944]:12	117	Anon 1934a:41
66	e.g. Anding and Robins 1954:134	118	Basham [1940]
67	Cameron 1929:91	119	Anon 1940c:8
68	'Tui' 1934:147	120	Anon [1958]:135
69	Kent-Johnston 1941:1	121	Anon 1964b:86
70	Kent-Johnston 1939; 1950	122	Gedye 1978:42
71	Kent-Johnston 1941:75	123	Anon [1955]:38; Anon 1965:109; Anon [1968]:90; Anon 1969b:63
72	Carter [1944]:151		
73	Galloway [1946–9]:44	124	Holst 1978:64
74	Anon 1947:55	125	[Flower] 1968:138
75	Anon 1947:56	126	Flower 1998
76	Anon 1948:9	127	Flower 1971:168
77	Hirschfeld 1999:97	128	Anon 1977:48
78	Innes et al. 1990:46	129	Gray 1978:50, 52
79	Rowe [1993]:20	130	Boardman 1927:13
80	e.g. Anon 1970:61	131	e.g. Anon 1937b:58S
81	McGee 2004:161; Leach 2008:142	132	Turner 1922:9
82	Anon 1675:2	133	Turner 1922:7
83	Stevenson and Davidson 1997:181	134	Carter [1916]:55
84	Lamb 1716:33	135	Turner 1922:148
85	E. Smith 1728:137	136	Anon 1952:22; Anon 1953a:141
86	Glasse 1995 [1747]:138	137	[Flower] 1968:137
87	Smith 1810:228	138	Dempsey [1969?]:70
88	Adams and Adams 1825:89–90	139	Anon 1974:63
89	Dods 1826:309	140	Anon 1969c:139
90	Leslie 1847:109	141	Anon [1968 1973]
91	Leslie 1850:453	142	Anon [1974]:10; Anon 1982:28
92	Leslie 1857:486	143	[Flower] 1969:51
93	Anon [1901]:157–8	144	Anon 1972:102
94	Harman and Gard'ner [1904]:131	145	Anon [1970]:82

146 Anon [1972]:28
147 Anon 1983:39; Anon [1983]:46; Anon 1985:95
148 Anon 1985:95
149 Basham [1947]:184
150 Basham 1961
151 Basham [1943]:124
152 Perry 1970
153 Dempsey [1970]:39
154 Bishop 1987:20
155 Holst 1991:243; 1995:11
156 Anon 1936d:4
157 Davidson 1999:163
158 Marris et al. [1965]:65
159 Anon 1954:89
160 Anon 1958:64–5; Anon 1961:43; Anon 1962a:80; Anon 1963:71
161 Anon 1969c:141
162 Flower 1971:168
163 Holst 1985:66
164 Holst 1991:243
165 Holst 1995:11
166 Bishop 1987:20
167 Flower 1971:168
168 Anon 1967:57
169 Law 1987:16
170 Anon 1953b:12
171 Acton 1860:540
172 J.B.R.P. 1870:488
173 Kellogg 1893:346
174 Beeton [1869]:890, 896
175 Beeton [1869]:865
176 Anon 1927b:15
177 Basham [1940]:149
178 Anon 1962b:134
179 Reeves 1985:76; Anon 1986:89
180 Clifford 1991:53; Anon 1993:120; Stockdill 1996; Anon 1998:17
181 Bishop 2002:24

Chapter 6 Icing box
1   Anon 1923:opp. p.16
2   Anon [1931]:27
3   Anon [1936]:opp. p.20
4   Harman and Gard'ner [1904]:162–3
5   Anon [1901]:194; 'Tui' [1936]:213; Sherriff 1961:15
6   Anon 1955:48
7   Sherriff 1961:14
8   Holst 1967:5.5
9   Holst 1967:5.5
10 Daish 2005:131; Pedersen 1992:233

Bibliography

'A Lady Resident', 1864, *The Englishwoman in India*. London: Smith, Elder & Co. [Google Books].

[Abbot, Edward], 1970, *The Colonial Cook Book*. Sydney: Paul Hamlyn Pty. Ltd.

Acton, Eliza, 1845, *Modern Cookery, in all its Branches: Reduced to a System of Easy Practice, for the Use of Private Families*. 2nd ed. London: Longman, Brown, Green and Longmans. [Google Books].

Acton, Eliza, 1860, *Modern Cookery, for Private Families, Reduced to a System of Easy Practice*. Revised & enlarged edition [1855]. London: Longman, Green, Longman, and Roberts.

Adams, Samuel and Sarah, 1825, *The Complete Servant*. London: Knight and Lacey. [Google Books].

Anding, Blanche and Joan Robins, 1954, *Modern Home Cookery in Pictures*. London: Odhams Press Ltd.

Anon, 1675, *The Gentlewomans Cabinet Unlocked*. 7th impression [1st ed. 1664?]. EEBO [Early English Books Online]: Electronic Book.

Anon, 1733, *The Cook's and Confectioner's Dictionary: or, the Accomplish'd Housewife's Companion*. 4th ed. ECCO [Eighteenth Century Collections Online, Gale CW3307472369].

Anon, 1769, Intelligence for the Gazeteer. *Gazeteer and New Daily Advertiser,* Issue 12434 (January 7, 1769): 4. Gale NewsVault.

Anon, 1773a, A Scene in the Trip to Portsmouth. *Lloyd's Evening Post*, Issue 2524 (September 1–3, 1773): 6. Gale NewsVault.

Anon, 1773b, Twelfth Day [advertisement]. *Public Advertiser*, Issue 11791 (January 6, 1773): 3. Gale NewsVault.

Anon, 1775, *The Christmas Frolick; or, Mirth for the Holidays*. ECCO [Eighteenth Century Collections Online, Gale CW111372180].

Anon, 1796, *The Chances; or, Sport for Twelfth-Night*. ECCO [Eighteenth Century Collections Online, Gale CW111765096].

Anon, 1800, Ranelagh [advertisement]. *Oracle and Daily Advertiser*, Issue 22 199 (January 20, 1800): 1. Gale NewsVault.

Anon, 1841, Refreshment Rooms! [advertisement]. *The Australian* (December 30, 1841): 3. [http://trove.nla.gov.au/].

Anon, 1843, Four Children Poisoned. *The Times*, Issue 18199 (January 21, 1843): 5. Gale NewsVault.

Anon, 1847, Christmas Cakes! Christmas Cakes! [advertisement]. *Moreton Bay Courier* (December 18, 1847): 3. [http://trove.nla.gov.au/].

Anon, 1848a, Old Christmas [advertisement]. *Sydney Morning Herald* (January 6, 1848): 3. [http://trove.nla.gov.au/].

Anon, 1848b, Sydney Heart Cake Union [advertisement]. *Sydney Morning Herald* (January 5, 1848): 1. [http://trove.nla.gov.au/].

Anon, 1851, Punch's Sermons to Tradesmen. To the Confectioner. *Punch* XX: 27. Google Books.

Anon, 1857a, Christmas Cake [advertisement]. *Daily Southern Cross*, Vol. XIV, Issue 1093 (December 18, 1852): 2. Papers Past.

Anon, 1857b, The Crystal Palace. *The Times*, Issue 22872 (December 24, 1857): 7. Gale NewsVault.

Anon, 1858, The Analytical Sanitary Commission. Records of the Results of Microscopical and Chemical Analyses of the Solids and Fluids Consumed by All Classes of the Public. On Poisonous Sugar Confectionery. *The Lancet* (December 18, 1858) II: 641. Google Books.

Anon, 1859, The Housewife. *Ballou's Dollar Monthly Magazine* IX(6) (June 1859): 591. Google Books.

Anon, 1860a, Police. Bow Street. *The Times*, Issue 23814 (December 27, 1860): 9. Gale NewsVault.

Anon, 1860b, Theatre Royal, Marylebone. *The Times*, Issue 23531 (February 1, 1860): 8. Gale NewsVault.

Anon, 1861, Court of Bankruptcy, Basinghall Street. *The Times*, Issue 23822 (January 5, 1861): 12. Gale NewsVault.

Anon, 1866, Christmas! (advertisment). *Daily Southern Cross*, Vol. XXII, Issue 2933 (December 19, 1866):1. Papers Past.

Anon, 1869, Christmas! Christmas!! (advertisement). *Taranaki Herald*, Vol. XVII, Issue 942 (December 18, 1869): 1. Papers Past.

Anon, 1870, Splendid Christmas Cake (advertisement). *Taranaki Herald*, Vol. XVIII, Issue 1046 (December 17, 1870): 3. Papers Past.

Anon, 1873, Recipes. *Daily Southern Cross*, Vol. XXIX, Issue 5017 (September 20, 1873): 2. Papers Past.

Anon, 1874, Cakes. *Peterson's Magazine* [Philadelphia] 65:162. Google Books.

Anon, 1882, The Christmas Holidays. Christmas at Waitara. *Taranaki Herald*, Vol. XXX, Issue 4224 (December 26, 1882): 2. Papers Past.

Anon, 1883, Home Interests. *Otago Witness*, Issue 1672 (December 8, 1883): 27. Papers Past.

Anon, 1885, Christmas Cookery. *Otago Witness*, Issue 1776 (December 5, 1885): 26–7. Papers Past.

Anon, 1890, Geraldine Floral, Horticultural and Industrial Society. *Timaru Herald*, Vol. L, Issue 4748 (January 20, 1890): 3. Papers Past.

Anon, 1892a, Items for Ladies. Recipes. *Evening Post*, Vol. XLIII, Issue 1 (January 2, 1892): 1. Papers Past.

Anon, 1892b, Recipes. Christmas Dishes. *Western Mail* (December 17, 1892): 49. [http://trove.nla.gov.au/].

Anon, 1892c, Christmas Cookery. *Otago Witness*, Issue 2025 (December 15, 1892): 43. Papers Past.

Anon, 1892d, An Old-Time Wedding. *Bruce Herald*, Vol. XXIII, Issue 2375 (May 20, 1892):5. Papers Past.

Anon, 1894a, Recipes. *Morning Bulletin* (December 13, 1894): 3. [http://trove.nla.gov.au/].

Anon, 1894b, Golden Bay Agricultural & Pastoral Show. *Colonist* Vol. XXXVII, Issue 7854 (February 3, 1894): 3. Papers Past.

Anon, 1895a, Horticultural Show. *Bay of Plenty Times*, Vol. XXII, Issue 3231 (February 15, 1895):4. Papers Past.

Anon, 1895b, Home Interests. Christmas Bakery. *Otago Witness*, Issue 2181 (December 19, 1895): 32. Papers Past.

Anon, 1897, Christmas Cookery. *Otago Witness*, Issue 2285 (December 16, 1897): 16. Papers Past.

Anon, 1899a, Recipes. *Clutha Leader*, Vol. XXVI, Issue 1362 (December 22, 1899): 3. Papers Past.

Anon, 1899b, School of Domestic Instruction. *Star*, Issue 6668 (December 14, 1899):4. Papers Past.

Anon, 1900, Book Notices. *Otago Daily Times*, Issue 11642 (January 27, 1900): 2. Papers Past.

Anon, [1901], *Colonial Everyday Cookery*. [1st ed.]. Christchurch: Whitcombe and Tombs Ltd.

Anon, 1902a, Home Interests. *Otago Witness*, Issue 2544 (December 17, 1902): 63. Papers Past.

Anon, 1902b, *The Royal Baker and Pastry Cook. A Manual of Practical Cookery. By the Chefs of the New York Cooking School*. New York: Royal Baking Powder Co.

Anon, 1903, *Cookery Book* [St Paul's Jubilee Fete]. Christchurch.

Anon, 1904a, Local and General News. *Marlborough Express*, Vol. XXXVII, Issue 31 (February 6, 1904):2. Papers Past.

Anon, 1904b, Ladies' Column. *Evening Post*, Vol. LXVII, Issue 37 (February 13, 1904): 11. Papers Past.

Anon, 1904c, Christmas Cooking. *Star*, Issue 8188 (December 10, 1904): 3. Papers Past.

Anon, 1905a, Christmas Recipes. *Star,* Issue 8487 (December 2, 1905): 3. Papers Past.

Anon, 1905b, The N.Z. Domestic Cookery Book. *Otago Witness*, Issue 2691 (October 11, 1905): 66. Papers Past.

Anon, 1906, Christmas Cookery. *Star*, Issue 8798 (December 8, 1906): 3. Papers Past.

Anon, 1908, *The "Sure to Rise" Cookery Book* [T. J. Edmonds]. [1st ed.]. Christchurch: Smith & Anthony, Limited.

Anon, 1911, Christmas Recipes. *Evening Post*, Vol. LXXXII, Issue 151 (December 23, 1911): 19. Papers Past.

Anon, 1915, *Our Boys' Cookery Book in Aid of Wounded Soldiers' Fund*. Wellington: Whitcombe and Tombs.

Anon, 1920, Egg Market. Big Fall in Prices. *Evening Post*, Vol. XCIX, Issue 119 (May 20, 1920): 8. Papers Past.

Anon, 1923, *The "Sure to Rise" Cookery Book* [T. J. Edmonds Ltd.]. 4th ed. Christchurch: Whitcombe & Tombs Limited.

Anon, 1925, Some Household Uses of Glycerine. *N.Z. 'Truth'*, Issue 1006 (March 7, 1925): 14. Papers Past.

Anon, 1927a, Advertisement. Fruit Cake [Wesson Oil]. *Good Housekeeping*, Vol. 84, No. 1 (January, 1927): 120. Home Economics Archive [http://hearth.library.cornell.edu/h/hearth/]

Anon, 1927b, Recommended Recipes. The Use of Wholemeal. *Evening Post*, Vol. CIV, Issue 68 (September 17, 1927): 15. Papers Past.

Anon, 1929, Some Dainty Dishes for the Yuletide Table. *N.Z. 'Truth'*, Issue 1254 (December 12, 1929): 23. Papers Past.

Anon, 1930, Eat Drink and Be Merry on Christmas Day. *Evening Post*, Vol. CX, Issue 149 (December 22, 1930): 21. Papers Past.

Anon, [1931], *The "Sure to Rise" Cookery Book* [T.J. Edmonds]. 5th ed. Christchurch: Whitcombe and Tombs Ltd.

Anon, 1934a, Best Recipes. Prize-winners in Our Special Pineapple Contest. *The Australian Women's Weekly*, Vol. II, No. 24 (November 10, 1934): 41. [http://trove.nla.gov.au/].

Anon, 1934b, Best Recipe Prizes. *The Australian Women's Weekly*, Vol. II, No. 28 (December 15, 1934): 54S. [http://trove.nla.gov.au/].

Anon, 1935, Advertisement [Fuller Fultons]. *Evening Post*, Vol. CXX, Issue 136 (December 5, 1935): 20. Papers Past.

Anon, 1936a, Edmonds Latest Cooking Book 6th edition [T.J. Edmonds]. *N. Z. Dairy Exporter and Farm Home Journal*, Vol. XII, No. 5 (December, 1936): 65.

Anon, 1936b, Advertisement. N.Z. *Dairy Exporter and Farm Home Journal*, Vol. XII, No. 3 (October 1, 1936): 81.

Anon, 1936c, Advertisements [Grand Hotel and Rivoli Theatre]. *Evening Post*, Vol. CXXI, Issue 4 (January 6, 1936): 1, 2. Papers Past.

Anon, 1936d, Advertisement [Self Help]. *Evening Post*, Vol. CXXII, Issue 145 (December 16, 1936): 4. Papers Past.

Anon, [1936], *The "Sure to Rise" Cookery Book* [T.J. Edmonds Ltd.]. 6th ed. Christchurch: Whitcombe & Tombs Ltd.

Anon, 1937a, Lower Egg Prices. Producers Concerned. *Evening Post*, Vol. CXXIII, Issue 126 (May 29, 1937): 25. Papers Past.

Anon, 1937b, Pineapple Cake. *The Australian Women's Weekly,* Vol. 5, No. 20 (October 23, 1937): 58S. [http://trove.nla.gov.au/].

Anon, 1938, Advertisement [Rathbone's]. *Evening Post*, Vol. CXXVI, Issue 132 (December 1, 1938): 1. Papers Past.

Anon, 1939, *Home Cookery Book* [New Zealand Women's Institutes]. New series, 1st ed. Wellington.

Anon, 1940a, The Homemaker. *The Australian Women's Weekly*, Vol. 7, No. 39 (March 2, 1940): 54S. [http://trove.nla.gov.au/].

Anon, 1940b, The Homemaker. *The Australian Women's Weekly*, Vol. 7, No. 50 (May 18, 1940): 50. [http://trove.nla.gov.au/].

Anon, 1940c. Advertisement for Whitcombe and Tombs Ltd. *Evening Post*, Vol. CXXX, Issue 148 (December 19, 1940): 8.

Anon, [1947], *Papanui Parish Cookery Book*. Christchurch: Bascands Ltd., Printers.

Anon, 1948, *Approved Recipes and Household Hints* [Grocers' United Stores Ltd.]. Christchurch: Simpson & Williams Ltd.

Anon, 1951, *League of Mothers, 1926–1951 Cookery Book and Household Hints*. Wellington: Digest Printing Company Limited.

Anon, [1951], *700 Neeco Tested Recipes* [National Electrical and Engineering Co. Ltd.]. 3rd ed. revised and enlarged. Auckland: Abel, Dykes Ltd.

Anon, 1952, *Borden's Eagle Brand 70 Magic Recipes*. U.S.A.: The Borden Company.

Anon, [1952], *Recommended Cooking. A Recipe Book of Proven Country Recipes* [Springs-Ellesmere Plunket Society]. Leeston: The Ellesmere Guardian.

Anon, 1953a, Advertisement. *Life* (November 16, 1953):141.

Anon, 1953b, Country Cookin'. *United Farmers News* [United Farmers of New England, USA], Vol. 13 (December, 1953): 12.

Anon, 1954, Your Christmas Cake. *The Australian Women's Weekly*, Vol. 22, No. 27 (December 1, 1954): 89. [http://trove.nla.gov.au/].

Anon, 1955, *Edmonds "Sure to Rise" Cookery Book*. De Luxe Edition, 1st printing. Christchurch: Whitcombe and Tombs Limited.

Anon, [1955], *Our Favourite Recipes* [Takanini Nursery Play Centre]. Auckland.

Anon, 1958, Christmas Cakes For Every Taste. *The Australian Women's Weekly*, Vol. 26, No. 24 (November 19, 1958): 64–5. [http://trove.nla.gov.au/].

Anon, [1958], *Further Reliable Tested Recipes Book 2* [Hora Hora Free Kindergarten Association]. Whangarei: The Northern Publishing Co. Ltd.

Anon, 1961, Christmas Cookery—Cakes and Puddings. *The Australian Women's Weekly*, Vol. 29, No. 22 (November 1, 1961): 43. [http://trove.nla.gov.au/].

Anon, 1962a, Christmas Cakes and Puddings. *The Australian Women's Weekly*, Vol. 30, No. 19 (October 10, 1962): 78–81. [http://trove.nla.gov.au/].

Anon, 1962b, Readers' Recipes. *New Zealand Woman's Weekly* (December 10, 1962): 134.

Anon, 1963, 30 Years of Favourite Recipes. *The Australian Women's Weekly*, Vol. 31, No. 17 (September 25, 1963): 61–75. [http://trove.nla.gov.au/].

Anon, 1964a, *Edmonds "Sure to Rise" Cookery Book* [T. J. Edmonds]. De Luxe ed., 6th printing. Christchurch: Whitcombe and Tombs Ltd.

Anon, 1964b, *What's Cooking* [Oamaru Intermediate School Parent Teacher Association]. Oamaru: Comet Print.

Anon, 1965, *Up-To-The-Minute Cookery Book* [Mayfield Branch of the Association of Presbyterian Women]. Revised ed. Ashburton: Higgins & Co. Ltd.

Anon, 1967, The Collector's Cookbook: Holiday Cakes. *Woman's Day* [USA] (November, 1967): 53–60.

Anon, 1968a, *Edmonds "Sure to Rise" Cookery Book* [T.J. Edmonds]. De Luxe ed., 9th printing, new revised edition. Christchurch: Whitcombe and Tombs Ltd.

Anon, 1968b, Bake-Off Enters Final Phase. *The Australian Women's Weekly*, Vol. 36, No. 10 (August 7, 1968): 32. [http://trove.nla.gov.au/].

Anon, [1968], *Tried Recipes* [Gordon Cub Pack]. Gore: Gore Publishing Company Ltd.

Anon, [1968–1973], *Catering Recipes. Nestlé's Catering Service*. Volume Two. Auckland: Decal Harvison Seymour Ltd.

Anon, 1969a, *Willow Cookery Book. Simple Recipes of Good Quality Plain Cooking* [Wilson Bros. Pty. Ltd.]. Melbourne: McCarron Bird Pty. Ltd.

Anon, 1969b, *Family Favourites* [Temuka Free Kindergarten Association]. Temuka.

Anon, 1969c, Readers' Recipes. *New Zealand Woman's Weekly* (November 24, 1969): 139–41.

Anon, 1970, Best-of-the-Week Awards. *The Australian Women's Weekly*, Vol. 38, No. 9 (July 29, 1970): 61. [http://trove.nla.gov.au/].

Anon, [1970], *Recipe Rendezvous* [Gladstone Scout Mothers' Committee]. Invercargill: Times Printing Service.

Anon, 1972, Readers' Recipes. Baking Using Sweetened Condensed Milk. *New Zealand Woman's Weekly* (January 31, 1972): 102.

Anon, [1972], *Our Favourite Recipes* [Bay of Plenty Plunket Mothers' Clubs]. Tauranga: Don Kale Printing Company.

Anon, 1974, Prize Recipes. *The Australian Women's Weekly*, Vol. 42, No. 14 (September 4, 1974): 63. [http://trove.nla.gov.au/].

Anon, [1974], *Highlander Quick 'n' Easy Cookbook*. Auckland: Nestlé Company (New Zealand) Limited.

Anon, 1977, *Favourite Recipes 1953–1977* [Women's Section Carterton Returned Services Association]. Carterton: Roydhouse & Son Ltd.

Anon, 1978, *Edmonds Cookery Book* [T.J. Edmonds]. De Luxe ed., 16th printing, centennial edition. Christchurch: Whitcoulls Ltd.

Anon, 1982, *Baking At Its Best*. Auckland: Nestlé Company (New Zealand) Limited.

Anon, 1983, *Gonville Kindergarten Recipe Book*. Wanganui: Hanton and Andersen.

Anon, [1983], *The Festive Lion—More Good Food From the Parish of St Mark* [St Mark's Parish, Opawa]. Christchurch.

Anon, 1985, *Kitchen Carnival* [Eastern Districts, South Island Swimming Centre]. Waimate: Waimate Publishing Co. Ltd.

Anon, 1986, *Centennial Cookbook* [Clinton Rugby Club Ladies' Committee]. Invercargill: Atlas Print.

Anon, 1988, *'Waitaki Favourites'. Four Hundred and Eleven Recipes for Everyday Use* [Waitaki Girls' High School Parent Teacher Association]. Dunedin: University of Otago Printing Department.

Anon, 1993, *'A Taste of Waverley'* [Rotary Park School]. Dunedin: Dunedin Photoengravers.

Anon, 1997, *Festive Recipes. Christchurch Hospitals Nurses' Reunion 1997*. Christchurch: Terrace Marketing.

Anon, 1998, *A Christmas Treasury* [Central Southland College History Group].

Austin, Thomas (ed.), 1888, *Two Fifteenth-Century Cookery-Books*. Oxford: Oxford University Press (1964 reprint).

A. W., 1591, *A Book of Cookrye*. London: Edward Allde. [Transcribed by Mark and Jane Waks, Early English Text microfilms reel 1613:9] http://jducoeur.org/Cookbook/Cookrye.html

Bailey, Ray with Mary Earle, 1999, *Home Cooking to Takeaways. Changes in Food Consumption in New Zealand During 1880–1990*. 2nd ed. Palmerston North: Massey University.

Bain, Priscilla, 1995, 'Recounting the Chickens: Hannah Further Scrutinized', pp. xxxv–xxxvii in Hannah Glasse *"First Catch Your Hare..." The Art of Cookery Made Plain and Easy*. Facsimile of 1st edition [1747]. Totnes, Devon: Prospect Books.

Bakels, Corrie and Stefanie Jacomet, 2003, Access to Luxury Foods in Central Europe during the Roman Period: the Archaeobotanical Evidence. *World Archaeology* 34(3): 542–57.

Basham, Maud R., [1934a], *"Aunt Daisy" Cookery Book Containing over 700 Recipes and Hints*. Auckland: Harvison & Marshall Ltd.

Basham, Maud R., [1934b], *The N.Z. "Daisy Chain" Cookery Book Containing over 800 Recipes and Hints*. Auckland: Harvison & Marshall Ltd.

Basham, Maud R., [1935], *Aunt Daisy's Book of Selected Special Recipes From California, Canada, France, Australia and New Zealand*. Auckland: Whitcombe & Tombs Ltd.

Basham, Maud R., [1940], *Aunt Daisy's Cookery Book of Selected Recipes [Aunt Daisy's Radio Cookery Book No. 4]*. Christchurch: Whitcombe & Tombs Limited.

Basham, Maud R., [1943], *Aunt Daisy's Cookery Book of 1,150 Selected Recipes Broadcast by Aunt Daisy. No. 5—Limited Edition*. Christchurch: Whitcombe & Tombs Ltd.

Basham, Maud R., [1947], *Aunt Daisy's New Cookery No. 6*. Christchurch: Whitcombe and Tombs Ltd.

Basham, Maud R., 1959, *Aunt Daisy's Ultimate Cookery Book*. Christchurch: Whitcombe and Tombs Ltd.

Basham, Maud R., 1961, Aunt Daisy, More Christmas Cakes, This Week's Special. *N.Z. Listener* (December 8, 1961).

Beecher, Catharine E., 1850, *Miss Beecher's Domestic Receipt Book*. New York: Harper & Brothers. Feeding America: http://digital.lib.msu.edu/projects/cookbooks/

Beeton, Isabella, 1861, *The Book of Household Management*. London: S. O. Beeton.

Beeton, Isabella, 1863, *The Book of Household Management*. (60th thousand). London: S. O. Beeton.

Beeton, Isabella, 1869, *The Book of Household Management*. (229th thousand). London: Ward, Lock, and Tyler.

Beeton, Isabella, 1899, *The Book of Household Management*. (660th thousand). London: Ward, Lock & Co., Limited.

Bell, Muriel, 1960, *Notes on Normal Nutrition for Nurses*. 4th ed. Dunedin: John McIndoe for Government Printer.

Beresford, John (ed.), 1924–1931, *The Diary of a Country Parson: The Reverend James Woodforde*. 5 vols. [1758–1803]. London: Humphrey Milford, Oxford University Press.

Beveridge, Sir William, 1939, *Prices and Wages in England from the Twelfth to the Nineteenth Century. Vol. I. Price Tables: Mercantile Era*. London: Longmans, Green and Co.

Bishop, Joan, 1987, Spice Up Traditional Fare. *Otago Daily Times* (December 8, 1987); 20.

Bishop, Joan, 2002, Delicious Low-Fat Cake Perfect for Christmas. *Otago Daily Times* (December 4, 2002): 24.

Boardman, R.E. 1927, Pineapple Canning. Methods in Hawaii. *The Brisbane Courier* (August 27, 1927): 13. [http://trove.nla.gov.au/].

Bradley, Richard, 1762, *The Country Housewife, and Lady's Director*... 6th ed. ECCO [Eighteenth Century Collections Online, Gale CW108975650].

Brandon, L.E. and Christine Smith, 1905, *"Ukneadit"* [Home for Incurables Bazaar]. Wellington: Geddis and Blomfield.

Briscoe, John P., 1876, *Nottinghamshire Facts and Fictions*. Nottingham: Shepherd Brothers. Google Books.

Browicz, Kazimriez and Daniel Zohary, 1996, The Genus *Amygdalus* L. (*Rosaceae*): Species Relationships, Distribution and Evolution under Domestication. *Genetic Resources and Crop Evolution* 43: 229–47.

Browne, Mary, Helen Leach and Nancy Tichborne, 1996, *The New Zealand Bread Book*. Revised and updated ed. Auckland: Godwit.

Cameron, Ethel M., 1929, *The Ideal Cookery Book* [Wellington Branch Plunket Society]. Wellington: Watkins Print.

Cappellini, Enrico, M. Thomas P. Gilbert, Filippo Geuna, Girolamo Fiorentino, Allan Hall, Jane Thomas-Oates, Peter D. Ashton, David A. Ashford, Paul Arthur, Paula F. Campos, Johan Kool, Eske Willerslev, and Matthew J. Collins, 2010, A Multidisciplinary Study of Archaeological Grape Seeds. *Naturwissenschaften* 97: 205–17.

Carter, Charles, 1730, *The Complete Practical Cook: or, a New System of the Whole Art and Mystery of Cookery*. ECCO [Eighteenth Century Collections Online, Gale CW3310514988].

Carter, Charles, 1749, *The London and Country Cook; or, Accomplished Housewife* ... 3rd ed. revised. ECCO [[Eighteenth Century Collections Online, Gale CW110796481].

Carter, Una I., [1916], *Home Made Sweets Recipes*. Wellington: Watkins, Tyer & Tolan, Ltd.

Carter, Una, [1944], *Una Carter's Famous Cookery Book Containing 800 Well-Tested and Latest Recipes*. 9th edition. Wellington: Hutcheson, Bowman & Johnson Ltd.

Cartwright, Caroline R., 2003, Grapes or Raisins? An Early Bronze Age Larder under the Microscope. *Antiquity* 77: 345–8.

Charsley, Simon R., 1992, *Wedding Cakes and Cultural History*, London: Routledge.

Chase, Alvin W., 1886, *Dr Chases's Third, Last and Complete Receipt Book and Household Physician*. Ann Arbor: Chase.

Clark, Gregory, [2007], English Prices and Wages, 1209–1914. Data-file provided on the International Institute of Social History (IISG) website: http://www.iisg.nl

Clark, Gregory, 2007, The Long March of History: Farm wages, Population, and Economic Growth, England 1209–1869. *Economic History Review* 60(1): 97–135.

Clifford, Rex D. (ed.), 1991, *One Hundred and One Diabetic Recipes* [Diabetes Wakatipu Society]. Alexandra.

Cole, Mary, 1789, *The Lady's Complete Guide; or Cookery and Confectionary in All Their Branches*. New edition improved. London: G. Kearsley.

Copley, Esther, 1838, *The Housekeeper's Guide, or A Plain & Practical System of Domestic Cookery*. London: Longman & Co. [Google Books].

Copley, Mark S., Robert Berstan, S.N. Dudd, S. Allaud, A.J. Mukherjee, V. Straker, Sebastian Payne and Richard P. Evershed, 2005, Processing of Milk Products in Pottery Vessels through British Prehistory. *Antiquity* 79(306): 895–908.

Cosman, Madeleine and Linda G. Jones, 2008, *Handbook to Life in the Medieval World*. New York: Infobase Publishing.

'Cosmopolita', 1762, To the Printer. *St James's Chronicle or the British Evening Post*, Issue 131 (January 12 – 14, 1762): 4. [17th–18th Century Burney Collection Newspapers. Gale Z2001254749].

Cox, Nancy and Karin Dannehl, 2007, *Dictionary of Traded Goods and Commodities, 1550–1820*. British History Online website: http://www.british-history.ac.uk/report.aspx?compid=58886

Croly, Jane C. 1866, *Jennie June's American Cookery Book*. New York: The American News Company. [Google Books].

Daish, Lois, 2005, *A Good Year*. Auckland: Random House.

Dalby, Andrew (transl.), 1998, *Cato On Farming De Agricultura. A Modern Translation with Commentary*. Totnes, Devon: Prospect Books.

Dalby, Andrew and Sally Grainger, 1996, *The Classical Cookbook*. London: British Museum Press.

David, Elizabeth, 1979, A True Gentlewoman's Delight. *Petits Propos Culinaires* 1: 43–53.

Davidson, Alan, 1995, 'Glossary and Notes', pp. 173–207 in Hannah Glasse *"First Catch Your Hare..." The Art of Cookery Made Plain and Easy*. Facsimile of 1st edition [1747]. Totnes, Devon: Prospect Books.

Davidson, Alan, 1999, 'Cherry', p.163 in *The Oxford Companion to Food*. Oxford: Oxford University Press.

Dempsey, Rosemary, [1969?], *1,001 Ways With Food*. Auckland: Wilson and Horton Ltd.

Dempsey, Rosemary, [1970], *Homeways Modern Recipes* [Four Square Stores]. Auckland.

Dickens, Charles, 1853, Slang. *Household Words*, VIII (September 24, 1853): 74. [Google Books].

Dickson, Camilla, 1996, Food, Medicinal and Other Plants from the 15th Century Drains of Paisley Abbey, Scotland. *Vegetation History and Archaeobotany* 5(1–2): 25–31.

Dods, Margaret [pseudonym of Christian Isobel Johnstone], 1826, *The Cook and Housewife's Manual*. Edinburgh: The Author. [Google Books].

Donahue, John F., 2004, *The Roman Community at Table During the Principate*. Ann Arbor: University of Michigan Press.

Downes, Peter, 1998, 'Basham, Maud Ruby 1879–1963', pp. 36–7 in *The Dictionary of New Zealand Biography. Volume Four 1921–1940*. Auckland: Auckland University Press with Bridget Williams Books and the Department of Internal Affairs.

Driver, Christopher (ed.), 1997, *John Evelyn, Cook. The Manuscript Receipt Book of John Evelyn*. Totnes, Devon: Prospect Books.

Driver, Christopher and Michelle Berriedale-Johnson, 1986, *Pepys at Table. Seventeenth Century Recipes for the Modern Cook*. London: Unwin Hyman.

Ellet, Elizabeth F., 1857, *The Practical Housekeeper; A Cyclopaedia of Domestic Economy*. New York: Stringer and Townsend. Feeding America: http://digital.lib.msu.edu/projects/cookbooks/

Evershed, Richard P., Sebastian Payne, Andrew G. Sherratt, Mark S. Copley, Jennifer Coolidge, Duska Urem-Kotsu, Kostas Kotsakis, Mehmet Özdoğan, Aslý E. Özdoğan, Olivier Nieuwenhuyse, et al., 2008, Earliest Date for Milk Use in the Near East and Southeastern Europe Linked to Cattle Herding. *Nature* 455: 528–31.

Faas, Patrick, 2003, *Around the Roman Table. Food and Feasting in Ancient Rome*. New York: Palgrave Macmillan.

Flower, Barbara and Elisabeth Rosenbaum, 1958, *The Roman Cookery Book. A Critical Translation of the Art of Cooking by Apicius*. London: Harrap.

[Flower, Tui], 1968. Close-Up On Christmas Cakes. *New Zealand Woman's Weekly* (December 9, 1968): 137–9.

[Flower, Tui], 1969. Test Kitchen. *New Zealand Woman's Weekly* (February 17, 1969): 51.

Flower, Tui (ed.), 1971, *The New Zealand Woman's Weekly Cookbook*. Auckland: Paul Hamlyn/Beckett Sterling Ltd.

Flower, Tui, 1998, *Self-Raising Flower*. Auckland: Viking (Penguin Books).

Flower, Tui (co-ordinator), 2000, *The Cookbook*. Auckland: New Zealand Guild of Food Writers.

Forbes, Judith (ed.), 1991, *A Taste of Karori. A Collection of Tried and True Recipes from the Karori Community*. Wellington.

Frazer, Mrs, 1791, *The Practice of Cookery, Pastry, Pickling, Preserving, &c*. ECCO [Eighteenth Century Collections Online, Gale CW3308292026].

Galloway, S., [1946–9], *Better Baking* [Imperial Chemical Industries (N.Z.) Ltd.]. Wellington: Whitcombe & Tombs Ltd.

'Gambolio', 1774, To the Printer. *St James's Chronicle or the British Evening Post*, Issue 2016 (January 15–18, 1774): 4. Gale News Vault.

Garrett, Theodore F. (ed.), [1894], *The Encyclopaedia of Practical Cookery: A Complete Dictionary of All Pertaining to the Art of Cookery*. 8 vols. London: L. Upcott Gill.

Gedye, Ruth, 1978, *Cooking with Ruth Gedye and Atlas Thermowave*. Wanganui: Wanganui Newspapers Ltd.

Gilchrist, J. (ed.) *The New Zealand Official Yearbook, 1946*. Fifty-fourth Issue. Census and Statistics Department of the Dominion of New Zealand. Wellington: E. V. Paul, Government Printer.

Gillette, Fanny L., 1887, *White House Cook Book*. Chicago: R. S. Peale & Co. Feeding America: http://digital.lib.msu.edu/projects/cookbooks/

Glasse, Hannah, 1995, *"First Catch Your Hare..." The Art of Cookery Made Plain and Easy*. Facsimile of 1st edition [1747]. Totnes, Devon: Prospect Books.

Gray, Eleanor, 1978, *Basic New Zealand Cookbook*. Dunedin: John McIndoe.

Gye, Eve, [1939], *"Woman's" Tested Recipes*. Sydney: Halstead Press Pty Limited.

Hale, Sarah J., 1852, *The Ladies' New Book of Cookery*. New York: H. Long & Brother. Feeding America: http://digital.lib.msu.edu/projects/cookbooks/

Harman, Mrs R.D. and Mrs S. Gard'ner, [1904], *The New Zealand Domestic Cookery Book*. 4th ed. Christchurch: Whitcombe and Tombs Limited.

Harris, E.A., 1977, *Social Trends in New Zealand*. Dept of Statistics Publication. Wellington: Government Printer.

Harrison, Sarah, 1738, *The House-keeper's Pocket-Book, and Compleat Family Cook*. ECCO [Eighteenth Century Collections Online, Gale CW3307304775].

Harvey, Elsie, [1933], *The Prizewinner Recipe Book. Prize Recipes by New Zealand's Leading Chefs Dainty and Wholesome*. Auckland: Brookdale Press.

Hassall, Arthur H., 1855, *Food and its Adulterations: comprising the reports of the Analytical Sanitary Commission of the* Lancet .... London: Longmans. Google Books.

Henderson, Mary N.F., 1877, *Practical Cooking and Dinner Giving*. New York: Harper & Brothers. Feeding America: http://digital.lib.msu.edu/projects/cookbooks/

Henisch, Bridget A., 1984, *Cakes and Characters. An English Christmas Tradition*. London: Prospect Books.

Herrick, Robert, 1648, *Hesperides or, The Works Both Humane & Divine of Robert Herrick, Esq*. EEBO [Early English Books Online]: Electronic Book.

Hess, Karen, 1981, *Martha Washington's Booke of Cookery*. New York: Columbia University Press.

Hirschfeld, Gisi, 1999, *Gisi's Cooking Book*. Wellington: Steele Roberts.

Holland, Mary, 1843, *The Complete Economical Cook, and Frugal Housewife; an Entirely New System of Domestic Cookery*. 14th ed. London: Thomas Tegg.

Holst, Alison, 1967, *Meals with the Family*. Auckland: Hicks Smith and Sons Ltd.

Holst, Alison (ed.), 1974, *The New Zealand Radio and Television Cookbook*. Auckland: Paul Hamlyn Ltd.

Holst, Alison, 1978, *Alison Holst's Kitchen Diary: A Book of Seasonal Recipes*. [Vol. 1]. Wellington: INL Print.

Holst, Alison, 1985, *Alison Holst's Kitchen Diary. Volume 8*. Wellington: Inprint Ltd.

Holst, Alison, 1986, *Alison Holst's Kitchen Diary. Volume 9*. Wellington: Inprint Ltd.

Holst, Alison, 1991, *The Best of Alison Holst*. Auckland: Premier Books.

Holst, Alison, 1995, *Alison Holst's Cooking For Christmas: Christmas Baking & Edible Gifts*. Dunedin: Hyndman.

Hone, William, 1838, *The Every-day Book and Table Book*. 3 vols. London: Thomas Tegg and Son. Google Books.

Hooper, William D. (transl.), 1934, *Marcus Porcius Cato On Agriculture. Marcus Terentius Varro On Agriculture*. London: William Heinemann Ltd.

'Housewife', [1944], *War Economy Recipe Book Containing Excellent Economical Cake, Pudding and Savoury Recipes*. Christchurch: Whitcombe & Tombs Limited.

Howard, Henry, 1717, *England's Newest Way in All Sorts of Cookery, Pastry, and All Pickles that are Fit to be Used*. 4th edition. ECCO [Eighteenth Century Collections Online, Gale CW108045296].

Hughes, Kathryn, 2006, *The Short Life & Long Times of Mrs Beeton*. London: Harper Perennial.

Inglis, Raelene M., 2007, The Cultural Transmission of Cookery Knowledge. From Seventeenth Century Britain to Twentieth Century New Zealand. Unpublished Ph.D. dissertation, Anthropology, University of Otago.

Innes, Diana, Anna Guild and Glenda Stone, 1990, *The Windwhistle Cookery Book*. Timaru: Pope Print Ltd.

Jarrin, William A., 1827, *The Italian Confectioner; or, Complete Economy of Desserts*. 3rd ed. London: William H. Ainsworth. [Google Books].

J. B. R. P., Notes From Practice: Sugar in Dyspepsia. *The Medical and Surgical Reporter*, Vol. XXII, No. 24 (June 11, 1870): 488. [Google Books].

Jenks, James, 1768, *The Complete Cook: Teaching the Art of Cookery in All Its Branches*. ECCO [Eighteenth Century Collections Online, Gale CW107289978].

Jewry, Mary (ed.), 1869, *Warne's Model Cookery and Housekeeping Book*. London: Frederick Warne and Company.

Jonson, Benjamin, 1641, [The Workes of Benjamin Jonson. The Second Volume.] EEBO [Early English Books Online]: Electronic Book.

Kellogg, Ella E. 1893, *Science in the Kitchen: A Scientific Treatise on Food Substances and Their Dietetic Properties*. Chicago: Modern Medicine Publishing Co. Feeding America: http://digital.lib.msu.edu/projects/cookbooks/

Kent-Johnston, Nan, [1939], *Christchurch Boys' High School Cookery Book*. Christchurch: Whitcombe and Tombs Limited.

Kent-Johnston, Nan, [1941], *Everyday Recipes. Tried and Tested by Mrs W. F. Kent-Johnston*. Christchurch: Willis & Aiken Ltd.

Kent-Johnston, Nan, 1950, *The Diocese of Waiapu Cookery Book. Everyday Recipes*. Napier: Daily Telegraph Co. Ltd.

Kirkland, John (ed.), [1907], *The Modern Baker Confectioner and Caterer*. Vol. II. London: The Gresham Publishing Company.

Knoppers, Laura L., 2007, Opening the Queen's Closet: Henrietta Maria, Elizabeth Cromwell, and the Politics of Cookery. *Renaissance Quarterly* 60: 464–99.

Kuijper, W.J. and H. Turner, 1992, Diet of a Roman Centurion at Alphen aan den Rijn, The Netherlands, in the First Century AD. *Review of Palaeobotany and Palynology* 73: 187–204.

'Ladies of the First Presbyterian Church, Dayton, Ohio', 1873, *Presbyterian Cook Book*. Dayton: Oliver Crook & Co., Printers. Feeding America: http://digital.lib.msu.edu/projects/cookbooks/

Ladizinsky, Gideon, 1999, On the Origin of Almond. *Genetic Resources and Crop Evolution* 46: 143–7.

Lamb, Patrick, 1716, *Royal-Cookery: or, The Compleat Court-Cook*. 2nd ed. ECCO [Eighteenth Century Collections Online, Gale CW3310510767].

Larkins, Joy, 1985, *Favourite Recipes* [Eastern Otago Federation of Country Womens Institutes]. Dunedin: Taieri Print/S. N. Brown Printing.

Laroque, François, 1993, *Shakespeare's Festive World. Elizabethan Seasonal Entertainment and the Professional Stage*. Cambridge: Cambridge University Press.

Latham, Robert and William Matthews, 1970–6, *The Diary of Samuel Pepys*. Vols I–IX. London: G. Bell and Sons Ltd.

Law, Digby, 1987, Christmas Lunch. *Cuisine*, Issue 6 (December 1987–January 1988): 14–17.

Leach, Helen M., 2008a, *The Pavlova Story. A Slice of New Zealand's Culinary History*. Dunedin: Otago University Press.

Leach, Helen M., 2008b, *Culinary Treasures of the Hocken Collections*. Hocken Lecture 3, 2007. Dunedin: Hocken Collections/Uare Taoka O Hakena, University of Otago.

Leach, Helen M., 2010, The Pavlova Wars. How a Creationist Model of Recipe Origins Led to an International Dispute. *Gastronomica* 10(2): 24–30.

Leach, Helen M. and Raelene Inglis, 2003, The Archaeology of Christmas Cakes. *Food & Foodways* 11: 141–166.

Lehmann, Gilly, 2003, *The British Housewife. Cookery Books, Cooking and Society in Eighteenth-Century Britain*. Totnes, Devon: Prospect Books.

Leslie, Eliza, 1832, *Seventy-Five Receipts for Pastry, Cakes, and Sweetmeats*. 4th ed. Boston, Mass.: Munroe and Francis. Feeding America: http://digital.lib.msu.edu/projects/cookbooks/

Leslie, Eliza, 1840, *Directions for Cookery, in its Various Branches*. 10th ed. Philadelphia: Carey and Hart. Feeding America: http://digital.lib.msu.edu/projects/cookbooks/

Leslie, Eliza, 1847, *The Lady's Receipt Book*. Philadelphia: Carey and Hart. Feeding America: http://digital.lib.msu.edu/projects/cookbooks/

Leslie, Eliza, 1850, *Miss Leslie's Lady's New Receipt Book*. 3rd ed. enlarged Philadelphia: A. Hart. Feeding America: http://digital.lib.msu.edu/projects/cookbooks/

Leslie, Eliza, 1857, *Miss Leslie's New Cookery Book*. Philadelphia: T.B. Peterson and Brothers. [Google Books].

Liu, Yi-Ping, Gui-Sheng Wu, Yong-Gang Yao, Yong-Wang Miao, Gordon Luikart, Mumtaz Baig, Albano Beja-Pereira, Zhao-Li Ding, Malliya Gounder Palanichamy and Ya-Ping Zhang, 2006, Multiple Maternal Origins of Chickens: Out of the Asian Jungles. *Molecular Phylogenetics and Evolution* 38: 12–19.

MacInnes, M. (ed.), 1896, *Cookery Book of Good and Tried Receipts*. [Women's Missionary Association of the Presbyterian Church of New South Wales]. 3rd ed. Sydney: S. T. Leigh & Co.

Marris, Katherine, Jeanette Hunt, Janie Denton and Kathleen McIntyre (eds), [1965], *What's Cooking? 300 Favourite Recipes of Queen Margaret College Old Girls*. Wellington: Organ Bros., Ltd.

Massey, John and W.J. Massey, 1866, *Massey & Son's Biscuit, Ice, & Compote Book; or, the Essence of Modern Confectionery*. London: Simpkin, Marshall, & Co. [Google Books].

May, Robert, 2000, *The Accomplisht Cook, or the Art and Mystery of Cookery*. Facsimile of 1685 edition [1st edition 1660]. Totnes, Devon: Prospect Books.

McGee, Harold, 2004, *On Food and Cooking. The Science and Lore of the Kitchen*. Revised and updated ed. New York: Scribner.

McGovern, Patrick E., 2003, *Ancient Wine. The Search for the Origins of Viniculture*. Princeton: Princeton University Press.

McGovern, Patrick E., Donald L. Glusker, Lawrence J. Exner and Mary M. Voigt, 1996, Neolithic Resinated Wine. *Nature* 381: 480–81.

'Meta', 1891, Ladies' Column. *Clutha Leader*, Vol. XVIII, Issue 910 (December 25, 1891): 7. Papers Past.

M. H., 1683, *The Young Cooks Monitor: or, Directions for Cookery and Distilling*. EEBO [Early English Books Online]: Electronic Book.

Miller, Naomi F., 2008, Sweeter than Wine? The Use of the Grape in Early Western Asia. *Antiquity* 82: 937–46.

Moffett, Lisa, 2006, 'The Archaeology of Medieval Plant Foods', pp. 41–55 in Christopher M. Woolgar, Dale Serjeantson and Tony Waldron (eds) *Food in Medieval England. Diet and Nutrition*. Oxford: Oxford University Press.

Mollard, John, 1802, *The Art of Cookery Made Easy and Refined*. London: The Author. [Google Books].

OED, 2011, Entries for 'icing', 'marchpane' and 'marzipan'. *Oxford English Dictionary*. 2nd ed. [1989] on-line version March 2011.

Palmer, David J. (ed.), 1972, *Shakespeare Twelfth Night. A Casebook*. London: Macmillan Press Ltd.

Parkinson, Eleanor, 1864, *The Complete Confectioner, Pastry-Cook, and Baker: Plain and Practical Directions for Making Confectionary and Pastry, and for Baking...* [1st ed. 1849]. Philadelphia: J.B. Lippincott. Feeding America: http://digital.lib.msu.edu/projects/cookbooks/

Parloa, Maria, 1882, *Miss Parloa's New Cookbook: A Guide to Marketing and Cooking*. New York: C.T. Dillingham. Feeding America: http://digital.lib.msu.edu/projects/cookbooks/

[Payne, Arthur G. (ed.)], [1878], *Cassell's Dictionary of Cookery*. London: Cassell Petter & Galpin.

Payne, Arthur G., 1882, *Choice Dishes at Small Cost*. London: Cassell, Petter, Galpin & Co. Open Library: http://www.archive.org/details/choicedishesatsm00payn

Pedersen, Elisabeth, 1992, *The Really Reliable New Zealand Cookbook*. Auckland: C.J. Publishing.

Piperno, Dolores R., Ehud Weiss, Irene Holst and Dani Nadel, 2004, Processing of Wild Cereal Grains in the Upper Palaeolithic Revealed by Starch Grain Analysis. *Nature* 430: 670–73.

Plat, Sir Hugh, 1602, *Delightes for Ladies, to Adorn their Persons, Tables, Closets, and Distillatories*. EEBO [Early English Books Online]: Electronic Book.

Pool, Ian, Arunachalam Dharmalingam and Janet Sceats, 2007, *The New Zealand Family from 1840: A Demographic History*. Auckland: Auckland University Press.

Raffald, Elizabeth, 1769, *The Experienced English House-keeper, for the Use and Ease of Ladies, House-keepers, Cooks &c*. ECCO [Eighteenth Century Collections Online, Gale CW107051996].

Rayne, Jenny, Margaret Dore, Wendy Weir, Bev Garrow (eds), 1985, *Mackenzie Muster. "A Century of Favourites"*. Timaru: Pope Print.

Reeves, Ann (ed.), 1985, *N.P.G.H.S. Centennial Cookbook* [New Plymouth Girls' High School]. New Plymouth.

'Rita', 1891, Home and Fireside. *Bush Advocate*, Vol. VII, Issue 529 (October 3, 1891): 7. Papers Past.

Roberts, I., 1836, *The Young Cook's Guide; with Practical Observations*. London: Laking. [Google Books.]

Roose, Mikeal L. and Timothy J. Close, 2008, 'Genomics of Citrus, a Major Fruit Crop of Tropical and Subtropical Regions', pp. 187–200 in Paul H. Moore and Ray Ming (eds) *Genomics of Tropical Crop Plants*. New York: Springer.

Rowe, Liz (ed.), [1993], *A Taste of Mid Canterbury*. Ashburton: Higgins Print Ltd.

Roxburgh, Alison (ed.), 1996, *The NCW Centennial Recipe Book* [National Council of Women]. Nelson: Nelson Bays Print Agency.

[Rundell, Mrs], 1808, *A New System of Domestic Cookery, Formed Upon Principles of Economy, and Adapted to the Use of Private Families by a Lady*. 3rd ed. Exeter: Norris & Sawyer. Google Books.

Salmon, William, 1705, *The Family-Dictionary: or, Household Companion*. 3rd edition. ECCO [Eighteenth Century Collections Online, Gale CW109819693].

Scaife, Katharine and Molly Scurr, 1972, *Souvenir Recipe Book* [Wanaka Improvement Society].

Scully, Terence, 1995, *The Art of Cookery in the Middle Ages*. Woodbridge, Suffolk: The Boydell Press.

Serjeantson, Dale, 2009, *Birds*. Cambridge: Cambridge University Press.

Sherriff, Sybil D., 1961, *GHB Cookery Book* [Good Housekeeping Bureau Stores]. [1st ed.]. Christchurch: Bascands Ltd.

Simmonds, P. L., 1877. *Tropical Agriculture. A Treatise on the Culture, Preparation, Commerce, and Consumption of the Principal Products of the Vegetable Kingdom*. London: E. and F. N. Spon.

Smith, E[liza?], 1728, *The Compleat Housewife: or, Accomplished Gentlewoman's Companion*. 2nd edition. ECCO [Eighteenth Century Collections Online, Gale CW3307271552].

Smith, E[liza?], 1973, *The Compleat Housewife: or, Accomplish'd Gentlewoman's Companion*. Facsimile of 15th edition [1753]. London: Literary Services and Production Limited.

Smith, Mrs, 1810, *The Female Economist; or, A Plain System of Cookery*. 2nd ed. London: Mathews and Leigh. [Adam Matthew Publications: Women Advising Women, Part 6: Advice Books, Manuals and Journals for Women 1450-1837].

Stead, Jennifer, 1995, 'Preface', 'Introduction', and 'Quizzing Glasse: or Hannah Scrutinized', pp. iii–xxxiv in Hannah Glasse *"First Catch Your Hare..." The Art of Cookery Made Plain and Easy*. Facsimile of 1st edition [1747]. Totnes, Devon: Prospect Books.

Stevenson, Jane and Peter Davidson (eds), 1997, *The Closet of the Eminently Learned Sir Kenelme Digbie Kt. Opened*. Totnes, Devon: Prospect Books.

Stockdill, Julie (ed.), 1996, *Festive Eats. Recipes for Christmas*. [Diabetes Life Education]. [Auckland].

Stuart, Alexander, [1863–6]. Diary and recipe book pages. Misc MS 0607, Hocken Library Archives and Manuscripts, Dunedin.

Taylor, E., 1769, *The Lady's, Housewife's, and Cookmaid's Assistant*. ECCO [Eighteenth Century Collections Online, Gale CW108326338].

Taylor, Leah, 1996, 'Gard'ner, Elizabeth Anne 1858-1926', pp. 168–9 in *The Dictionary of New Zealand Biography. Volume Three 1901-1920*. Auckland: Auckland University Press with Bridget Williams Books and the Department of Internal Affairs.

Taylor, Nancy M., 1986, *The New Zealand People at War. The Home Front*. Wellington: Historical Publications Branch, Department of Internal Affairs.

Teal, F. Jane, 2010, 'Changing Kitchen Technology', pp. 71–96 in Helen M. Leach (ed.) *From Kai to Kiwi Kitchen. New Zealand Culinary Traditions and Cookbooks*. Dunedin: Otago University Press.

Tell-Truth, Tommy [pseudonym], [1765?], *Christmas Holidays A Poem...* ECCO [Eighteenth Century Collections Online, Gale CW111218597].

Terral, Jean-Frédéric, Elidie Tabard, Laurent Bouby, Sarah Ivorra, Thierry Pastor, Isabel Figueiral, Sandrine Picq, Jean-Baptiste Chevance, Cécile Jung, Laurent Fabre, Christophe Tardy, Michel Compan, Roberto Bacilieri, Thierry Lacombe and Patrice This, 2010, Evolution and History of Grapevine (*Vitis vinifera*) under Domestication: New Morphometric Perspectives to Understand Seed Domestication Syndrome and Reveal Origins of Ancient European Cultivars. *Annals of Botany* 105: 443–55.

Thomas, Richard and Sue Stallibrass, 2008, 'For Starters: Producing and Supplying Food to the Army in the Roman North-West Provinces', pp.1–17 in Sue Stallibrass and Richard Thomas (eds) *Feeding the Roman Army; the Archaeology of Production and Supply in NW Europe*. Oxford: Oxbow Books.

Thompson, D'Arcy Wentworth, 199-?, *History of Animals by Aristotle*. Boulder, Colorado: NetLibrary Electronic Book.

Thompson, Roger, 1976, Samuel Pepys's Penny Merriments: A Check List. *The Library* S5-xxxi(3): 223–234.

Thomson, Jessie (ed.), 1927, *The Amuri Cookery Book of Well Tried Recipes Kindly Given by Amuri Ladies and Their Friends*. 2nd ed. Christchurch: The Sun Print [pp 1–96 correspond to 1st ed.]

Toynbee, Claire, 1995, *Her Work and His: Family, Kin and Community in New Zealand 1900–1930*. Wellington: Victoria University Press.

'Tui', [1933], *Tui's Practical Cookery Book*. Wellington: The N. Z. Dairy Produce Exporter Newspaper Company Ltd.

'Tui', 1934, *Tui's Annual 1934*. (N. Z. Dairy Exporter, October 12, 1934).

'Tui', [1936], *Tui's Second Cookery Book: Over 1000 Tested Prize Recipes*. Wellington: C. M. Banks Ltd.

Turner, M.S., 1922, *The Highlander Economical Cookery Book*. 2nd ed. Invercargill: N.Z. Milk Products Limited.

Vaisey, David (ed.), 1984, *The Diary of Thomas Turner 1754–1765*. Oxford: Oxford University Press.

Van der Veen, Marijke, Alexandra Livarda and Alistair Hill, 2008, New Plant Foods in Roman Britain—Dispersal and Social Access. *Environmental Archaeology* 13(1): 11–36.

Veart, Dave, 2008, *First Catch Your Weka. A Story of New Zealand Cooking*. Auckland: Auckland University Press.

'Villette', 1934, Women's Column. *The Mercury*, Vol. CXLI, No. 21,003 (December 1, 1934): 6. [http://trove.nla.gov.au/].

W. G____N, 1820, Letter to the Editor [advertisement]. *The Times*, Issue 11129 (December 28, 1820): 3. Gale News Vault.

W. J., 1653, *A True Gentlewomans Delight*. 2nd ed. EEBO [Early English Books Online]: Electronic Book.

W. M. 1655, *The Queens Closet Opened*. EEBO [Early English Books Online]: Electronic Book.

Warren, Eliza, 1858, *The Economical Cookery Book*. London: Piper, Stephenson, and Spence.

Wilkins, John, David Harvey and Mike Dobson (eds), 1995, *Food in Antiquity*. Exeter: University of Exeter Press.

Willcox, George, 2002, Charred Plant Remains from a 10th Millennium B.P. Kitchen at Jerf el Ahmar (Syria). *Vegetation History and Archaeobotany* 11: 55–60.

Wilson, C. Anne, 1976, *Food and Drink in Britain from the Stone Age to Recent Times*. Harmondsworth, Middlesex: Penguin Books Ltd.

Woolley, Hannah, 1664, *The Cook's Guide: or, Rare Receipts for Cookery...* EEBO [Early English Books Online]: Electronic Book.

Yost, Genevieve, 1938, The Compleat Housewife or Accomplish'd Gentlewoman's Companion: A Bibliographical Study. *The William and Mary Quarterly*, 2nd series, 18(4): 419–35.

Zohary, Daniel and Maria Hopf, 1994, *Domestication of Plants in the Old World*. 2nd ed. Oxford: Clarendon Press.

Index

1,001 Ways With Food (Dempsey, c. 1969) 141
700 Neeco Tested Recipes (c. 1951) 105, 106, 109

Abbott, Edward 70
Acton, Eliza 74, 76, 152
Alcohol, in cakes 92 (*see also* Spirits; Wine)
Alison Holst's Kitchen Diary (1978–1986) 11, 111–12, 134
All-Bran 87
Allspice (Jamaica pepper) 76, 92
Almonds 19, 27, 46, 70, 73, 76, 88, 98, 99, 109, 114, 122, 147, 149, 160, 165, 169; domestication of 15, 17, 19; ground 40, 46, 48, 76, 88, 147, 160; in Greece and Rome 20; luxury import 21; sliced 76, 88, 111–12, 140, 147; Tutankhamun's tomb 17 (*see also* Icings, types)
Ambergris 40
America, as source of recipes 62, 64, 65, 70, 72–4, 99, 104, 105, 108–9, 110, 132–3, 138–9, 165, 166
Analysis of recipes 9, 11–12, 13, 47, 77–8, 95; spreadsheet 12, 13, 126
Anatolia, prehistoric dairying 15
Angelica 94
Anise 20
Apicius, Roman cookbook 18–19, 20
Appert, Nicolas 139
Apple, dried 90; grated 90, 132; stewed 90
Apricots, candied or dried 131, 149
Arabs, introduction of cane sugar by 19
Aristotle 18
Art of Cookery Made Easy and Refined, The (Mollard, 1802) 62
Art of Cookery, Made Plain and Easy, The (Glasse, 1747) 46, 48, 50, 55
Aunt Daisy (*see* Basham, Maud)
Aunt Daisy's Book of Special Recipes From California, Canada, France, Australia and New Zealand (Basham, 1935) 113, 116, 132
Aunt Daisy's Radio Cookery Book No. 4 (Basham, c. 1940) 130, 133, 153
Aunt Daisy's Cookery Book ... No. 5 (Basham, c. 1943) 130
Aunt Daisy's New Cookery No. 6 (Basham, c. 1947) 105, 109, 146
Australia, as source of recipes 86, 87, 118, 125, 127, 130–31, 133, 138–9, 148–9, 152, 165

Australian Women's Weekly 118, 127, 131, 133, 141, 148, 149, 152

Bain, Priscilla 47
Bake-stone 14, 33
Baking At Its Best (Nestlé, 1982) 144
Baking powder (*see* Raising agents)
Baking soda (*see* Raising agents)
Bananas 94
Barker, Lady 56
Barley 14, 15, 16
Barm (*see* Yeast)
Basham, Maud (Aunt Daisy) 105, 109, 113, 115, 116, 130, 132–3, 146
Basic New Zealand Cookbook (Gray, 1978) 138
Bay (bark, leaves) 20
Beeton, Isabella 11, 64–5, 66–7, 68–9, 70, 73, 74, 75, 76, 153, 161
Better Baking (Galloway, 1946–9) 121
Biscuit, crumbs as cake base 87
Bishop, Joan 149, 151, 155, 156–7, 158, 160, 163
Book of Household Management, The (Beeton 1861; 1863; 1869; 1899) 64, 66–7, 68–9, 73, 75, 84–5, 153
Borden, Gail 139
Borden's Eagle Brand 70 Magic Recipes (1952) 140
Bracciano, Duke of 23
Brandy 46, 48, 63, 91, 92, 98, 99, 104, 106, 108, 113, 114, 134, 144, 146
Brazil nuts 88, 147–50, 152
Bread, flat 14; leavened 14, 20; Roman 20
Britain, as source of recipes for New Zealand 65, 70; early dairying 15
Browne, Mary 10, 142
Browning, gravy 86
Brunel, Isambard 60
Buckland, Jessie 85
Burnard, Norah 113
Butter, early evidence of manufacture 15, 19, 20; in cake, methods of incorporation (creaming, melting, rubbing in) 27, 38, 43–5, 46, 47, 50, 53, 81–3, 119, 166, 168; rationing (*see* War); use in 20th century cakes 82, 118–9, 120, 155
Button, G. 57

INDEX

Cake, fruit; cooling 168; ingredients, variations in 83–94 (*see also* individual items); methods of mixing (boil-and-bake 82, 86, 87, 91, 144, 146, 155, creaming 38, 43–5, 46, 47, 50, 53, 81–82, custard 119–120, kneading 27, melting butter 82, 141, 142); preparation of tins 167; size, variation in 62, 74, 76, 78–9; storing 163, 168; testing for doneness 168

Cakes, festive (*see also* Recipes, named; Trends), 16th century 22; 17th century 22, 23, 25–31, 35–40, 42, 43, 44, 53, 79, 153; 18th century 38, 39, 40, 41–7, 50–55, 81, 82; 19th century 56–8, 63, 71, 73–4, 76, 81; 20th century 76, 77–94, 95–152 (*see also* Trends); 21st century 155–60; black 102–105, 108–9; brazil nut date 80, 81, 82, 84, 88, 90, 112, 147–50, 151, 152, 154, 160, 166; bread-type 22, 27, 32–4, 38, 40, 44, 45, 50, 53, 94, 125, 166; bride (*see* Cakes, wedding); cathedral (*see* Cakes, brazil nut date); christening 11; Christmas, earliest named 59–60, 62, 64; Classical era 18, 20–21; condensed milk 79, 84, 86, 92, 140–6, 166; custard 82, 92, 119–25, 146; diabetic 84, 88, 155; fruit 11–12, 14, 15, 17, 19, 20, 22, 25, 26, 29, 31, 35–41, 43, 45, 46, 50, 51, 53, 62, 65, 74–6, 108; giant 22, 26, 27, 29, 32, 35, 42, 57, 59–61, 63; ginger ale 125, 127, 128, 130–31, 152, 155, 165; Greek, ancient (see Cakes, Classical era); low fat 155–8, 160; medieval 21–2; microwaved 155; pavlova 10, 11, 12, 78, 113; pineapple 90, 112, 131–9, 145, 165, 166; plum (*see* Cake, fruit); pound 44, 45, 50, 51, 53, 55, 62, 74, 76, 81–3, 87, 94, 99, 102, 114, 125, 147, 152–3, 154, 161, 166; prehistoric 14–15; Roman (see Cakes, Classical era); safflower 19; twelfth 11, 12, 21, 23, 28, 30, 31, 35, 36, 41–3, 50, 51–2, 53, 57–9, 60–3, 71–2, 74, 125, 166; unbaked 84, 86, 87, 88; wedding 11, 12, 43, 53, 62, 66, 71–4, 75, 76, 102–3, 105–6, 108–9, 110, 149, 161, 166; white 76, 89, 108, 111; wholemeal 153–5

Callaghan, D. 59
Canning, Charles 59
Canterbury Tales 21
Caramel 86
Caraway 43
Cardamom 92
Caroline, Queen 57
Carrot 94, 132
Carter, Charles 61
Cashews 88, 147, 149
Cassell's Dictionary of Cookery ([Payne], 1878) 62
Cassia 92
Catering Recipes (Nestlé, 1967–74) 141

Cato 20
Charles I, King 26, 27
Charles II, King 27
Charsley, Simon 108
Chaucer 21
Cheese (in cakes) 20
Cherries, candied (glacé) 89, 90, 91, 98, 104, 111–12, 114, 122, 131, 134, 140, 147–8; colouring, artificial 148, 160; maraschino 148; preservative in 148
Chicken, domestication in China 18; distribution 18
Chocolate 86
Choice Dishes at Small Cost (Payne, 1882) 70
Christchurch Girls' High School 104
Christmas Cake, first recipes named 64, 67
Christmas Cake in Four Quarters, A (Barker, 1872) 56
Christmas Day 43; 19th century innovations 12, 60–61; season 12
Christmas, His Masque (Jonson, 1616) 25
Cinnamon 19, 20, 22, 30, 39, 50, 92, 98, 102, 108
Citron, candied peel of 18, 19, 22, 76, 104, 109, 148
Citrus fruit, candied peel of (*see* Peel); juice 90–91; rind 90 (*see also* Citron, Lemon, Orange)
Civil War, English 26
Closet of the Eminently Learned Sir Kenelme Digbie Kt, The ([1669]) 31, 32
Cloves 20, 22, 30, 31, 39–40, 50, 92
Clutha Leader 65, 70
Cocoa 86, 135
Coconut 94
Coffee 86
Cole, Mary 47, 54–5
Colonial Everyday Cookery [1901] 126
Compleat Cook, The (1655) 29
Compleat Housewife, The (Smith, 1728) 45–6
Complete Cook, The (Jenks, 1768) 50, 51
Confectioners 57, 58, 59, 60, 62, 70, 71–2, 74
Cookbook, The (N.Z. Guild of Food Writers, 2000) 142
Copley, Esther 62
Cookbooks, 14th–17th century 22, 26, 27, 29, 31, 43–4; 18th century British 43–7, 50–3, 61–62; 19th century American 62, 72–3, 99, 104, 108–9; 19th century Australian 65, 70; 19th century British 62–3, 64, 66–7, 70, 74, 152, 153; 20th century American 140; 20th century Australian 70, 127; 20th century New Zealand 77, 95–152
Cookery Book (Presbyterian Women's Missionary Assoc. NSW, 1895, 1896) 65, 99
Cook's Oracle, The (Kitchiner, 1823) 62
Coriander 92
Cornflour 87

Cream 27, 38, 39, 92, 153
Cream of tartar (*see* Raising agents)
Croly, Jane 74
Currants (dried grape variety) 15, 16, 19, 22, 25, 27, 30, 40, 62, 76, 88–9, 104, 125–6, 131; black, red, white (*Ribes* spp.) 118
Cumin 20
Curry powder 92, 146

Daish, Lois 112
Dates 40, 90, 98, 131, 134, 147, 149, 158, 169
David, Elizabeth 26
Davidson, Alan 61
Decorations on Christmas cakes 101, 110; on twelfth cakes 36, 41, 42, 52, 57, 71–2; toxic paint on 58, 60–61
Dempsey, Rosemary 141, 147
Depression (1930s), adjustment in cakes 78, 104, 113, 125, 147, 165; cookbooks 113, 120; prices 118
Dethier, Louis 60
Dickens, Charles 60
Digby, Sir Kenelm 31, 32, 37, 43, 125
Dods, Meg (*see* Johnstone, Christian)
Dole, James 138
Dr Chase's Third, Last and Complete Receipt Book and Household Physician (1886) 99
Dripping (*see* Fat)

Edmonds, cookery book series 95–8, 100–101, 110–11, 162
Eggs, basic ingredient 22, 27, 39, 78, 80, 86–7, 114, 125, 155, 167, 168; earliest availability 17, 18, 19; eggless cakes 86, 118, 119, 141, 144; preserved 119; prices 118–9; separation of whites and yolks 39, 53, 70, 74, 76, 87, 102, 134; rationing (*see* War)
Elizabeth I, Queen 23
Ellet, Elizabeth 62–3, 64, 109
Encyclopaedia of Practical Cookery, The (Garrett, [1894]) 63, 102–3
England's Newest Way in All Sorts of Cookery … (Howard, 1717) 45
English and Australian Cookery Book, The (Abbott, 1864) 70
Equipment (*see also* Oven) electric mixer 33, 48, 164; (see Hoops; Tins, cake)
Essences 39, 76, 98, 115, 131, 166, 167; multiple use 93, 146; almond 93, 122, 134, 160; brandy 93; cherry 93; gin 93; lemon 93, 122, 134; orange 93; Parisian 86; pineapple 93; rum 93; vanilla 93, 122, 134; whisky 93
Evelyn, John 35, 37, 39, 45

Evening Post (Wellington) 70, 153
Everyday Recipes (Kent-Johnston, 1941) 121
Evolution, biological 14, 145; cultural (exemplified in recipes) 11, 13, 40, 95, 112, 145, 166
Experienced English Housekeeper, The (Raffald, 1769) 53, 54–5

Family (and household), changing size of 13, 26, 78, 114
Family-Dictionary: or, Houshold Companion, The (Salmon, 1705) 44–5
Fat, as substitute for butter (*see also* Butter) 84; cod 84; dripping 84, 119, 121, 153; lard 21, 84; margarine 84, 121
Female Economist, The (Smith, 1810) 126
Figs 16, 21, 22, 90, 131, 147
Figures, as cake decorations 42, 57–8, 63, 72
Filberts 88
Fire of London, Great (1666) 27
Flour, self-raising 87; sifting 168; white or unspecified (bread, plain) 32, 35, 38, 39, 40, 87–8, 167; wheat 14, 19, 20, 21–2, 154; wholemeal 32, 87–8, 153, 154–5
Flower, Tui 133, 135, 136, 138, 140–41, 152
Frazer, Mrs 52
Fruit, candied 89, 90, 148, 151, 160 (*see also* Cherries, Ginger, Peel, Pineapple); dried 11, 15, 16, 39, 40, 74, 79–80, 81, 83, 84, 88–90, 114, 160 (*see also* Currants, Figs, Prunes, Raisins, Sultanas); mixed, pre-packed 89, 90, 126, 131, 144; Australian 81, 88, 102, 160; Californian 88, 102; colouring, artificial 160; preparation 89, 125–7; preservatives used 160; pre-soaking 91, 92, 126–7; sinking 126–7
Fuller Fultons, grocers (Wellington) 89
Further Reliable Tested Recipes Book 2 [1958] 133

Galloway, S. 121
Gard'ner, Elizabeth 102, 104–5, 109, 110, 112, 126, 161
Garrett, Theodore 63, 102–3
Gentlewoman's Cabinet Unlocked, The (1664) 29, 31
George IV, King 57
GHB Cookery Book (Sherriff 1961-8) 98, 111
Gill, M. 59
Gillette, Fanny 73
Ginger, ground 19, 20, 22, 65, 76, 92, 98, 134; preserved 90, 91, 104, 114, 115, 131, 134, 149, 160
Ginger ale 90, 91, 125, 127, 128, 130
Gingerbread, soft, source of Beeton's Christmas Cake 65, 68, 76, 161, 166

Glasse, Hannah 46–7, 48, 50, 51, 55, 102, 125, 161
Glaze (under icing or topping) 111, 163
Glycerine (glycerol) 87, 127, 130, 164
Golden syrup 76, 86, 119, 131
Good Housekeeping (USA) 133
Goudie, Thomas 59
Grape vine, domestication of 15–16, 17, 19
Grapes, archaeological remains of 16, 21, 22
Gray, Eleanor 138
Grindstones for cereal grains 14, 15
Grocers' United Stores (G.U.S.) 122

Hajji Firuz (Iran) 16
Harman, Alice 102, 104–5, 109, 110, 112, 126, 161
Hartman, George 31
Harvey, Elsie 105, 109
Hawaiian Pineapple Company 138
Hazelnuts 17, 88, 147, 160, 169
Hearths, cooking (prehistoric) 14
Henderson, Mary 72–3
Henisch, Bridget Ann 60–61
Henrietta Maria, Queen 27
Herrick, Robert 25
Highlander, brand of condensed milk 139–140
Highlander Economical Cookery Book, The (Turner, 1922) 140
Highlander Quick 'n' Easy Cookbook (c. 1974) 144
Holst, Alison 11, 87, 111–2, 134, 135, 138, 149
Home Cookery Book (N.Z. Women's Institutes, 1939–1950) 98, 115
Home Science (*see* School of Home Science)
Honey 19, 20, 84
Household, size (*see* Family)
Housekeeper's Guide, The (Copley, 1838) 62
Howard, Henry 45

Icings, additions to (bluing agents 71, 110; citric acid 110; colourings 73; gelatine 110; glucose 110; glycerine 110); Elizabethan 36; in 17th century 36–7; in 18th century 41, 43, 51–2; in 19th century 62, 71–4; in 20th century 110–12; on twelfth cakes 51–2, 71–2; types (almond 36, 51–2, 72, 73, 74, 110, 112, 161, 163, 166; butter 52, 110–11; frosting 52; royal 33, 36–7, 51–2, 71–4, 110, 112, 161, 164, 166; Vienna 111) (*see also* Recipes, named)
Ideal Cookery Book, The (Cameron, 1929) 120
Inflation, economic (1970–80s) 146
Inglis, Raelene 9

Jam or jelly 86, 94, 135, 169; blackcurrant 86, 114, 116, 117, 118, 165, 169

James I, King 25, 26
Jarrin, William 70, 71–2
Jenks, James 50, 51, 61
Jennie June's American Cookery Book (Croly, 1866) 73
Jerf el Ahmar (Syria) 14–15
Johnstone, Christian 126
Jonson, Ben 25–6

Kellogg, Ella 153
Kent-Johnston, Nan 121, 122
Kidder, Edward 38
King Henry the Eighth (Shakespeare) 22
Kitchens, prehistoric 15
Kitchiner, William 62, 63, 71
Kiwi Kitchen (Till, 1st series) 156

Lady's Complete Guide, The (Cole, 1789) 54–5
Lady's, Housewife's and Cookmaid's Assistant, The (Taylor, 1769) 50, 53
Lamb, Patrick 125
Lard (*see* Fat)
Law, Digby 152
Lawrence, B.C. 59
League of Mothers 130
Lehmann, Gilly 44
Lemon, candied peel 18, 22, 76, 148; grated rind 90; juice 90
Leslie, Eliza 109, 126
Life, magazine (U.S.A.) 140
Liqueur, orange 92
London and Country Cook, The (Carter, 1749) 61
Lotteries (and raffles), involving twelfth and Christmas cakes 63; Australian 59–60; British 58, 60–61; New Zealand 59–60

Mace 20, 22, 30, 39–40, 50, 92, 98, 102, 108, 169
Mango, candied 149
Marchpane 36–7
Margarine (*see* Fat)
Marmalade 86, 144, 160, 169
Marzipan 36–7
Massey, John and son 72
Mawditt, Mr 57
May, Robert 29
Meals with the Family (Holst, 1967) 111
Measures, change in system 21–2, 97, 122; imperial 32, 35, 77, 97, 114, 115, 144, 152; metric 97–8, 122, 134, 142, 144
Mercury, The (Tasmania) 133
Middle East, as source of cake ingredients 14–18
Milk, condensed 79, 84, 86, 92, 139–146; evaporated 139; fresh 27, 76, 92, 119, 145

Miller, Naomi 17
Mixing, methods of (*see* Cake, fruit)
Modern Cookery (Acton 1845, 1855) 152
Mollard, John 62
Musk 30, 40
Mustacei (Roman must cakes) 20
Mustard seed, cakes 15

NCW Centennial Recipe Book, The (Roxburgh, 1996) 115
Nestlé Maggi Recipe Club 146
New Year's Day, present-giving on 61
New Zealand Dairy Exporter and Farm Home Journal 113
New Zealand Domestic Cookery Book, The (Harman & Gard'ner, 1900) 102
New Zealand Herald 141
New Zealand Radio and Television Cookbook (Holst, 1974) 131
New Zealand "Truth" 105
New Zealand Weekly News 141
New Zealand Woman's Weekly 132, 135, 136, 140, 141, 144, 149, 154
New Zealand Woman's Weekly Cookbook (Flower, 1971) 136, 138, 152
Nutmeg 20, 22, 27, 39–40, 92, 98, 102, 108
Nuts 15, 17, 79, 80, 81, 84, 88, 148, 151, 160 (*see also* Almonds, Brazil nuts, Cashews, Hazelnuts, Pecans, Pistachios, Walnuts)

Ohalo II site (Sea of Galilee) 14, 17
Oil, edible 84, 133, 139
Olive 15, 16, 21
Orange, candying of peel 18, 22, 76, 148; grated rind 90–1; juice 90, 104, 135, 158
Orange-flower water 37, 39, 48, 51, 91, 103, 104, 109
Otago Daily Times 149, 151, 156, 163
Otago Witness 70, 73, 74
Our Favourite Recipes (c. 1972) 145
Ovens, bread 13; coal-range 97; electric 97; microwave 168; temperature control 13, 77, 97, 134, 167

Paisley Abbey (Scotland) 22
Pans (*see* Tins)
Papanui Parish Cookery Book (1947) 121
Parkinson, Eleanor 62
Parloa, Maria 73
Pastry-cooks 22, 42, 52, 53, 57–62, 72, 74
Payne, Arthur 70
Peach, candied 149
Pecans 147, 160

Pedersen, Elisabeth 112
Peel, candied 40, 41, 76, 86, 89, 90, 98, 104, 114, 122, 131; processing 148 (*see also* Citron, Lemon, Orange)
Pepper, cayenne 92; unspecified 92
Pepys, Samuel 27–31, 35, 42, 125; household accounts 30; servants 28–9, 40; wife Elizabeth 28, 30, 39, 40
Pineapple, candied (crystallised, glacé) 89, 111, 131, 133; canned 87, 132, 133, 134, 135, 138; juice 91, 132, 133, 134, 138; production (Australia, Hawaii) 138
Pistachios 160
Plague, Great (1665) 27, 31
Plat, Hugh 36, 37
Plum, term for dried fruit 25, 41
Poisoning, of children from painted decorations 58, 60, 61
Practical Cooking and Dinner Giving (Henderson, 1877) 72–3
Practical Housekeeper, The (Ellet, 1857) 62
Presbyterian Cook Book (Dayton, Ohio, 1873) 104
Prices, of cake ingredients, 17th century 28, 29–31, 39–40; 18th century 50; 20th century 80–81, 89, 114, 118–9, 130, 147
Prizewinner Recipe Book, The (Harvey, c. 1933) 105, 109
Prunes 25, 90, 131, 149, 158
Pudding, Christmas 12; plum 25

Queens Closet Opened, The (W. M., 1655) 27, 40

Raffald, Elizabeth 53, 54–5
Raising agents, chemical (baking powder 76, 87, 98, 99, 121, 122, 144, 166; baking soda 65, 76, 87, 92, 99, 122, 144, 153; cream of tartar 87, 121, 122)
Raisins 15, 16, 17, 19, 20, 21, 22, 25, 40, 62, 88–9, 118, 126, 131, 147, 149 (*see also* Sultanas)
Rationing (*see* War)
Recipe, as artefact 9; as code 13, 165–6; books (*see* Cookbooks); historical value 12–13, 77–8, 166; lineages 10, 12, 45, 50, 78, 83, 95, 161, 169
Recipes, named and quoted in full: 2-Egg Custard Christmas Cake (1948) 122, 123, 165; Almond Paste (2002) 163; Another Plum Cake With Almonds (1728) 44, 46, 47; Butter Icing for Christmas Cake (1955) 111; Cakes, Queens, call'd Portugal Cakes (1705) 44; Cheap Fruit Cake (c. 1944) 119; Christmas Cake (1861) 11, 64, 65, 68, 76, 153, 161; Christmas Cake (1929) 120; Christmas Cake (1985) 146; Christmas Cake (Economical and Delicious) (c. 1970) 145,

165; Christmas Cake [Edmonds'] (1908) 96, 100, 161; Christmas Cake [Low-fat] (2002) 156, 158, 165; Christmas Cake or Bride Cake (1904) 103, 110, 161; Christmas Cake (Wholemeal) (c. 1940) 154; Christmas Jewel Cake (1987) 149–50, 151, 165; Christmas or Wedding Cake (c. 1951) 105, 106; Dark Xmas Cake (1936) 114; Dark Christmas Cake (1968) 135, 136, 165; Delicious Uncommon Christmas Cake (1935) 132; Easy Mix Cake (1968) 140; Economical Fruit Cake (1941) 121; Frosting (1877) 72–3; Ginger Ale Cake (1939) 127; Ginger Ale Christmas Cake (c. 1943) 130; Ginger Ale Christmas Cake (1972) 128, 131; Holiday Cake (1859) 65; Howick Christmas Cake (1935) 115, 116, 165, 169; Marchpane (1602) 36; Most Marvellous Christmas Cake (1969) 141; New Style Christmas Cake (1954) 148; Plum Cake (1896) 99; Rich Fruit Cake (1934) 120–21; Royal Icing (1836) 71; Royal Icing (2002) 164; Sweetened Condensed Milk Christmas Cake (2000) 142; To Make A Cake (1653) 26, 30; To Make A Good Cake (1664) 29, 30; To Make A Rich Cake (1747) 47, 48, 50, 161; To Make A Spice Cake (1653) 26, 30; To Make Almond-Iceing for the Bride Cake (1769) 52; To Make An Excellent Cake (1669) 31, 32, 161; To Make Sugar Iceing for the Bride Cake (1769) 52; Twelfth Cake (1866) 72; Wholemeal Xmas Cake (1962) 154
Recipe Rendezvous (c. 1970) 144
Restoration, of Monarchy (1660) 23, 27
Rice, ground 87
Roberts, I. 71
Rosewater 36–7, 39, 40, 51
Royal Baking Powder Company (New York) 99
Rum 92, 98, 114
Rundell, Mrs 74
Rye 14

Sack (*see* Wine)
Sackville, Edward 31
Saffron 30, 40
Salmon, William 44–5
Salt 93–4; in butter 167
Saturnalia (Roman festival) 21, 23, 166
Scales, weighing 114, 115
School of Domestic Instruction (Christchurch) 104, 112
School of Home Science, University of Otago 134, 135, 138
Science in the Kitchen (Kellogg, 1893) 153
Shakespeare, William 22, 25

Sherriff, Sybil 98, 111
Sherry (*see* Wine)
Shipley, Jenny 122
Shows, agricultural and horticultural, cake competitions 112
Smith, E[liza?] 45–6, 47, 50
Smith, Mrs 126
Souvenir Recipe Book (Scaife and Scurr, 1972) 128, 131
Spice, mixed 76, 92, 98, 144
Spices, use of 11, 19, 20, 21, 27, 29, 30, 39–40, 41, 48, 63, 70, 76, 92, 104, 106, 108, 114, 115, 144, 167 (*see also* Cinnamon, Mace, Nutmeg &c)
Spirits 11 (*see also* Brandy, Rum, Whisky)
Stanley, Venetia 31
Star (Christchurch) 104
Station Life in New Zealand (Barker, 1870) 56
Statius 21
Stead, Jennifer 47
Stuart, Alexander 65
Sugar, origins of 18–19; rationing (*see* War); specified types (beet, brown, cane, caster, demerara, raw, refined) 19, 37, 84; unspecified 22, 29, 38–9, 41, 43, 44, 77, 79, 80, 81, 155 (*see also* Golden syrup, Honey, Treacle)
Sultanas 88–9, 99, 102, 104, 166
"Sure to Rise" Cookery Book, The (Edmonds', 1908) 95 (*see also* Edmonds, cookery book series)
Sweetener, artificial 84
Sweetmeats (*see* Peel)

Taming of the Shrew, The (Shakespeare) 22
Taste of Mid-Canterbury, A (Rowe, c. 1993) 122
Taylor, E. 50
Teal, Jane 97
Tell es-Sa'idiyeh (Jordan) 16
Tell Sweyhat (Syria) 18
Thomson, Noeline 130
Tins, cake 13, 149, 167; lining 13, 77, 127, 134, 167; sizes 77, 106, 167
Toppings, alternative to icing 111–12
Treacle 76, 86, 114
Trends, in New Zealand Christmas cakes 77–94; proportions of main ingredients 77, 78, 79–81, 83, 127; sizes (weights) 77, 78–9, 82–3, 130, 131, 155
Troilus and Cressida (Shakespeare) 22
True Gentlewomans Delight, A (W.J., 1653) 26
Trusler, Mrs 42
Tui's Practical Cookery Book ([Burnard], 1933) 113
Tui's Second Cookery Book ([Burnard], 1936) 113
Turner, Thomas 42
Twelfth cake (*see* Cakes, twelfth)

Twelfth Night (or Day), characters 27–8, 42, 59, 60, 63; revelries 12, 21, 22–3, 25, 26, 27, 36, 42, 53, 57, 58, 60, 166; tokens 25, 28, 42, 59
Twelfth Night (Shakespeare) 22, 23

Una Carter's Famous Cookery Book (Carter, c. 1944) 121
United Farmers News 152
United States (*see* America)

Varro, Marcus 18
Victoria, Queen 57
Vi-max 87
Vinegar 144

Wafers, iced 36
Walnuts 17, 88, 114, 140, 147, 160, 165, 169
War (influence on cakes), Seven Years War 41; World War I 78, 80, 81, 118; World War II 78, 81, 88, 93, 119, 121, 130, 147; rationing 78, 81, 84, 90, 118–9, 121, 125, 130, 154, 165
War Economy Recipe Book (c. 1944) 119, 121
Warne's Model Cookery and Housekeeping Book (Jewry, 1869) 70, 115
Warren, Eliza 64
Wassail 25–6
Wedding Cakes and Cultural History (Charsley, 1902) 108

Weekly News, The 133
Weighing machine (*see* Scales)
Wesson Oil Company (USA) 133
Wetherell, Mrs 153
What's Cooking? 300 Favourite Recipes of Queen Margaret College Old Girls (Marris et al. c. 1965) 148
Wheat, bran 87, 88; early use of 14, 17, 19; flour, extraction rate 88 (*see also* Flour, white or unspecified, wholemeal); germ 87, 88, 155; proteins 14
Whisky 92, 98
White House Cook Book (Gillette, 1887) 73
Wholemeal (*see* Flour)
Williams, Edmund 42
Willow Cookery Book (1969) 70
Windwhistle Cookery Book, The (Innes et al., 1990) 122
Wine, origins 16; port 92, 98, 145; sack 32, 39, 46; sherry 32, 39, 92, 98, 104, 106, 115; use in cakes 15, 16, 19, 20, 21, 27, 92, 93; resinated 16
Woman's Day (U.S.A.) 152
"*Woman's*" *Tested Recipes* (1939) 127
Woodforde, James 43

Yeast, ale 21, 22, 27, 32, 35, 39, 44, 45, 50, 53, 61, 62, 74, 76, 125; bread 14, 20, 22, 32, 87, 153
Young Cook's Guide, The (Roberts, 1836) 71–2